St Thérèse of Lisieux
by those who knew her

Edited and translated by Christopher O'Mahony

St Thérèse of Lisieux
by those who knew her

Testimonies from the process of beatification

Veritas Publications

CA
248.242
OMS

First published 1975 by
Veritas Publications
Pranstown House, Booterstown Avenue, Co. Dublin.
Reprinted 1977, 1989
This translation © 1975 Christopher O'Mahony.

Originally published in French:
Procès de beatification et canonisation de Ste Thérèse de L'Enfant-Jesus
et de la Sainte Face. I Procès informatif ordinaire. Rome, Teresianum, 1973.

Set in 10/11 pt Baskerville and
printed and bound in the Republic of Ireland by
The Leinster Leader.
Designed by Liam Miller.
Cover by Eddie McManus.

NIHIL OBSTAT:
Richard Sherry, D.D.
Censor Deputatus.

IMPRIMI POTEST:
Jerome Lantry, O.C.D., Provincial.
April 6, 1975.

IMPRIMATUR:
✠ Dermot,
Archbishop of Dublin.
February 15, 1975.

ISBN 0 901810 84 3

Contents

Preface

For some years now there has been a determined effort to present "the real St Thérèse" to the public. Conflicting interpretations of her life and character led to a desire for access to more authentic sources regarding her. A great step in this direction was taken when, in 1956, P. François de Sainte Marie published his photographic edition of the manuscripts of her autobiography. Critical work of this kind was also done on the various versions of her sayings, and resulted in a two-volume edition of *Derniers Entretiens* in 1973.

The present book is also a contribution to this return to primary sources of information. It makes public in their original form the testimonies given by witnesses at the diocesan inquiry into the life and virtues of Sister Thérèse which was held in Lisieux in 1910 and 1911: a necessary and important preliminary stage of any process of canonisation.

The movement to have Sister Thérèse's cause for canonisation introduced grew gradually as her *Story of a Soul* and the amazing power of her intercession spread her fame for holiness round the world. By 1908 the initial reluctance of some important people like Thérèse's uncle and the bishop of Bayeux had been overcome. The Cause could now be officially introduced, and officials appointed in Rome and in France to investigate and examine thoroughly the person and the writings of the candidate.

A diocesan tribunal was set up by the bishop of Bayeux and Lisieux in 1910. For a full year it interviewed a total of forty-eight witnesses, some of whom had known Thérèse personally, while others were concerned only with the investigation of alleged miracles.

The full text of these proceedings was never published; all that was available was the *Summary*: a selection of extracts from testimonies, arranged under various headings. The present French edition makes no pretence at completeness either, but it is not an edition of extracts. It publishes the full text of thirty-seven testimonies out of the forty-eight; those it omits are concerned purely with the verification of certain miracles attributed to Sister Thérèse's intercession.

Besides the actual testimonies, each of which is preceded by a presentation of the witness by the editors (pp. 129-588), the French edition includes legal documents connected with the setting up of the tribunal (pp. 1-7); a document called *Articles* (pp. 8-114), which comprises a biography of Sister Thérèse and an account of the wonders attributed to her intercession up to 1910; a list of all the witnesses (pp. 115-120); detailed instructions concerning the questions to be asked of the witnesses (pp. 121-128); and the text of St Thérèse's autobiography, as it is preserved in the proceedings of this tribunal (pp. 589-720). All of this is prefaced by an erudite twenty-six page introduction.

My task has been to reduce this rich and erudite volume to a size that would suit a wider public (and translate it), without impairing its invaluable worth as a first-hand source of information about the life, virtues and spiritual teaching of St Thérèse of the Child Jesus.

I first omitted everything in the volume outside of the actual testimonies (in French) and the document (in Latin) outlining how the witnesses were to be questioned. A closer look at the thirty-seven witnesses revealed that only twenty-three knew the Saint personally, some of them very slightly. Only thirteen could be said to have known her well enough to have something interesting to say about her. I have translated fully all that these witnesses have to say about St Thérèse, and have retained a simplified version of the introduction to each testimony.

Two other witnesses have been included for special reasons: Fr Thomas Taylor for his information about her early impact on the English-speaking world; and Fr Godefroy Madelaine for his work in preparing the *Story of a Soul* for publication.

In conclusion, I wish to thank Fr Alberic Fowler, o.c.d., for providing me with a useful first draft of two of the longest chapters in the book, chapters 3 and 4.

Christopher O'Mahony

Introduction

The interrogator's instructions

If it is the duty of the Postulator of the Cause to gather every possible piece of information available on the life and writings of the Servant of God, it is the duty of the Promoter of the Faith to scrutinise carefully the evidence on which such information rests. The latter's persistence sometimes gives the impression that he is opposed to the Cause—hence the name "Devil's Advocate" by which he is popularly (but very unofficially) referred to.

The Promoter of the Faith in this case was Canon Pierre-Théophile Dubosq. Born in 1860, Canon Dubosq obtained doctorate degrees in Theology and Canon Law in Rome before joining the Society of St Sulpice. He was a professor at the Major Seminary at Bayeux for eighteen years, and superior of it from 1905 till 1931. He was also for many years vicar-general of the diocese of Bayeux and Lisieux. He died at Lisieux on 10 May 1932.

Having played a very important role throughout the whole process of Thérèse's canonisation, Canon Dubosq became deeply imbued with her doctrine and spirit, and remained her humble disciple for the rest of his life. When in 1926 a Capuchin wrote a rather derogatory article about the new Saint, called *St Thérèse of the Child Jesus as I knew her,* Canon Dubosq replied with a pamphlet called *St Thérèse of the Child Jesus as she was.*

The document that follows is a set of instructions drawn up by Canon Dubosq for the interrogator. All the questions that each witness will be asked are grouped under thirty points, under the following eight headings:

1. General questions (1-9).

2. The life of the Servant of God (10-19).

3. Heroism of her virtues, in general and in particular (20-21).

4. Extraordinary gifts (22).

5. Reputation for holiness during her lifetime (23).

6. Death and burial (24-26).

7. Reputation for holiness after death (27-28).

8. Favours attributed to her intercession (29), and a concluding request concerning any additions or corrections the witness might wish to make (30).

General questions

1. Each witness shall first be admonished about the nature, gravity, and object of an oath, and the penalties for perjury in so grave a matter as this. To be specific:

> 1. His very grave obligation to tell the whole truth sincerely, just as he sees it, about everything that has a bearing on this case.
>
> 2. The crime of perjury he would otherwise be guilty of, and the automatic excommunication attendant thereon—an excommunication reserved to the Supreme Pontiff alone—should anyone deliberately conceal relevant information, especially such information as would be unfavourable.
>
> 3. The obligation to observe secrecy concerning both the questions asked and the answers given, until such time as the results of the enquiry are made public.

Each witness shall be asked:

2. His name, surname, parents' names, age, place of birth, profession, and other particulars.

3. Whether he observes the precepts of the Holy Roman Church concerning the confession of his sins and the reception of holy

communion at Easter, and whether he does so at any other time during the year.

4. Whether he has ever been accused of or tried for any crime. If so, what crime, how often, when, before what judge, and what the verdict was.

5. Whether he has ever incurred an ecclesiastical censure. If so, which one, how often, when, and whether or not he has been absolved.

6. Whether anyone has instructed him, verbally or in writing, as to how he is to testify. That is to say, whether anyone has suggested to him what he should say, or what he should perhaps pass over in silence, or modify. Should the witness admit to such influence, he shall supply the name(s) of the person(s) involved, and say how it was done and when, etc.

7. For what motive and in what frame of mind he is coming forward to testify. That is to say: whether the witness is moved by some such human motive as fear, hate, love, etc. Should it happen (as it very often will in this case) that the witness is related to the Servant of God by consanguinity or affinity, then he shall be asked whether he is being careful to leave all family considerations aside when giving evidence.

8. What source of information he is chiefly relying on for his knowledge of the Servant of God, namely: (a) whether he acquired his knowledge of her from others (from whom, when, etc.); (b) whether he acquired this knowledge from books or other writings; if so, he shall name them.
     Should he say that he knows a certain amount about the Servant of God's thought, character and life from the *Histoire d'une âme écrite par elle-même,* he shall be asked what he knows of the origin, intention, truth, etc. of this work, and whether it has been tampered with.

9. Whether he has a special devotion to and affection for her, and why; whether he desires and works for her beatification— for what motive, and how.

The life of the Servant of God

10. Each witness shall be asked if he knows the place and date of the Servant of God's birth, her parents' names and surnames, place of origin, and state in life; whether they had any children, how many and when; whether both parents were equally responsible for her upbringing. Should the witness say that the Servant of God's mother died rather early, he is to be asked if he knows or has heard who then reared the Servant of God— with circumstances of time, places, names, and the source of his information.

11. He shall be asked whether he knows anything about the reputation, faith, conduct, character or piety of her parents.

12. He shall be asked whether he knows where she was baptised.

13. He shall be asked how her parents loved their children, and how they reared them, with special reference to the Servant of God. Should he say that her father was especially fond of her, he shall be asked whether the Servant of God ever took advantage of this to have her own way, or took an unjustifiable pride in it.

14. He shall be asked where the Servant of God spent her childhood—with her family or elsewhere. Should the witness say that she went to the Benedictine nuns in Lisieux as a child, he shall be questioned about the reason for this, the kind of education she received there, who taught her, how long she remained there, and what she was like at the time. Finally, he shall say when it was she made her first holy communion, and with how much awareness and piety she did so; also when and where she was confirmed, adding necessary details as above.

15. He shall be asked whether to his knowledge the Servant of God completed her education at the aforesaid abbey of Benedictine nuns. Should he say that she was taken home earlier than usual, he shall be asked if he knows why this was so. Also, what kind of progress she made at home, what she was like then, what

good qualities or natural defects she had, how she behaved in spiritual matters, whether she frequented the sacraments, especially holy communion, how often and with what fervour. He shall add all relevant details and give the source of his information.

16. He shall be asked if he knows whether the Servant of God intended embracing a particular way of life. Should he say that she had decided to consecrate herself to God in the Lisieux Carmel, he shall be asked if he knows how this decision originated; what age she was at the time; whether she showed any signs of a divine vocation, and, if so, what signs; whether she succeeded in doing what she had proposed to—how and when. He shall add circumstances and source of information as above.

17. He shall be asked whether, to his knowledge, the Servant of God entered the novitiate of the Lisieux Carmel, whether she persevered and made her profession there, what vows she took, when and how. Should the witness mention that her ecclesiastical superior postponed her profession for a while, he shall be asked if he knows the reason for this delay. The witness shall also be asked whether he has anything to say about the state of her soul and her assiduity in practising virtue while in the Carmelite novitiate, adding circumstantiated examples and the source of his information.

18. He shall be asked if he knows or has heard that she exercised some office or function in her Order. Should the witness answer that she exercised the functions of a novice-mistress but without *the title of novice-mistress,* he shall be asked whether or not he knows the reason behind this restriction. Besides, the witness shall be asked if he knows when she was elected to this office, how she acquitted herself in it and for how long, and what her method of training novices was. Finally, he shall say whether to his knowledge she held any other office in the community— what, when, how well, etc., with details and source of information as above.

19. He shall be asked whether he knows or has heard of her writing anything, and, if so, what.

Heroism of her virtues generally

20. He shall be asked whether to his knowledge the Servant of God displayed uncommon fervour, constancy, and eagerness throughout her life for the practice of virtue generally. If his answer is affirmative, he shall illustrate by what deeds of hers can this excellence or "heroism" be proved, suitably circumstantiating his examples and including the source of his information.

Regarding specific virtues

21. *The theological and cardinal virtues*

Heroic faith

The witness shall be asked whether the Servant of God did or said anything which showed that she submitted to divine revelation, Holy Church, or the infallible authority of the Pope with more than ordinary faith, and especially what words or actions of hers throw light on this. He shall also be asked whether she had suffered temptations against the faith; if so, he shall say what they were, and how she coped with them.

Heroic hope

The witness shall be asked if he knows what she thought about future happiness, or about the joys of this life. Also, what kind of trust she had in God. The witness shall state what basis he has found in her conduct for his judgment.

Heroic love of God

The witness shall be asked if he knows anything about her love of God; whether or not she had an especial horror of sin, and was zealous for God's glory. Should the witness state that she was unusually virtuous on these points, he must not omit examples and the source of his information. He shall also be asked if he knows anything of her love for our Lord Jesus Christ, what the chief object of this love was, and what form of expression she gave it; whether the love shown by the Servant of God was more intense than that usually displayed by devout people, and, if so, how he knows this.

Heroic love of neighbour

The witness shall be asked if he has anything to say about her behaviour towards her neighbour: whether or not she was especially solicitous for the material welfare of the poor and the sick, in what way, and when; likewise, whether or not she especially cared about people's spiritual welfare, in what way, and when; also whether she was not sometimes insulted, or at least treated rudely or contradicted by certain people—in what way, by whom, and when; how she behaved towards people who opposed her in any way; whether her love was only for some, or embraced everybody; whether or not this love for her neighbour was free of carnal or sensible attraction. The witness shall add relevant circumstances and give the source of his information regarding all these points.

Prudence

The witness shall be asked whether to his knowledge the Servant of God met with difficulties in her personal life, what they were and how she coped with them. Also, if he knows whether or not she was careful not to waste time, and in what way; whether or not she adopted suitable means to avoid what was dangerous to her spiritual well-being, and to foster her own spiritual growth: he shall state what these means were. He shall also be asked what he knows about her way of guiding others, giving circumstances, etc., as above.

Justice and its parts

The witness shall be asked if he has anything to say about the way the Servant of God expressed her devotion to God, our Lady, or any of the saints; whether or not she showed an especial respect and obedience to her superiors; by what words or deeds she showed this, when and for what motive. Whether the Servant of God was particularly careful about telling the truth—how and when. Whether she faithfully observed the laws of friendship, and was affable in her daily dealings with people. He should give circumstances, etc., as above, and state whether on all these points she displayed an uncommon degree of perfection.

Fortitude

The witness shall be asked if he knows or has heard that the Servant of God had to bear a certain amount of *harsh treatment,* what form it took, by whom inflicted, when, for how long; with how much patience, constancy, and perseverance it was borne. Whether he knows or has heard that she undertook some *difficult things* for God's sake, what they were, when undertaken, and with how much generosity and constancy. Whether he knows her attitude to work, bodily mortification, interior mortification of the feelings and other faculties, with relevant details, etc., as above, and the sources of his information.

Temperance

The witness shall be asked if he knows how the Servant of God behaved in the matter of food and drink; whether or not she was modest in bearing and speech, etc. Should the witness give too general an answer, he shall be asked for facts to prove his statements. He shall be asked whether or not she was naturally short-tempered, or vehement in her feelings; whether she nevertheless practised meekness and was in control of herself. He is to add relevant circumstances as above, and give the source of his information.

The vows and related virtues

The witness shall be asked if he knows any facts that would illustrate the way the Servant of God kept her vows and observed the rules of her Order; particularly whether she was outstanding in her practice of obedience, poverty and chastity. He shall be asked separately and searchingly about her humility: whether she had a poor opinion of herself, and especially whether she willingly suffered others to despise and belittle her. With relevant details, etc., and source of information as above.

Supernatural gifts

22. The witness shall be asked if he knows or has heard whether the Servant of God was at any time of her life favoured with supernatural gifts, such as: apparitions, revelations, prophecy, the ability to read people's thoughts, rapture, ecstasy, etc. If so,

the witness shall very carefully tell what he knows, with all the relevant details, as well as accounting for his own knowledge.

Reputation for holiness

23. The witness shall be asked if he knows or has heard anything about the opinion those who lived with the Servant of God had of her outstanding holiness at various stages of her life, and particularly: (a) while she was a girl in the world; (b) during the time she spent in the Lisieux Carmel. If the witness answers affirmatively, he shall say what that opinion was in either period, and in particular whether people were unanimously agreed about her eminent holiness, or if there were some who disagreed; how widely held either opinion was, who were for or against it, to what extent, why, and what kind of people—how well-informed, whether or not they were prudent, virtuous, etc. Details and sources of information to be given as above.

Death and burial

24. The witness shall be asked whether he knows the date of the Servant of God's death, and what disease it was she died of; whether she gave signs of eminent piety and faith; what signs; whether she was fortified by the rites of the Church, and was resigned to the divine will. Finally, the witness shall state what opinion the members of her community entertained of her holiness at the time of her death. Details and source of information to be given as above.

25. The witness shall be asked if he knows where the Servant of God's body was buried, whether it has remained there or has since been transferred. If the latter, he shall state when this happened, by what authority, and where her body is now kept. Details, etc., as above.

26. The witness shall be asked whether he has ever visited the Servant of God's grave—when, how often, why. Whether he

knows or has heard of others doing likewise—how many, for what purpose, whether they often do so, what kind of people they are: educated and prudent, or simple, uneducated people, or all sorts. If he can do so, he shall name the principal visitors. He shall also say when this practice began, whether it still continues, whether the number is increasing or decreasing, and give relevant details, etc., as above.

Reputation for holiness after death

27. The witness shall be asked whether he knows what reputation the Servant of God had after her death for holiness and heroic virtues. If the witness says that such a reputation indeed existed, he shall be asked whether it is growing or otherwise; whether it exists only where she lived, or elsewhere as well, and, if the latter, where. He shall be asked whether this fame is spreading only, or chiefly, among simple, ignorant, inexperienced and immature persons, or also among educated, serious-minded people. If he can, he shall name some of the more outstanding people who subscribe to the view that her sanctity is heroic. The witness shall finally be asked if he knows where this reputation originated, the cause of it, whether it was deliberately contrived, fostered and spread; what has been done, and is still being done, to this end, and by whom. Details, etc., and sources of information as above.

28. The witness shall be asked whether he knows of people who disagree with this reputation for holiness by word, deed, or in writing. If so, he shall say what kind of people they are— whether they are good-living, serious and educated; whether they disagreed by some passing, almost jesting, remark, or opposed this reputation seriously and out of personal conviction, and whether they still do so. If he says there are people who seriously and conscientiously disagree, he shall be asked to provide their names and addresses, so that they may be summoned here to testify according to the law, and to explain their reasons for regarding this reputation as suspect, doubtful or false.

Favours and miracles after death

29. The witness shall be asked if he knows or has heard whether at the time of the Servant of God's death or afterwards any prodigy or miracle was worked by God through her intercession. If so what, where, when, in what way, etc., with all the necessary and relevant details, and the sources of information.

30. Finally, the witness shall be asked if he has anything else to say or to clarify about the Servant of God's life, death, reputation for holiness, or miracles, if any; it may be some point he was not asked about specifically before, or something he forgot to mention, or would like to modify; whether it enhances her reputation or is contrary to it does not matter. Should the witness wish to add something he shall do so simply and faithfully, with an accurate account of all useful circumstances and the sources of his information.

Should anything else be necessary the piety, integrity and diligence of the judge and his associates will supply it.

I Agnes of Jesus, O.C.D.

The series of testimonies collected in this inquiry opens fittingly with that of Mother Agnes of Jesus. No one knew Thérèse better than this elder sister of hers who was a mother to her in her childhood, and again as prioress of the Lisieux Carmel. It was to Mother Agnes she once said: "You and you alone know me through and through." Thérèse always looked up to Mother Agnes, and loved her deeply. In the course of her last illness she called her her "light", her "telephone" and her "support".

Agnes of Jesus was Marie-Pauline Martin, the second of nine children born to Louis Joseph Stanislas Martin (1823-94) and Marie-Zélie Guérin (1831-77). She was born at Alençon on 7 September, 1861. After spending nine years (1868-77) at the boarding-school of the Visitation nuns at Le Mans, during which she imbibed much of the teaching of their founder, St Francis de Sales, it was nevertheless the Carmelite convent in Lisieux that she entered on 2 October, 1882. She made her profession on 8 May, 1884, the day of Thérèse's First Holy Communion.

The future saint followed in her footsteps four years later, and had her as prioress from 1893-96. It was during this time that Mother Agnes ordered her to commit her childhood memories to writing. Thus came into being the first of the three manuscripts that constitute her autobiography. Thérèse presented it to her for her feastday in 1896. It was also thanks to Mother Agnes that Thérèse wrote the third manuscript in 1897, during Mother Marie de Gonzague's term of office. Before she died, she gave Mother Agnes a free hand to edit the work as she thought fit, and in this testimony we shall hear all about that from Mother Agnes herself.

Mother Agnes published the autobiography for the first time in 1898, and it quickly became a best-seller in several languages. Convinced of the good it would do in the Church,

Mother Agnes publicised her sister's book boldly from the start;
she appreciated her true spiritual stature and the value of her
teaching earlier than most.

After Thérèse's death, Mother Agnes was several times
elected prioress, and in 1923 she received from Pope Pius XI the
unusual honour of being appointed prioress for life. She died
on 28 July, 1951, after a painful illness.

She testified before the tribunal from 12-19 August and
from 27 August—15 September, 1910. The interruption was
caused by the judge's desire to hear Fr Thomas Taylor from
Glasgow, while he was in Lisieux on pilgrimage.

The testimony

7. I am happy to testify; it is for God's glory. Naturally, I
am glad that it is a sister of mine who is involved, but I found
her life so edifying that even had she not been my sister, I would
still be very happy to testify in exactly the same way.

8. My knowledge of the Servant of God stems from having
lived with her at home from 1877-82, and here in Carmel from
1888 till her death. During the first five years of her life I was
away at boarding-school. We were separated too from 1882, when
I entered Carmel, till 1888, when she entered herself. But we
kept in touch. I knew everything she says in the *Story of a Soul*
myself; reading it added very little to my knowledge of her life.
On her deathbed she said to me: "You and you alone know me
through and through."

9. I am very fond of her and have great confidence in her,
because I think she is very near God and has great power over
his Sacred Heart. I pray to her a great deal, not because she is
my sister, but because of her holiness. I have a real respect for
her; during her life I respected her too, but then it was mostly
a question of affection. I want to see her beatified because she
will bring God great glory, and will make his mercy known
especially. People will put more trust in his mercy and fear his
justice less: that is the secret of the "humble path of trust and
self-surrender" that she hoped to make known to everybody
once she was dead.

10. She was born on 2 January, 1873, in the Rue Saint-
Blaise, Alençon. Our father's name was Louis Joseph Stanislas

Martin, and he was born in Bordeaux on 22 August, 1823. Our mother was Marie-Zélie Guérin; she was born in Gandelain on 23 November, 1831. Our father was a jeweller and mother made and sold Alençon lace. At the time of the Servant of God's birth, father had retired from business, and we were comfortable.

Our parents had nine children, all born in Alençon: Marie-Louise, born 22 February, 1860; Marie-Pauline, born 7 September, 1861; Marie-Léonie, born 3 June, 1863; Marie-Hélène, born 13 October, 1864, died aged four and a half; Marie-Joseph-Louis, born 20 September, 1866, died five months later; Marie-Joseph-Jean-Baptiste, born 19 December, 1867, died nine months later; Marie-Céline, born 28 April, 1869; Marie-Mélanie-Thérèse, born 16 August, 1870, died three months later; Marie-Françoise-Thérèse (the Servant of God), born 2 January, 1873.

The children were educated partly at home and partly at 'the boarding-schools of the Visitation nuns at Le Mans for older girls, and of the Benedictine nuns at Lisieux for the little ones, because of our change of residence following mother's death. This was so particularly in the case of Léonie, Céline and Thérèse.

11. Our parents were looked upon as religious, even very devout, people. In spite of her hard-working life, mother attended half-past five Mass every morning with father, and they both went to holy communion four or five times a week. Towards the end of his life father became a daily communicant; he was also a member of the St Vincent de Paul Society, the nocturnal adoration sodality, etc. Both observed the Lenten fast and abstinence, despite mother's delicate health. Father observed Sunday rest strictly, even though closing his shop on that day was particularly damaging to his business.

12. Thérèse was baptised in the church of Our Lady in Alençon on 4 January, 1873.

Asked how she knew this, she replied:

Because I was present.

The judge then asked her why the child had been baptised two days after her birth. She said:

We had to wait for her god-father. Our devout mother was very worried about this; she disliked the delay, and was afraid something might happen to the baby: she was convinced that the baby was in some danger. All the other children had been baptised the day they were born. Anyway, the vice-postulator must have the baptismal certificate.

13. One might say that our spiritual welfare was our parents' only concern. Mother would have liked all her daughters to be nuns, though she did not try to influence us.

Asked if she could be a little more specific about this, she said:

Mother made us raise our hearts to God often during the day, and brought us on visits to the Blessed Sacrament. She brought us up rather strictly, and let nothing pass, especially anything that savoured of vanity, etc. Father was gentler, and was particularly fond of his little Thérèse; mother used to say: "You'll ruin her!"

Asked why her father was especially fond of the Servant of God, she replied:

First of all because she was the youngest, but also because she was particularly bright and affectionate. Even at a very early age she was aware of my father's feelings, and after mother's death he found his greatest comfort in her.

The judge wanted to know if this paternal favour did not result in her being a bit spoiled.

Not at all; father loved her, but he did not spoil her. One day (she was about three) she took the liberty of saying to him: "Come here yourself!" He reprehended her and made her see that she had done wrong. For her once was enough; she was always very respectful from that on. I never knew her to take pride in her position at the expense of her sisters; quite the contrary. After her mother's death she regarded her elder sisters, especially me, as her mother. I cannot remember her disobeying me even once; she asked permission for everything. When father asked her to go for a walk with him, for instance, she would say: "I'll go and ask Pauline." Father himself insisted on this obedience, and if I refused to let her go, she obeyed instantly. Sometimes, though, she would cry because she knew what pleasure it gave father to go out with her.

14. After mother's death, on 28 August, 1877, father moved to Lisieux. This was because his brother-in-law, M. Guérin, lived there; Mme Guérin was a particularly kind and devout woman, and father thought she would be a great help to him in bringing up his daughters. Thérèse was reared and taught at

home by father, Marie and myself until she was eight and a half years old. She then attended the boarding-school of the Benedictine nuns in Lisieux as a day pupil. Her two sisters, Léonie and Céline, had been educated there, and when Léonie finished, Thérèse took her place. Céline was with her there, and can fill in the details about it better than I could.

During the years previous to her going to the Abbey, it was mainly I who taught her. She was very diligent, and profited a great deal from the lessons I gave her. She strove, too, to gain self-control; she trained herself from that time never to complain or to make excuses. At the Abbey she gave every satisfaction, as her weekly reports showed. She confided to me at a later date that a class-mate's jealousy had caused her a lot of suffering, but at the time she never complained of it. At school she noticed that some of her companions made a practice of getting well in with one or other of the teachers; Thérèse thought she would do the same, but found she was unable to. She has often told me that she considered this a special grace from God. In fact she tells it in her autobiography as well: "I did not know how to ingratiate myself with people, so I never succeeded. But I'm glad, because this blessed ignorance saved me from many a pitfall."[1]

She made her first holy communion at the Benedictine Abbey on 8 May, 1884. I was already in Carmel at the time, and it was chiefly Marie who prepared her for this. Three months before her first communion, I gave her a little notebook in which she was to write down every evening her sacrifices and little acts of love for Jesus. Her total for the three months was: 818 sacrifices and 2,773 acts of love or aspirations. She was confirmed at the same Abbey on 14 June, 1884.

15. Shortly after her first communion she passed through an attack of scruples. It looked as if her health would give way, so father thought it prudent to withdraw her from school and resume tuition at home.

Asked whether this withdrawal was entirely due to ill-health, or was not perhaps due rather to some disapproval on the part of her teachers, or even Thérèse's own dislike of the school, she said:

Oh, no! It was her frailty alone that made father afraid that school was proving too much for her. However, my sisters know more about this than I do.

Asked what kind of life the Servant of God lived after she had been withdrawn from the school, she replied:

I was in Carmel; my sisters will know that better, because they were at home. I could only repeat what she wrote in her autobiography.

16. From a very early age the Servant of God used to say that she wanted to live in a desert so as to be able to pray to God more freely. When out walking in the country with her father she used to ramble off by herself, while he was fishing, and think of eternity, as she put it. When I became a Carmelite in 1882 her thoughts then turned towards that form of religious life, and from the time she was nine she was determined to be a Carmelite herself. This determination became clearer as the years passed, and she took the first steps towards realising her ambition when she was fourteen.

The judge suggested that the prospect of rejoining her sisters, or perhaps her love of Pauline, might have been the cause of all this.

At the time I am talking about, neither Marie, Céline nor Léonie showed any inclination towards the religious life. Marie especially gave quite the opposite impression. I was afraid Thérèse might have been thinking of Carmel because of me, so one day I asked her if this was so. This suggestion pained her, and she exclaimed: "Oh, no! It's for God alone." Anyway, she has amply proved that since.

I was the only one who encouraged her when she tried to become a Carmelite; whenever she mentioned the subject to Marie she met with opposition, for Marie thought her too young, and did her best to prevent her from entering. Just to test her I, too, sometimes tried to dampen her enthusiasm; if she had not had a true vocation the obstacles she met with in her efforts to respond to God's call would have made her give up the idea immediately.

Eventually Marie joined me in Carmel and Léonie became a Poor Clare in Alençon. Thérèse did not know how to break the news of her decision to my father, who had already sacrificed his three elder daughters. She was then fourteen and a half years old. She chose Whit Sunday for the revealing of her great secret, and spent the whole day praying to the saints to help her find the right words. Father told her she was too young, but her arguments finally won him over and he announced that he considered it a great honour to have God ask him for his children. But there were still some painful trials in store for her.

When her uncle, M. Guérin, was consulted on the matter, he said that as far as he was concerned she must never mention the subject again until she was seventeen. It was most imprudent, he said, to let a child of fifteen enter Carmel: letting an inexperienced child embrace that kind of life would greatly harm religion in the eyes of the world. He assured her that it would take a miracle to change his mind. Thérèse sought comfort in prayer, and asked Jesus for this miracle. Shortly afterwards she suffered a severe interior trial: for three days she felt totally abandoned. On the fourth day my uncle unexpectedly gave his consent. A few days later she came to the convent to tell me her joy, only to suffer another bitter disappointment when I told her that the ecclesiastical superior would not hear of her entering before she was twenty-one.

The judge asked her who this ecclesiastical superior was, and why he objected to her entering.

It was Fr Delatroëtte, parish priest of St Jacques in Lisieux. He told me himself that he thought she was too young, and that was the only reason he gave.

The judge suggested that it might have been because she already had two sisters in that Carmel.

He did not say so to me.

The witness then continued with what she had been saying:

Nobody had expected opposition from this quarter; Mother Prioress was quite favourable. Thérèse did not lose heart. She asked father to take her to see the superior, and Céline went along as well. She did her best to convince him that she had a Carmelite vocation, but he remained cold and unmoved. He told her that waiting would not do her any harm, that she could lead a Carmelite life at home, that not being able to take the discipline, etc., would not be much of a loss. He added, however, that of course he was only the bishop's delegate, and that if the bishop did not have any objections, then he would have nothing further to say.

Asked if all this was based on her reading of the autobiography, she answered:

She often told me all this herself.

At her request, father promised to take her to see the bishop. "If the bishop does not give me permission," she said, "I will go and ask the Holy Father."

She told me the whole story of this journey, and afterwards wrote of it in her autobiography. What worried her most was where she was going to find the courage to explain to the bishop the object of her visit and her reasons for wanting to enter. Whenever she had gone visiting before, it was with her elder sisters and she did not speak unless spoken to, which was seldom. But she overcame her shyness and pleaded her cause as best she could. The bishop suggested she might remain with her father for several years more and be a comfort to him, but to his surprise, father supported his daughter's request. The vicar-general, Fr Révérony, could not help expressing his admiration. The bishop asked her when it was she had first thought of becoming a nun. "A long time ago," was the reply. "Still, it can't be as long as fifteen years," interposed the vicar-general with a smile. "You don't have to subtract many years from that," she replied, "because I've wanted to be a nun since I was three, and a Carmelite for as long as I've known this Order." The bishop said he would have to discuss the matter with Fr Delatroëtte, the superior of the Carmel, and that he would give his answer later. The Servant of God, knowing Fr Delatroëtte's attitude, was broken-hearted, and the tears flowed. In the course of the conversation M. Martin mentioned that he was thinking of paying a visit to Rome; the bishop approved.

When she returned from Bayeux, she came to visit me. I was struck by the fact that in spite of her real disappointment she nevertheless displayed a great peace of soul, founded on her complete surrender to God's will. That conversation inspired me with such respect for her that I can still remember it all quite vividly.

Before going to Rome she made a pilgrimage to Our Lady of Victories in Paris. There she put her mission in the hands of the Blessed Virgin and fervently beseeched her to keep her virtue ever intact. "I also asked her," she says, "to keep far from me all occasions of sinning. I knew that I would be likely to find many things on the journey that could trouble my conscience. I did not know evil, and I was afraid of discovering it."[2] She wrote this in her autobiography, but she often told it to me herself too, just as she did the rest of the story of her life.

As her letters testify, she was not insensible to the beauty of nature or of the masterpieces of art she saw on her journey, and her admiration of them always led to some pious thought. But what occupied her mind most was the audience she was going to have with the Holy Father. You will find a detailed account of the journey in her autobiography, and Céline, who was with her, can tell it again. I know only what I have heard, and I can state that this corresponds exactly with what she wrote. I intend to present a copy of it for inclusion among the documents of this Cause.

The judge asked if she had anything to add to what the Servant of God had written about this journey in the Story of a Soul.

No, everything she told me is there. In her audience with the supreme pontiff she overcame great timidity and asked him for his permission to enter Carmel at fifteen years of age. Fr Révérony was present at the audience and told the supreme pontiff that the matter was being studied by the superiors; Pope Leo XIII's answer to the Servant of God was: "Do what the superiors tell you to." She insisted: "But, Holy Father, if you were to say yes, they would all agree." "Come, come," replied the Pope, "you will enter if God wills it." She wanted to insist further, but the vicar-general and the guards cut short the audience by dragging her away from the Holy Father's feet.

Here is an excerpt from a letter she wrote to me after this audience: "I think I have done God's will; there is nothing for it now but to pray. My heart is full, but I know that God cannot give me trials that are too much for my strength. He has given me the courage to bear this one. Oh! Pauline, this is a very great trial, but I am the Child Jesus's little ball; if he wants to break his toy he is free to do so. Yes, indeed; I want only whatever he wants."[3]

After her return to France she confined herself, with perfect obedience, to acting on the advice I gave her after consultation with Mother Prioress: to obey, she assured me, was the only way to be certain of not making a mistake. Accordingly, she wrote again to the bishop of Bayeux just before Christmas, 1887. This time (28 December) he granted the longed-for authorisation. She did not enter, however, until the following April.

Asked by the judge why she had not entered as soon as she had received the bishop's permission, she said:

The immediate superior, Fr Delatroëtte, was so displeased at the steps that had been taken behind his back, and at an authorisation that was contrary to his own opinion, that we in Carmel thought it better to appease him by delaying the postulant's entry a while. She finally entered Carmel on 9 April, 1888, and was accompanied to the convent by father and all the family. This is how Fr Delatroëtte introduced her to the community: "Reverend Mother, you can sing the *Te Deum* now. As the bishop's delegate, I present this fifteen-year-old child to you. It was you who wanted her here, and I hope that she will not disappoint your expectations. I am reminding you that if she does, the responsibility will be entirely yours."

Asked how she knew this, Mother Agnes replied:

I was present.

The judge inquired if the superior had continued to hold this view afterwards.

It took this holy priest many years to change his mind, but he did eventually come to esteem the Servant of God, so much so that he once said to Mother Prioress: "Mother, that child is a real angel!" I heard him say this, and there were tears in his eyes as he did so.

17. When she entered the convent most of the sisters expected just an ordinary girl, but her presence soon compelled a certain respect. There was something so dignified, determined and modest about her whole person that I was surprised at her myself. One sister later admitted to me that when she saw me strongly supporting her entry she had said to herself: "How imprudent it is to let a young girl like that enter Carmel! What does Sister Agnes think she's doing? She's certainly in for a disappointment." She admitted that she had been mistaken.

Asked what nun had felt this way, and whether she was still alive, Mother Agnes said:

It was Sister John of the Cross; she died some years ago.

She then continued her testimony:

Since she had started her postulancy in April, at the age

of fifteen years and three months, the Servant of God should normally have been clothed six months later, before the end of October. But her clothing did not in fact take place until 10 January, 1889. The reason for this was that father was very ill at the time, and we hoped that the delay would enable him to be present.

On 11 January, 1890, a year and a day after her clothing, she was due to make her profession, but Mother Prioress asked her to postpone it; she was afraid that the superior would object on the grounds of her youth.

Asked how the Servant of God reacted to this delay, she said:

I was with the prioress when she informed her of this decision, and I supported this decision myself. Her first reaction was one of disappointment, but almost immediately she understood in prayer that the delay was God's will. She told me herself at the time what she wrote later in her autobiography: "I understood that my eagerness to be professed had a strong streak of self-love in it. I had given myself to Jesus for his pleasure and consolation, so I ought to have been doing what he wanted, and not trying to do what I wanted. 'Oh God,' I said to him, 'I am not asking you to allow me to make my profession; I will wait for as long as you wish. It's just that I do not want our union to be delayed through any fault of mine. Meanwhile, I am going to do my best to make myself a beautiful wedding-dress, all studded with jewels. I am sure, my Beloved, that when you consider it sufficiently adorned, no one will be able to prevent you from coming down and uniting me to you forever.' "[4]

She made her profession on 8 September, 1890. We could not vote on her admission to the vows without first obtaining the ecclesiastical superior's authorisation. He was still rather hesitant, and passed our petition on to the bishop; the latter granted it. Sister Thérèse's dispositions at the time of her profession are recorded in her autobiography, just as she had described them to me. The outstanding features of the period from her entry till she was put in charge of the novices were her humility and her fidelity to the very least of her obligations, despite continual aridity. I know all this from what she used to tell me of her state of soul on the days when the Rule permitted us to talk together.

The judge asked if she preferred to seek the company of her own sisters.

Quite the contrary, actually. At recreation or on other occasions she avoided us, and preferred to seek the company of those who were less friendly towards her.

18. She was entrusted with the training of the novices, as an assistant, when she was twenty years old. She first received this charge in 1893 when I was prioress, and she retained it till her death (1897), for Mother Gonzague confirmed her in it when she became prioress in 1896.

Asked why she was only made assistant and not novice-mistress, Mother Agnes said:

When I became prioress in 1893, I felt obliged to give the outgoing prioress, Mother Marie de Gonzague, the title of novice-mistress.

But why, insisted the judge, did you make the Servant of God her assistant?

Since Mother Gonzague was outgoing prioress, I found it expedient to appoint her novice-mistress. She had some good qualities, but she also had some unfortunate shortcomings and defects, which I hoped to counter-balance by associating Sister Thérèse with her in this work.

Asked why it was that when Mother Marie de Gonzague again became prioress she merely confirmed Sister Thérèse as assistant and did not appoint her novice-mistress, Mother Agnes replied:

Because Mother Gonzague decided to retain the title and influence of novice-mistress as well as being prioress.

She was then asked how Sister Thérèse acquitted herself in the charge entrusted to her.

She was not afraid of being hurt; she corrected fearlessly, whatever the cost to herself. But she did so prudently and wisely. As she humorously put it: "Some of them I have to catch by the scruff of the neck, others by their wingtips." She never spoke of her worries and troubles; she never asked the novices questions just to satisfy her curiosity; she never tried to be popular with them. In all her difficulties she put her whole trust in God, and had more fervent recourse to our Lady. In this connection she said something to me one day which I immediately went and wrote down: "I scatter the good seed that

God gives me among my little birds, and then let events take
their course without worrying any more about the outcome.
Sometimes one would think I had sown nothing, but God says:
Just go on giving and don't worry about anything else."

She let the novices say whatever they liked against her. The
fact that she was not really novice-mistress and that she was
younger than many of them gave her greater freedom to do this
of course. I met her one day after a novice had come and spoken
to her in a particularly humiliating way. Since she was looking
a bit flushed I asked if there was anything the matter with her
or if she was tired. "I am very happy," she said, "because God has
just provided me with an opportunity to remind myself that I
am a very, very ordinary person, and not at all virtuous. I
thought of Semei cursing David and said to myself: Yes, indeed,
it was the Lord who ordered Sister X to say such things. What
makes me still more certain that that is what happened is that
this morning I really desired to be humiliated."

*Asked what the Servant of God's relations with the novice-
mistress, Mother Gonzague, were like while she was her assistant, Mother Agnes answered:*

She was always very respectful and deferential, and coped
with what was a very delicate situation with consummate
prudence. When Mother Gonzague was on her deathbed in
1904, seven years after the Servant of God's death, she said to
me: "Mother, there is no one here as blameworthy as I am, but
I trust in God and in my little Thérèse: she will obtain salvation for me."

Asked how she knew all these things, she said:

I have seen all these things myself, and Sister Thérèse continually told me her thoughts; I made a note of whatever I considered interesting.

*Asked whether the Servant of God had exercised any other
office or function, she answered:*

She filled several of the ordinary offices in the convent: she
was successively sacristan, portress, refectorian, in charge of the
linen-room — more or less all the offices in the convent except
that of infirmarian, and she would have loved to have had that
office too. She showed no preference for one job rather than

another; she did whatever she was given to do very conscientiously as the expression of God's will for her at that particular time.

19. Her chief written work is the manuscript containing the
story of her life. Besides that, she wrote several letters to members
of her family and composed some pious poems either to express
her own feelings or, at their request, to please one or other of the
sisters on such occasions as professions, feastdays, etc. There are
also a few compositions entitled *Pious Recreations;* these are
little sketches intended for our own community celebrations.

As for how she came to write her life-story, it was like this:
one winter's evening early in 1895 (two and a half years before
Sister Thérèse's death), I was chatting with my two sisters, Marie
and Thérèse, and the latter was telling us a lot of stories about
her childhood. "Mother," said Sister Marie of the Sacred Heart,
"what a pity we haven't got all that in writing! If you asked
Sister Thérèse of the Child Jesus to write down her childhood
memories for us, I am sure we'd find them very entertaining."
"I couldn't ask for anything better," I replied. Then I turned to
Sister Thérèse, who was laughing at what she took to be a bit of
leg-pulling, and said, "I order you to write down all your childhood memories."

The Servant of God set to work on it out of obedience, for
I was prioress at the time. She wrote only during her free time,
and gave me her copy-book on my feastday — 20 January, 1896.
I was at evening prayer, and she gave it to me as she passed
my stall on the way to her own. I acknowledged it with a nod,
and put it down beside me without opening it. In fact, I did
not get round to reading it until after the elections in the
Spring. I noticed the Servant of God's virtue with regard to this:
once she had done what obedience had required, she thought
no more of it, and never even asked me if I had read it or what
I thought of it. One day I told her that I had not had time to
read it; she did not seem the slightest bit offended.

I found her account incomplete. She had dwelt on her
childhood and early youth, as I had asked, but had dealt with
her religious life only in barest outline. I thought it a pity that
she had not treated her religious life in the same detail, but I
was then no longer prioress — Mother Gonzague had returned
to that office. I was afraid the latter would not be so interested

B

in this manuscript as I was, and I dared not mention it to her. Then Sister Thérèse became seriously ill, and I decided to try the impossible. Towards midnight on 2 June, 1897, four months before Sister Thérèse's death, I went to Mother Prioress's room and said: "Mother, I cannot sleep until I tell you a certain secret. While I was prioress, Sister Thérèse wrote some memoirs of her childhood. She did so out of obedience and to please me. The other day I read them through again, and they are very charming, but they will not be of much use to you when it comes to writing her obituary letter because she says hardly anything about her life as a nun. Now, if you were to order her to do so, she could write something a little more serious, and I am sure it would be much better than the manuscript I have."

God blessed my endeavour: the following morning Mother Gonzague ordered Sister Thérèse to continue her account. I had already picked out a copy-book for her, but she thought it was too expensive-looking, though, as the tribunal can see for themselves (*and she showed them the copy-book*), it was ordinary enough. She was afraid she would be showing a lack of poverty by using this, and she asked me if I would at least draw the lines closer together so that she would use less paper. I told her she was too ill to tire herself by writing like that, and that she should rather space the lines out well and write in a good, big hand.

She set to work, and wrote away as it came to her, without any erasures. It was quite disorderly, however, because of her illness and of the interruptions caused by the constant coming and going of the infirmarians and the novices, these latter taking as much advantage as they could of her last days with them. So much so that one day she said to me: "I don't know what I'm writing." Another day, after she had been interrupted several times, she said: "I am writing about charity, but I have not been able to do it as well as I should have liked to; in fact, I couldn't have done it worse if I'd tried. Still, I have said what I think. But you must touch it all up, for I assure you it is quite a jumble." And another time: "Mother, whatever you see fit to delete or add to the copy-book about my life, it is I who have added or deleted it. Remember that later on, and have no scruples about it."

She stopped writing at the beginning of July, 1897. She was so weak that she had to use a pencil for the last page. The last paragraph she wrote was: "I am certain that if my conscience were burdened with all the sins it is possible to commit, I would still go and throw myself into the arms of Jesus, heartbroken with sorrow, because I know how much he loves the prodigal child who returns to him. It is not because God in his preventive mercy has preserved me from mortal sin that I approach him with such trust and love."[5] When she heard me say how sorry I was that she could not go on, she said: "There is plenty there: something for everybody, except those who travel along extraordinary ways."

That is where her manuscript ends. The pages that come after them in the *Story of a Soul*, as published in 1910, were added to round off the story of her life. They were taken from what the Servant of God herself had written during her last retreat (September, 1896) at Sister Marie's request, and with the permission of Mother Marie de Gonzague.

Asked if the Servant of God had any suspicion that what she was writing would be published some day, or would at least be used in her obituary circular, Mother Agnes replied:

She had no such suspicion when writing the first part, which was chiefly about her childhood and youth. She thought she was writing it just for me and our two sisters, Marie and Céline, who were with us in Carmel. In fact, that was what we thought ourselves at the time. The same is true of what has become the third part; her sister Marie had asked her for this, and it was written exclusively for her. But when Mother Gonzague asked her to write about her life in Carmel, I hinted to her that this might give edification to many people, and that its publication might well be the means that God would use to realise her ambition to do good on earth after her death. She accepted this quite simply. I also told her that Mother Prioress was liable to burn the manuscript. "That wouldn't matter," she said; "it would mean that God did not wish to make use of that means but there would be others."

Asked whether it was customary for Carmelite nuns to write such accounts of their lives, and whether prioresses usually made use of such accounts to write the obituary circular, at least in the Lisieux Carmel, she replied:

No, that had certainly never been done since the Lisieux convent was founded.

The judge asked if the Servant of God had written differently once there was a possibility that what she was writing might be published.

She wrote these last pages of her manuscript with exactly the same simplicity. One has only to read them to see that they flow spontaneously from her pen, with little semblance of order. She even asked me: "What do you want me to write about?" "About charity, about the novices, etc.," I said; and she just wrote away without any research.

Asked if the Servant of God's writings had already been published, she replied:

In October, 1898, a book entitled *Soeur Thérèse de l'Enfant Jesus et de la Sainte Face: Histoire d'une âme, écrite par elle-même* was published for the first time. The work contains her autobiography and a selection of her letters and poems. It was I who thought of publishing this book after her death. When I read over the manuscript, I felt I had a treasure that could do people a great deal of good. That was why, with Mother Prioress's permission, I decided to publish it. She gave the copy I had to Fr Godefroy Madelaine, O.Praem., the present abbot of St Michael's in Frigolet, then prior of Mondaye Abbey in the diocese of Bayeux. On his recommendation, Bishop Hugonin of Lisieux and Bayeux gave his *imprimatur*. It was published after a few emendations, suggested by Fr Godefroy, had been made.

Asked if this work would be a useful complement to her own testimony in this Cause, she said:

Certainly; she tells the story of her life much better than I do.

Asked if the published edition corresponded entirely to the original manuscript, so that one could take the former for the latter with complete security, she answered:

There are some changes, but they are unimportant and do not affect the substance or general meaning of the account. These changes are a) the suppression of some very short passages which relate intimate details about our family life during her childhood; b) the suppression of one or two pages that I thought would be of little interest to readers outside of Carmel; c) the manuscript is made up of three parts: one addressed to me, the second to her sister Marie, and the third (chronologically, that is) to Mother Marie de Gonzague, the then prioress. Since Mother Gonzague supervised the publication, she demanded some little changes in the parts addressed to the Servant of God's sisters; in order to give the whole work a greater unity, she made it look as if it was all addressed to herself.

When the judges heard this they ordered a copy to be made which would correspond exactly with what the Servant of God herself had written, and they directed it to be included among the official documents of the proceedings.

Mother Agnes was then questioned about the pictures of Sister Thérèse which had appeared in the above-mentioned volume.

Most of these portraits were drawn by Céline (Sister Genevieve of St Teresa) from old family portraits and from photographs. We had a camera in the convent, and Sister Genevieve was good at working it. She used it in connection with her drawing, and often photographed Sister Thérèse and other members of the community. The Servant of God always acceded to her demands with perfect simplicity, just to please her.

20. When she entered Carmel, I must admit there was a certain amount of laxity in the convent. Many nuns were, no doubt, quite observant, but there were not a few who were guilty of abuses. The Servant of God got on with her duty and took no notice of what others did. I have never seen her stop to hear the latest news from the groups that gathered round Mother Prioress outside the parlour, or listen to uncharitable conversations. In our family troubles she was much braver than the rest of us. After hearing painful news in the parlour, such as our father's state of health, she did not hang around to comfort herself by talking to us about it; she returned immediately to whatever she should have been doing in the community at the time.

She seemed so perfect to me from her very first years in religion that I have never been aware of the progress she speaks of when she writes: "When I look back on my novitiate days, how obvious my imperfection becomes!"[6] This imperfection was obvious only to herself. As far as I could see, she was always intent on pleasing God. Even amid the most distracting occupations one felt that the Servant of God did not give herself entirely except to the supernatural. I have never caught her in an unguarded moment of distraction; whenever I was with her, her recollection communicated itself to me even when she spoke of purely indifferent matters. She never complained about anything that made her suffer. With her, interior or exterior trials did not cause any lessening in the generosity of her efforts: it was when she was gayest at recreation, or working hardest, that one could guess there was something wrong. One day I asked her why she looked so exceptionally gay. "Because I'm suffering," she said, "and nothing gives me so much joy as suffering."

She was always serene despite her aridity and sufferings; she was so sweet-tempered that one might say grace played a perpetual smile on her lips. But more often than not, that smile was not the expression of natural joy. It was caused by a love for God that made her see a source of joy even in suffering. However, for all its generosity her fervour expressed itself with great simplicity and was entirely free of any affectation or stiffness.

21. *Faith*

Sister Thérèse saw everything from the standpoint of faith; she never confined herself to the worldly or human side of events. When she had charge of the novices, for instance, she never permitted them to criticise sermons or conferences. It was not that she thought all priests spoke equally well, but she could not bear for people to dwell on the shortcomings of their preaching. The same was true of the shortcomings of priests themselves: the spirit of faith did not allow these to be discussed, she said.

She went to confession for the first time when she was about six and a half years old. She regarded this as a great event in her life, and very carefully examined her conscience before me. I had told her that the tears of the Child Jesus would fall on her soul and purify it at the moment of the priest's blessing, so she looked forward to it as if it were a great feast. When she was examining her conscience aloud to me, she asked me what she should say in confession. I was hard put to it to find some sin for her to tell, because I had never seen her disobey or commit any other fault. So I urged her towards sentiments of love and gratitude rather than to contrition.

At the Benedictine school in Lisieux she did very well at her lessons, and was especially interested in religious knowledge. Fr Domin, the chaplain, called her his "little doctor". When I was preparing Céline for her first communion, Thérèse, who was seven, used to come and listen to the lessons. Sometimes I told her to go away, that she was too young. Later, she wrote, and indeed told me herself, too: "I used to be very disappointed, but I said to myself that four years were not too much preparation for receiving God."[7] Anything about God or the truths of religion found in her an immediate response, and her mind went to work on it effortlessly.

All her life she suffered from aridity. When her health was bad, spiritual authors left her cold, but the Gospel, which she always carried next to her heart, then became her spiritual nourishment. In 1895 she wrote: "When I was seventeen or eighteen years old, the works of our holy father, St John of the Cross, were my only nourishment. Later, all books left me cold, and I am still that way. In this impotence the Bible and the *Imitation of Christ* come to my aid. In these I find nourishment that is pure and solid; for prayer, however, it is the Bible I use mainly; everything I need for my soul is there. . . . I understand, and know from experience, that God's kingdom is within us (*Lk 17:21*). . . . I have never heard Jesus speak, but I feel he is within me. He guides me at every moment, and inspires me with the right thing to say or do. I discover new insights just when I need them, and not always during prayer either; usually it happens in the middle of my daily work."[8]

She never had what are called sensible consolations, but holy communion was her greatest desire and happiness. When the 1891 Decree[9] came out, she hoped confessors would at last be free to allow those whom they thought fit for it to receive holy communion daily. This was what the pope wanted, and she was delighted. She sounded triumphant: "It's not right for the frequency of holy communion to be regulated by the Mother Prioress; that is something that has always shocked me."

Towards the end of her life she was subjected to the terrible trial of being tempted to doubt the existence of heaven. She often confided her thoughts and impressions to me, but I cannot do better than to quote her own description of it. What she writes in her autobiography is exactly what she told me:

"I had such a vivid faith at the time that the thought of

heaven filled me with happiness. I could not imagine that there were really some godless people who had no faith. I thought they were not being honest when they denied the existence of heaven. But during those joyful days of Eastertide Jesus made me see that there really are people who have not got this faith, people who lose this precious treasure by abusing his grace. He permitted my soul to be covered in thick darkness, and allowed the thought of heaven, which had always been so dear to me, to become something that caused me torment and internal conflict. . . . This trial was not for a matter of a few days, or even weeks; it is something that is destined to go on until God sees fit to have things otherwise, and he has not done so yet. . . . Only one who has travelled through this dark tunnel can understand how dark it is. . . .

"The King of the land of the shining sun came to live in the land of darkness for thirty-three years; unfortunately, darkness did not understand that this Divine King was the light of the world. But, Lord, your child has understood your divine light; she asks your pardon for her brothers; she is willing to eat the bread of pain for as long as you wish, and will not leave this bitter table where poor sinners eat, until the day that you have decided on. Maybe she can also say, in her own name and in theirs: 'God have mercy on us poor sinners!' (Lk 18:13). May all those who are not enlightened by the flaming torch of faith some day see it shine! Oh Jesus, if the table they have dirtied must be cleaned by someone who loves you, I am more than willing to stay and eat the bread of trial alone until such time as it pleases you to bring me into your lightsome kingdom. The only favour I ask is never to offend you. . . .

"Whenever I try to rest my soul, wearied by the darkness that surrounds it, by remembering the lightsome country of my ambitions, my torment is doubled. The darkness seems to borrow the voice of sinners and jeer at me, saying: 'You dream of light and a land bathed in sweet fragrance; you dream of possessing the Creator of all these marvels; you think that one day you will emerge again from the surrounding darkness. Keep right on, then, and rejoice in the death he has in store for you; it will not be what you are expecting; it will be a night of still deeper darkness, the night of nothing. . . .' I don't want to write any more about this—I am afraid I might say something blasphemous.

. . . May Jesus forgive me if I have offended him. He knows well that although I find no enjoyment in the faith, I at least try to live by it. I think I have made more acts of faith in the past year than in my whole lifetime."[10]

I remember, *continued Mother Agnes*, one day during her last illness (11 July, 1897). The temptations against her faith were troubling her more than usual, and she kept repeating these lines from one of her poems:

> Since the Son of God wished his Mother
> to undergo darkness and heartfelt anguish,
> Mary, is it therefore a good thing to suffer here on earth?
> Yes, to suffer out of love is purest happiness.
> Jesus can take back everything he has given me,
> But tell him never to get angry with me.
> He can hide if he likes, and I will wait for him
> Till that undying day when my faith will cease to be.

Hope

As long as I knew her, the only part of her that touched the ground were the soles of her feet. When, as a little child, she used to go off by herself during her walks with father, it was, as she later told me, to think about heaven and eternity. On the evenings of Sundays and Holydays she was sad to see all the beautiful ceremonies come to an end, and used to comment that happiness was lasting only in heaven. When she was very little, she was known to say that she hoped her father or mother would die, though she was obviously very fond of them. When her words met with shock and reproaches, she said: "It's only so that you can go to heaven." I did not hear these words myself, as I was away at school at the Visitation convent in Le Mans; my mother told me of the incident in a letter.

When she was about ten, my father took her to visit some friends in Alençon during the holidays. Later on, both in the parlour and after she had entered, she often told me her impressions of this stay in a worldly environment. What she told me is exactly what she has written in her manuscript: "God has done me the favour of letting me know the *world* just enough to despise it and leave it. It was during our stay at Alençon that I made its acquaintance for the first time. All was joy and happiness around me; I was fêted, admired, and pampered. In a word, for a fortnight my life was all roses. I admit this life had its attractions for me. The Book of Wisdom is right when it warns us that the lure of worldly trifles leads the soul astray, even when there is no evil involved (*Wisdom 4:12*). I regard it as a great grace, too, that we did not go on living at Alençon; the friends we had there were too good at combining the joys of this world with the service of God. They did not think enough about death. . . . I love to look back and wonder where these people are now, and what satisfaction they have derived from the castles and parks where I saw them enjoy the good things of this life to the full. It makes me realise that there is nothing but vanity and disappointment under the sun (*Eccles 2:11*). I see now that *the only worthwhile thing* is to love God wholeheartedly and to be *poor in spirit* here below. Maybe Jesus wanted to show me what the world was like before paying me his *first visit,* so that when it came to promising to follow him I would be able to choose more freely."[11]

Asked if all this information was based on her reading of the autobiography, she answered:

Certainly not. There is nothing in her manuscript that I did not already know from our intimate conversations. In fact, when I ordered her to write her childhood memoirs, she said: "What can I write that you don't know about already?" I quote from the manuscript only because I could not say it as well myself.

She then resumed her testimony:

In Carmel, she was completely heavenly; earth no longer meant anything to her. She told me in a thousand different ways that when she thought of heaven what she really dwelt on was not so much the personal happiness she would find there, as the fact that she would then be able to love God more than ever; that she would be loved by God, and that she would be able to find a way there of making God better loved.

Trust in God had become her special characteristic. She felt attracted to this in early childhood, and I had done all in my power to develop this bent in her. She once told me that she had been struck from childhood by this verse from the Book of Job: "Even if he were to kill me, I would continue to hope in him." First, scruples came to paralyse this impetus, and she was very troubled, too, during her first years in Carmel. This was partly because she had heard it said in some sermons that it was very easy to offend God and to stain one's purity of conscience. This was a real torment to her. The preacher of the 1891 retreat restored her peace of mind. "He helped me especially," she writes, "by telling me that my faults did not offend God. This assurance made the exile of this life bearable. I know that God loves us more tenderly than any mother, and is a mother not always ready to forgive the involuntary little failings of her child?"[12]

From this retreat onwards her trust in God was complete, and she searched spiritual books for approval of her daring. She used to repeat happily St John of the Cross' saying: "You obtain from God as much as you hope for." She used also say that she had found a "lift" up to heaven, namely the arms of Jesus. She found complete security in this trust and the misfortunes of this life could not terrify her any more.

About her temptations against faith she used to say that they only removed some too natural elements from her desire for heaven. "Some might think," she said, "that it is only because I have not sinned that I have such confidence in God, but I feel that I would have just as much even if I had committed every possible crime."

She expected as much from God's justice as she did from his mercy. "How nice it is to think that God is just!" she said. "It means he takes our weakness into account and knows full well how frail we are by nature."[13] She also said that she would prefer to live without consolation, because in that way she could give God greater proof of her trust in him.

The Servant of God relied solely on God's help for everything. She told me herself how once, when she had tried in vain to comfort and encourage Céline in the parlour, she turned to God with complete confidence and asked him to console Céline himself and to make her understand a certain matter, telling him what it was. After that she worried no more about it. Her trust was never disappointed: every time Céline needed it, she received the necessary comfort and enlightenment. She told Sister Thérèse this herself at their next meeting in the parlour.

Love of God

In my opinion, Sister Thérèse breathed the love of God just

as I breathe air. When she was very little, mother used to make her offer her heart to God every morning, as is customary with children. But Thérèse was not satisfied with the morning recitation; she often repeated it by herself during the day. I remember thinking on the evening of her first communion day how like a seraph she looked; she was like someone who no longer lived on this earth. I have seen a great many devout young girls on their first communion day, but this was something different. Whenever she came to visit me in the parlour from then till the time she entered, her conversations were always about the love of God and the practices of a devout life.

Although she was very sensitive, affectionate, and spirited by temperament, she suffered from almost continual aridity during the whole of her religious life. Her love of God then found expression in a generous concern to seize every opportunity of doing what was pleasing to God. She let no opportunity pass. It was in the ordinary details of community living that she sought, and found, these opportunities for acts of charity. She always sought what was more difficult in order to show more love, but she always allowed herself to be guided by obedience. There was an elderly sister in the infirmary at the time, whom age and infirmity had rendered unusually difficult. Sister Thérèse would have liked to be infirmarian: "Oh, how I would have liked all that!" she said. "I would have had more to suffer for God."

In early childhood she used to worry about whether God was pleased with her or had something to reproach her with. Since I was a mother to her at the time, she would ask me every evening what I thought about this. When she was about twelve years old, she went through a year and a half of terrible scruples about every detail of her behaviour. She was all the time scared of offending God in some way or other. Twice in her life she confided to me that she was extremely happy. The first time was when she was about fifteen and a half, and Fr Pichon, s.j., assured her that she had never committed a mortal sin. The second was when, at the 1891 retreat, Fr Alexis, a Recollect, taught her that her imperfections, which were all due to frailty, gave no offence to God. This latter statement was a source of great joy to her, because the fear of offending God was poisoning her life. She composed a little prayer for her profession, and always carried it next to her heart. One phrase in that prayer was: "Take me, Jesus, before I commit the least wilful fault."

Before she entered Carmel, she told me that she wanted to be a Carmelite nun even if it was to save only one soul; a lifetime of suffering, she said, would not be too much for that. But afterwards her desires embraced a lot more than that: her constant preoccupation was to win souls for God; she never stopped talking to me about it. When she was due for profession, she was asked, in accordance with the requirements of Canon Law, what her motives were for embracing this way of life. "Above all," she replied, "it is to save souls and to pray for priests."

She told me she would like to have been able to share in the vocation of priests and missionaries, in order to bring God's name to all the countries in the world and die a martyr for Jesus Christ. But since she could not, she thought she would make up for it by the intensity of her love and desires; if her desires were sufficiently intense, she argued, they would be as effective as deeds.

One day, when she was sorely troubled by an interior trial, she said: "Oh, Mother, how fortunate for us that God became man, so that we could love him. It was well he did, for otherwise we would never have dared to love him." Her approach to our Lord was chiefly through the Childhood and Passion, an approach that is expressed in her double religious name—Sister Thérèse of the Child Jesus and of the Holy Face. Her love of the Child Jesus drew her to offer herself to him as a toy in the hands of a child. By this apparently childish expression she meant that she should surrender herself entirely to our Lord's will, and be prepared to be treated by him as he pleased. In the Holy Face she saw an expression of all the humiliations our Lord had to endure, and drew from it a constant willingness to suffer and be humiliated for love of him. One day we were standing in front of a picture of the Holy Face, and I said: "What a pity his eyes are lowered; we can't see the expression in them." "Oh, no!" she said. "It's better that way; we could not look at his divine expression without dying of love."

Asked how she knew all this, Mother Agnes replied:

From continual personal contact. If I were to tell everything I saw, and repeat all she told me, we would be here for ever. I have known a good many really fervent Carmelites, nuns who loved God and feared to offend him, but Sister Thérèse's state of soul was so different from what I have seen in others that they seem to have nothing in common. Such was the intimacy of her union with God that you would have thought she was always able to see him.

In the month of June, 1895 she was inspired to offer herself as a victim to the merciful love of God. She came to me for permission to do so, for I was then prioress. When she asked me this, her face was all lit up, as if she was on fire with love. I let her do it, but attached no great importance to it. Then she composed the formula of her self-dedication and submitted it to my approval, expressing at the same time the desire to have it checked by a theologian. Fr Le Monnier, superior of the Missionaries of Our Lady of Ransom, examined it. He said he found nothing in it that was contrary to the faith, but that one should speak of "immense desires" rather than "infinite desires". This was a sacrifice for the Servant of God, but she obeyed without question. The principal part of it had been approved, and she was delighted.

It was on 9 June, 1895, the Feast of the Holy Trinity, that she officially made this offering of herself. I find two quite extraordinary requests in the act of offering: 1. The favour of retaining the real presence of our Lord within her between one communion and the next: "Stay in me as you are in the tabernacle." 2. The favour of seeing the Holy Wounds of the Passion shining on her glorified body when she went to heaven.

The judge asked if these words about "real presence between one communion and the next" and "the Wounds on her glorified body" were meant in some metaphorical sense or were to be taken literally.

She often enlarged on these ideas when speaking to me, and I am certain she meant them literally. Her loving confidence in our Lord made her extraordinarily daring in the things she asked him for. When she thought of his all-powerful love, she had no doubts about anything.

Asked if she made this offering publicly, before all the nuns, she replied:

Oh, no; nobody knew about it. Later, she spoke of it to just two of her novices, and explained to them the advantages of it and the glory it would give to God. On the other hand, she also repeatedly insisted that to give yourself up to love was to give yourself up to suffering. She expressed this thought, too, in one of her poems:

> Here on earth, to live for love
> does not mean settling on Thabor;
> it means climbing Calvary with Jesus
> and looking on the Cross as a treasure.

Mother Agnes was then asked if she had the original formula of the offering. She produced the following document, and it was read to the tribunal:

"An offering of myself as a holocaust victim to the merciful love of God.

"O my God, Trinity ever-blessed, I want to love you and make you loved. I want to work for the glory of the Church by saving the souls who are here on earth and freeing those who are suffering in purgatory. I want to fulfil your will perfectly and to attain to that degree of glory which you have prepared for me in your kingdom. In a word, I would dearly like to be holy, but I feel incapable of it; so I ask you, my God, to be my holiness yourself.

"You have loved me to the point of giving me your only Son as my saviour and my spouse; the infinite treasury of his merits are all mine. I happily offer them all up to you, and beseech you to look at me only through the eyes of Jesus and in his ever-loving heart.

"I offer you, too, the merits of all the saints in heaven and on earth, as well as their acts of love and those of your holy angels. And, finally, Blessed Trinity, I offer you the love and merits of my dear mother, the Blessed Virgin; it is to her I hand up my offering, begging her to present it to you. When her divine Son, my beloved spouse, was here on earth he said: 'Anything you ask the Father in my name, he will give it to you' *(Jn 16:23)*. I am certain therefore that you will grant what I desire. I know, my God, that when you want to give us more, you increase our desires. My heart is full of immense desires, and I confidently invite you to come and take possession of it. I cannot receive holy communion as often as I would like to, Lord; but are you not all-powerful? Stay in me as you do in the tabernacle, and never leave this little host of yours.

"I would like to comfort you for the ingratitude of wrong-doers, so I ask you to take away from me the freedom to displease you. Should I fall now and again through frailty, may your divine glance immediately purify my soul, and burn up all my imperfections, just as fire turns everything into itself.

"I thank you, God, for all the favours you have granted me, especially for having put me through the crucible of suffering. I shall be happy to see you on the Last Day with the Cross as your sceptre, for you have deigned to share this precious Cross with me. I hope that when I get to heaven, I will be like you and will see the sacred marks of your Passion shining on my glorified body.

"After this exile here on earth I hope to enjoy your company in our heavenly home, but I have no desire to amass a fortune of merits for heaven. I want to work solely for love of you, with no other end in view but to give you pleasure, to comfort your Sacred Heart, and to save souls so that they can love you for all eternity. When the evening of life comes, I shall appear before you empty-handed, because I am not asking you to count my good deeds, Lord. In your eyes nothing we do is ever perfect (Is 64:5). I want to be clothed in your own goodness, and to receive from your love the eternal possession of yourself. You are the only throne or crown that I want, my Beloved. Time is nothing in your eyes, a thousand years are but a day (Ps 89:4); so in one instant you could make me ready to appear before you.

"In order to live in an act of perfect love, I offer myself as a holocaust victim to your Merciful Love, and I ask you to consume me unceasingly by allowing the waves of infinite tenderness which are shut up in you to overflow into my soul, so that I may become a martyr of your love, my God. May this martyrdom first prepare me to appear before you and then kill me, and may my soul fly without delay to the eternal embrace of your merciful love. My Beloved, I wish to renew this offering an infinite number of times with every beat of my heart, until the shadows pass (Cant 4:6) and I can tell you of my love face to face for all eternity.

"Marie Françoise Thérèse of the Child Jesus and of the Holy Face, Carmelite.
Feast of the Holy Trinity, 9 June, 1895."

The judge asked if Thérèse had made her offering just once and then forgotten about it.

Oh, no, never; she constantly repeated it, and her whole life revolved around it. On her deathbed she said to me one day: "I often repeat my act of consecration."

Love of neighbour

She was very sensitive to other people's sufferings, even as a child. At home it was she who was entrusted with the distribution of alms to the poor. Every Monday poor people would come to Les Buissonets (our house in Lisieux). Every time the bell rang, little Thérèse ran to open the door and came back to me saying: "Pauline, it's a poor old cripple!" "It's a poor woman with little children; one of them is only a baby and the woman looks very pale." I could see the deep compassion in her eyes. Then she ran off to them again with bread or money, as the case might be. Sometimes she would come back radiant: "Pauline, that poor man said: 'God will bless you for this, little girl.'" Father used to give her a few coins to reward her for various tasks, and her greatest happiness was to give these away in alms, too.

In Carmel she would have liked to be infirmarian, so as to comfort the sick. She used to tell the infirmarian: "You're lucky. You will hear our Lord say: 'I was sick and you comforted me'" *(Mt 25:36)*. There was an elderly lay-sister in the convent, who was ill and pretty cranky (she died in 1895). The Servant of God asked to be allowed to help and support her as she tried to get around from one community act to another. This was a very difficult task because the old sister was very odd and sharp-tempered. But Sister Thérèse fulfilled the task with such persevering kindness and gentleness that she won the old nun's complete confidence, though she had treated her very badly at the start. Sister Thérèse used to say that she took as much care about taking Sister X around as if it had been our Lord himself.

When she was a child, I taught her the practice of making little voluntary sacrifices for the conversion of sinners. She took to this with great fervour. But it was on Christmas Day, 1866, that she began to be really drawn to this particular expression of fraternal charity. "Jesus," she wrote, "made me a 'fisher of men' *(Lk 5:10)*. I felt a strong desire to work for the conversion of sinners."[14] She also told me, both in the parlour and later on in Carmel, all she had done for the conversion of Pranzini, the murderer, but Sister Genevieve knows more about this than I do; she was at home at the time.

Later on, she was more attracted to the spiritual welfare of priests, because she knew these were dearer to our Lord and better able to attract people to him. She spoke about this to me several times after her visit to Rome. It was then that she saw what weak and frail men priests were, in spite of the dignity that raised them above the very angels. She always prayed for priests after that, and spoke of the need of obtaining graces for them. It made her very happy to offer her prayers and sacrifices especially for two missionaries with whose work Mother Prioress had associated her. On 19 August, 1897, the feast of St Hyacinth in the Carmelite calendar, she offered up her holy communion, which was to be her last, for the conversion of the unfortunate priest who bears that name in our Order (Fr Hyacinth Loyson). This was something she longed for and often spoke to me about; she said she had made many sacrifices for this purpose.

On 12 July, 1897, she said to me: "Nothing sticks to my hands; all I have or receive is for the Church and for souls. Even if I live to be eighty, I shall always be just as poor. If I had been rich, I could not have borne to see a poor person without giving him something. In the same way, as soon as I earn any spiritual riches, I immediately feel there are souls in danger of going to hell, and I give them all I have. I have not yet experienced a time when I could say: now I will work for myself."

In the course of her religious life she often had to suffer from people's dislike of her, or from clashes of temperament or of mood, and, indeed, even from jealousy and spiteful behaviour on the part of other nuns. Not only did she bear all this with patient equanimity, but she always tried to excuse their behaviour. She also sought the company of such nuns in preference to that of others, and showed them the greatest kindness. I considered the conduct of one of these to be particularly reprehensible, but Sister Thérèse insisted: "I assure you that I have the greatest compassion for Sister X. If you knew her as well as I do, you would see that she is not responsible for all of the things that seem so awful to us. I remind myself that if I had an infirmity such as hers, and so defective a spirit, I would not do any better than she does, and then I would despair; she suffers terribly from her own shortcomings."

When Mother Genevieve, the foundress of the Lisieux Carmel, died, our relatives and people who worked for the convent sent lots of wreaths. Sister Thérèse arranged them around the coffin as best she could. When Sister X saw her, she exclaimed: "Ah! you're well able to put the wreaths sent in by your own relatives in a prominent place, aren't you! And you put those of the poorer families in the background." To this hurtful remark I heard her answer gently: "Thank you, Sister; you're right. Give me that cross of moss the workers sent, and I'll put it out in front." From that day forward Sister X regarded her as a saint, as she afterwards admitted.

She seemed to have a particular affection for those nuns who made her suffer, and she showed a preference for their company. Her eldest sister, Sister Marie of the Sacred Heart, often expressed her surprise at this, and was sometimes hurt by it. "I was a mother to her," she once complained, "and yet you'd think she loved that sister whom I can't stand better than she does me." At recreation she never went out of her way to meet her own three sisters. She chatted with any nun, no matter who she was, and especially with anyone she felt was lonely or left out. Though naturally very sensitive and affectionate, she was very reserved in external signs of affection and her manner imposed a certain respect. During her last illness someone was trying to kill the flies that were pestering her, when Sister Thérèse made this rather surprising remark: "They are the only enemies I have, and since God has told us to love our enemies I am glad they give me this opportunity to do so. That is why I always spare them."

Prudence

Before she entered Carmel she never felt the need to consult anyone about her spiritual life, except her sisters. These had been a mother to her and knew her inside out. It was to them that she turned when she suffered from scruples, and when

Marie told her that her fears were unfounded, she obeyed her and found peace. The question of her becoming a nun was so simple that she never even dreamt of looking on it as a problem that needed the enlightenment of a director. She had known what she wanted since she was ten; the only difficulty was how to obtain admission; it was on how to go about this that she came to consult me in the parlour.

At this time of her life (13-15 years of age) she saw clearly what God was asking of her. Beyond determining how often she could go to holy communion, she had nothing of consequence to discuss with her confessor. On this point she writes: "Jesus was giving himself to me in holy communion more often than I had dared hope. I had made it a rule to go to communion as often as the confessor allowed me to; I let him decide the frequency, and never asked for anything myself. I was not as daring then as I am now. If I had been, I would certainly have acted differently because I think that when one feels a desire to receive God, one ought to tell the confessor about it. . . . I took very little time over my confessions, and never said a word about my spiritual life. The way I was travelling was so straight and bright that I needed no other guide but Jesus. . . . I looked on directors as mirrors that reflected Jesus faithfully to souls. And I took the attitude that in my own case God was not using any intermediary; he dealt directly with me."[15]

After her entry into Carmel, Thérèse felt the need to submit the spiritual way to which she felt drawn to the opinion of an enlightened spiritual director. Hers was a combination of desire for the peaks of sanctity and a powerful attraction towards a childlike trust in and complete surrender to our Lord's kindness and love. It was God's will that she should find great difficulty in making her sentiments understood, and it was years before she found the director she was looking for. One director had just come to understand her when he had to leave for Canada, from where he wrote her a few lines once a year. Another was so astonished at the daring of her aspirations to an eminent degree of holiness that he told her it was sheer pride on her part to want to equal and even to surpass St Teresa. A third finally assured her in 1891 that she was not offending God, and that she could follow her way of trust and surrender with complete confidence.

In dealing with novices, it is remarkable that she never tried to win their affection by concessions that human prudence might suggest. All that mattered to her was their spiritual perfection, and she sought this even at the expense of popularity. Time and again I witnessed the way she faithfully followed her conscience in what concerned them.

About 1895 or 1896 she agreed, by order of the prioress, to enter into a kind of spiritual fraternity with two missionaries: Fr Bellière of the White Fathers, and Fr Roulland, a missionary in Sut-Chuen. She offered her prayers and sacrifices for both of them and exchanged several letters on spiritual matters with each of them. But during her last illness she made the following remarks and recommendations to me on this subject: "Later on, a great many young priests will come to know that I was given to two missionaries as a spiritual sister, and they will want the same favour. This could be dangerous. We can be useful to the Church only by prayer and sacrifice. Such correspondence ought to be a rare occurrence, and should not be allowed at all to some nuns, for they would become too engrossed in it. They would think they were working wonders, whereas in reality they would only be doing harm to their own souls, and might easily become a prey to the subtle snares of the devil. Mother, what I'm telling you is important; don't forget it later on."

Justice

When she was sacristan, she carried out her duties with great devotion, especially when she touched the sacred vessels or prepared the altar linen and vestments. This work acted as a spur to her fervour; she used to recall the words of the Bible: "Be holy, you who touch the vessels of the Lord." If she found the tiniest particle on the corporal, or in the ciborium, she was delighted. Once, when she found a fairly large particle, she ran off to the laundry, where the rest of the community was at the time, and made a sign to several nuns to come with her. She was the first herself to kneel down and adore the Lord; then she put the corporal back in the burse and had us all kiss it. Her emotion on that occasion was indescribable.

Another time, the priest dropped a host when he was distributing holy communion. Sister Thérèse stretched out the end of her scapular to prevent it from falling to the floor. Afterwards she joyfully announced that she had carried the Child Jesus in her arms, as the Blessed Virgin had.

When she was ill, someone brought her the chalice of a young priest who had just celebrated his first Mass. She looked into it and said: "My face is reflected in the bottom of this chalice where the blood of Christ has descended and will descend so many times more. I used to like looking into chalices like that when I was sacristan." She also had a very fervent and filial devotion to our Lady.

Because of her spirit of faith she had a religious respect for anyone in lawful authority. While she was in Carmel it so happened that a certain nun was elected prioress, notwithstanding notable defects which ought, perhaps, to have excluded her from this office. I know that the Servant of God was particularly apprehensive about this election. But once it was over, she not only gave this prioress the normal obedience, she even went out of her way to show her a filial and affectionate respect. And she tried to comfort her when the prioress was upset because the election had been so closely contested. She also used her influence with the novices whom she knew to be opposed to this election to try and instil into them a religious respect for their prioress.

Since I was no longer prioress, I accepted the frequent confidences of Sister X out of compassion for her. I asked Sister Thérèse what she thought of this, and without hesitation she replied: "Mother, if I were in your place I would refuse to listen to these outpourings. You are no longer prioress, and it is an illusion to think that one can do any good outside of obedience. Not only are you unable to help this poor soul by listening to her; you could harm her, and risk offending God yourself."

About 1894 there appeared in France a series of self-styled revelations of the secrets of Freemasonry, published by a certain Dr Bataille (Léon Taxil) and a woman called Diana Vaughan. These accounts gripped the imagination of the French public for a while. Later, they were found to be false. The Servant of God took a certain interest in them at first, but long before there was any official denial of them she told us that they were not to be believed. Her only reason for rejecting them was the fact that Diana Vaughan once spoke against episcopal authority. "That kind of thing cannot come from God," she said.

She had a horror of lies, even when they were spoken in jest. Indeed, she was uprightness personified. She used to correct the novices even for playful, good-humoured statements which no one believed, and she never indulged in them herself. She was so pleasant and cheerful that anyone who knew her could not help liking her. She was the life and soul of our recreations, and one got the feeling that her cheerfulness sprang from an inner joy. She said to me: "I am always cheerful and happy even when I am suffering. I prefer Bl. Théophane Vénard to St Aloysius Gonzaga, because I've read that the latter was sad even at recreation, whereas Théophane was always cheerful."

Fortitude

On this subject Mother Agnes was asked whether the Servant of God was ever sad, and, if so, how she behaved then.

She certainly was not lacking in causes for distress. I shall speak first of all about the physical sufferings which she bore with such extraordinary courage and strength. As a child she got bronchitis every winter, which brought with it high fever and congestion. But she continued uncomplainingly with her daily chores as long as she was able to, and resumed them as soon as she began to get better.

Her really heroic courage displayed itself in her last illness. She never excused herself from any of her tasks, even from those that must have been very hard on her, like sweeping out dust-filled rooms and laundry work, until on the night between Holy Thursday and Good Friday, 1896, a violent haemorrhage revealed the seriousness and true nature of her illness. That night, when she felt herself vomit blood for the first time, she did not light her lamp to see what was happening, just to mortify her curiosity. The following morning she found her handkerchief soaked with blood, and went along to the prioress. "Mother," she said, "look what has happened to me. Please don't attach any importance to it; it's nothing. I have no pain, so let me continue to attend the Holy Week ceremonies like everybody else." She did in fact attend all the Good Friday functions and performed all the mortifications customary in Carmel on that day. And she so convinced everybody that

there was nothing seriously wrong with her that she was allowed
to share in all the practices and work of the community for a
full year after that.

One of the greatest trials that she and ourselves ever had to
suffer was the particularly distressing and humiliating infirmity
that afflicted our father during the last five years of his life.
A paralysis that at first affected only some parts of his body
eventually reached his brain, and he had to be treated in a
mental home. Rather tactless people were wont to remark, even
in Sister Thérèse's presence, that this had been brought on by
the entry of his daughters into Carmel, especially that of his
youngest daughter whom he loved so much. Well-intentioned
people spoke to us about it in the parlour, without any consideration for our feelings. Even in the community, people
would often talk at recreation about this subject which was so
painful for us. But while Marie and I were often overcome by
our distress, the Servant of God, who unquestionably felt it very
keenly, bore this trial very calmly in a great spirit of faith. There
is a picture on which she listed all the favours God had done
her. Among them is 12 February, 1889 — the day our father was
admitted to the institution where he was cared for.

The sentiments she expressed at the time are perfectly
summed up in her autobiography: "There are no words to
express the anguish we suffered. No doubt, one day when we
are all in heaven, we will enjoy speaking of the *glorious* trials
we have been through. Are we not already glad to have suffered
them? Yes, I liked those three years of papa's martyrdom: they
were the most beneficial years of our lives, and I would not
exchange them for all the ecstasies and revelations enjoyed by
the saints. My heart overflows with gratitude when I think of
this priceless *treasure;* it must have caused even the angels of
the heavenly court a certain amount of holy envy. My desire
for suffering had been satisfied, but my attraction to it was in
no way diminished."[16]

She was very generous in practising the mortifications laid
down in the Rule. She would have liked to increase them, in
fact, and often asked to be allowed to do so, but she was refused
because of her delicate health. To make up for that, she availed
of every opportunity to suffer that came her way, but she did it
so skilfully that no one noticed it. It was only towards the end

of her life that we found out that, no doubt due to the state of her health, she had suffered a great deal from the cold. Yet she was never seen rubbing her hands in winter, or showing her discomfort in any other way. She never remarked, for instance, on how cold or warm the weather was. And it was the same with a thousand other little ways she found of suffering.

Temperance

Talking to me in 1897 about her childhood memories, she said: "Had God himself and the Blessed Virgin not gone to feasts, I couldn't see the point of inviting friends to such a thing. To invite them in for a chat, or to hear them tell of their travels, or to talk about science, etc., yes; but I used to think eating was something you ought to go aside to do, or at least stay at home: I found it embarrassing."

In Carmel, she always said that going to the refectory was like going to a place of punishment. Since she never complained, people thought she did not have the same likes and dislikes as the rest of us, and they served her food that had been left over or rejected at a previous meal. She took it all without protest. During the last illness she was unexpectedly assailed by a real temptation to gluttony. All sorts of exotic dishes flashed through her imagination, and she was obsessed with a desire for them. She said to me with a sigh: "To think that all my life eating has been a penance for me, and look at me now! I feel like I'm dying of hunger. How awful it must be to die of hunger! I have become immersed in matter. O God, come and take me away soon!"

By temperament she was a very sensitive person. As a child, and even later, it was extraordinarily easy to make her cry. That was the only fault I ever noticed in her. On 25 December, 1886, she said she would have to control this excessive sensitiveness for God's sake, and she did in fact achieve perfect self-control from that day on. In her autobiography she refers to that day as her "conversion". In Carmel she was just as sensitive as others, and found people who interrupted her in the middle of her work just as annoying. Yet, not only did she receive them politely, she seemed to put herself in the way of those who were most likely to disturb her.

Virtues connected with the vows

She was extraordinarily obedient. She took the least commands literally, and one had to be careful not to put her under undue strain. She said obedience was an infallible compass, and that anyone who ignored authority would stray far from the paths of grace. Out of obedience to Mother Prioress, she several times refrained from confiding her thoughts and feelings to me, though the habits of childhood made her feel the need to do so, and she would have found great comfort in this outlet as she had formerly done. One day I asked her what she would have done if it had been one of her three sisters who was ill instead of herself. "Would you have come to the infirmary during recreation?" I asked. "I would have gone straight to recreation without even asking how she was," she replied, "but I would have done so only so that no one would notice the sacrifice I was making."

She was very attentive to the practice of poverty. The ordinary poverty of Carmel was not enough for her; she was glad to do without the things we have in Carmel, even things she needed. If, for instance, someone forgot to serve her in the refectory, she was quite content and would not draw attention to the fact. "I am like the real poor," she would say; "it's not worth making a vow of poverty if you don't have to suffer for it." Sometimes a sister might steal an idea or a saying of hers. She found this quite natural, and said that because of her poverty she had no claim to these any more than she had to anything else.

She had a very correct notion of chastity: no scruples, but no illusions either. I found the advice she gave the novices in this matter very enlightened, and it was certainly not from her experience of evil that she got her light. She told me that, without trying to, she had learned everything herself from watching the flowers and the birds. "It's not knowing things that's wrong," she added. "God has made everything good. Marriage is a very fine thing for those whom God has called to it; the only thing that can disfigure or dirty it is sin."

She was deliberately very faithful to the practice of this virtue, but her natural simplicity helped too. I do not think she ever had any serious struggle in this matter. There were times, however, when her delicacy and vigilance showed themselves: 1. Before she went to Rome she was aware of the dangers she could encounter, and she recommended her innocence to the special protection of Our Lady of Victories in Paris. 2. She never permitted her novices any signs of affection that could be mixed with the slightest trace of sensuality. 3. She was just as reserved and modest when she was alone, because, as she put it, she was in the presence of angels.

Humility

When she was a child we took great care to train her in humility, and carefully avoided praising her. At school she was sometimes congratulated on her success at studies. She says herself that she knew then that her heart would not be indifferent to praise, and she thanked God that when she returned home, or even more so if she went to her uncle's, she would find something to counter-balance the praise she received elsewhere. She came to the convent parlour one day when she was ten years old, and one of the nuns rather thoughtlessly admired the pretty little girl aloud to other people in the room. The Servant of God was hurt and a little shocked at this, and as she was already thinking of becoming a Carmelite, she said: "If I enter Carmel it will not be to hear myself praised. If I leave the world, it will be for Jesus alone."

She often told me that when she entered Carmel, our Lord showed her that true wisdom consisted in desiring to be ignored. In the midst of the humiliations which our father's illness caused us, she told me that her desires had been fulfilled, because suffering and contempt had become her lot. The day of her profession she carried a note next to her heart, saying: "May nobody take any notice of me; may I be trodden underfoot like a grain of sand." During her 1892 retreat (she was then nineteen) she wrote me a note saying: "How good it is to be hidden away and unknown even to people who are living with us! I have never wanted fame; contempt attracted me, but I found that even that brought me too much notice, and I longed to be forgotten." The further she advanced in perfection, the humbler she became. There were still some little involuntary faults that she could not overcome, but she did not let this discourage her: "I am resigned to being always imperfect." she said, "and I even find happiness in it. I keep an eye on myself to see if I can discover any new imperfections."

On 28 May, 1897, four months before her death, she was running a very high temperature. While I was with her, some-one came and asked her to help in a very delicate piece of paint-ing. Just for an instant a very slight blush betrayed her effort to keep her patience. That evening she sent me a little note humbly admitting her weakness. Here are some phrases from it: "This evening I showed you my *virtue,* my *treasures of patience!* I who am so good at preaching to others! I am glad you noticed my imperfection. It does me good to have been naughty, you know. . . . I much prefer to have been imperfect than to have been a model of gentleness with the support of grace. It does me so much good to see that Jesus is always so gentle and tender towards me."[17]

During the worst period of her last illness a lay-sister brought her some broth. She gently refused it, pleading that it would make her vomit. I do not remember whether or not she eventually drank it, but she did humbly ask the sister's pardon. The latter was disedified by her refusal, however, and went off and told another sister: "Sister Thérèse is no saint; she is not even a good religious." This remark came back to the Servant of God, and she felt such a holy delight that she could not refrain from telling a sister who understood her about it. That sister later said to me: "This is the most edifying memory I have of Sister Thérèse."

There were plenty of occasions during her last illness when she might well have been annoyed or impatient. But she hardly ever showed the slightest feeling. When she did, she admitted her weakness, and asked the person concerned to forgive her and pray for her. Later on she said to me: "The fact that people find me imperfect brings me real joy, and what brings me even more joy is to realise this myself and to feel the need for God's mercy at the moment of dying."

Her humility did not prevent her from acknowledging God's gifts. When she was asked what she thought of the graces she had received, she said simply: "I think God's Spirit breathes where he wills." (Cf. *Jn 3:8.*) As she progressed towards more perfect humility, the simplicity with which she acknowledged God's gifts became greater, until it became quite daring. But no matter how precious these gifts were, one felt that when she spoke about them, she did so in utter simplicity and without a trace of pride.

I could say lots more about her humility, and indeed about the other virtues I saw in her, but then I would never finish.

22. Generally speaking, the Servant of God led a very simple life; otherwise she could not be a model for "ordinary people"[18] which, as she said herself, was "her way". Some isolated facts could be pointed out here, however, which had all the appearance of being extraordinary favours.

When she was six or seven years old she had a vision, which she describes in her autobiography.[19] Father was away, and was not due back for several days. About 2.30 p.m. Thérèse was looking out of the window overlooking the garden. Suddenly, she saw a man walking along a well-lighted path about twenty yards away. In build and appearance he resembled father, but he walked as if bent by the weight of years, and had a veil of some nondescript colour over his head. She followed his progress silently for a few moments, and then called out: "Papa, Papa!" Marie and I ran in immediately from the next room, and Thérèse told us about the apparition, which by then had disappeared. The garden was encircled by a wall, and no one could get into it. We went down and searched it, but could find no trace of human presence. We told our little sister to forget it and not even to talk about it. But she remained convinced both of the reality of the vision and of the fact that it had a definite meaning which would be revealed to her later—that it was a sign of some future trial or misfortune. When father suffered that humiliating cerebral paralysis during the last five years of his life, the illness I've already spoken of, she realised that it was these sad events that were presaged by that childhood vision.

Asked if the Servant of God understood the vision only when she knew of her father's illness, Mother Agnes answered:

It was then that she realised its *precise* meaning. But for a long time previously, from the time of the vision itself in fact, she was absolutely convinced that the vision foreboded some painful event.

The judge asked if the Servant of God had at any time suffered from an over-lively imagination, or showed some neurotic symptoms.

Not at all; she was a child who weighed things up very calmly, and she was not a bit imaginative. When she was about ten and a half she had a rather strange illness (I shall speak about that in a moment, but my sisters know more about it because they were at home at the time). But the vision which I have just related happened three years prior to that, and anyway the said illness was a passing thing, and left no trace.

At the age of ten and a half she was struck down by a strange illness, which my sisters will be able to describe in greater detail. I was already in Carmel and knew only what I was told in the parlour. It consisted of attacks of terror, with horrible visions and an urge to throw herself head-first off the bed. She said afterwards that she never lost the use of her reason for one moment, and that when she seemed to be unconscious she actually heard and understood everything that was being said around her. She was always convinced, too, that the devil had a lot to do with these phenomena. Whatever about that, the illness disappeared suddenly on 10 May, 1883, and never troubled her again.

The circumstances attending this sudden end were as follows: during a novena we were making to Our Lady of Victories, she had a more violent attack than usual. Those of my sisters who were present started to pray to the Blessed Virgin before a statue in the room. In spite of the attack, Thérèse joined them in invoking Mary's help. She told me that she suddenly saw the statue come to life, and that the Blessed Virgin moved towards her, smiling. From that moment there was no further trace of her illness.

During her last illness I placed this same statue near her in the infirmary. She looked at it and was obviously pleased to see it. I was by her bed at the time, with Sister Marie of the Sacred Heart. "She has never looked so beautiful," she said, "but today it is only the statue; the other time, you know well it was not the statue."

Several times during her life she confided to me that she had sometimes felt extraordinary impulses of love. Before she entered Carmel she several times experienced what she called "transports of love", without any effort on her part to bring them about. She just felt in her heart certain impulses till then unknown to her. She told me how on these occasions she would not know what to say to Jesus to express her love and the desire she had to see him loved and glorified everywhere. So she used to tell God that "to please him she would be willing even to be plunged into hell, if that would make someone in that blasphemous place love him". In this connection, she writes in her autobiography: "I knew well that that could not give him glory, because all he wants is our happiness; but when you love, you feel the need to say all sorts of silly things."

She also told me that while she was still a novice she once spent nearly a week feeling as if she was separated from her body. "I was no longer on earth; I did my work in the refectory as if someone had lent me a body. I just cannot express it. It was as if a veil had been thrown up between me and everything around me."

Asked if such states were different from a period of particularly deep recollection, she said:

They certainly were. She was always very recollected, and if it had been only that, she would not have spoken to me about it as something special. When I asked her if in the course of her religious life she had experienced extraordinary manifestations of grace, she said: "In the garden during night silence, I have often felt so deeply recollected and my heart so united with God that I used to make very intense, yet effortless, acts of love; I think these graces must have been what St Teresa calls 'flights of the spirit'."

In 1895, when I was prioress, she spoke to me about a grace she called "a wound of love". No doubt to test her, God permitted that I should pay no attention to this at the time. I even appeared not to believe her, and I admit that I did not. But when I thought about what she had said, I wondered how I could have doubted her statement. Still, I did not say a word to her until her last illness. I then wanted her to repeat what she had said in 1895 about this wound of love. She looked at me with a sweet smile and said: "I told you about it the day it happened, and you hardly even listened to me." I told her I was sorry, and then she went on: "You didn't hurt me; I just said to myself that God permitted that for my greater good. What happened was this. It was a few days after my consecration to Merciful Love. I was just beginning to make the Stations of the Cross in choir when I felt myself suddenly wounded by a flash of fire so intense that I thought I would die. I don't know how to describe this experience; there is no comparison which could give an adequate idea of the intensity of this heavenly flame. Another second, and I would surely have died. Look, Mother, it's something that the saints have often experienced. You know what it is; you've read it in their lives. In my whole life I experienced it only just that once, and then aridity returned immediately to take possession of my soul. You might say, I have spent all my religious life in that aridity. Only very rarely have I been consoled, nor have I ever wanted to be. On the other hand, I am very proud of the fact that God was not annoyed with me. Extraordinary graces have never tempted me; I prefer to say to God over and over again:

'I have no desire
to see him here below'."

Towards the end of her life (during the last three months), when my two sisters and I were at her bedside, she revealed to us with great simplicity the strange presentiment she had about what would happen in her own regard after she died. She gave us to understand that people would be looking for relics of her, and that she would have a spiritual mission to accomplish propagating her "ordinary way of trust and surrender". She specifically urged us to keep even her nail clippings carefully. During the last weeks of her life we brought her roses, so that she could pluck the petals and put them on her crucifix. If any fell on the floor, she would say: "Don't lose those, sisters; you will give pleasure to people yet with those roses."

She also said: "The manuscript (her autobiography) must be published without delay after my death. If you delay, the devil will set all sorts of traps to stop its publication, important though it is."

"So you think it is by means of the manuscript that you are going to benefit people?" I said.

"Yes, it is one of the means which God will use to make me heard. It will benefit all kinds of people, except those who travel by extraordinary ways."

"But what if Mother Prioress throws it in the fire?" I insisted.

"That's all right. It won't hurt me in the least, or make me doubt my mission in the slightest. I would merely think that God was going to satisfy my desires in some other way."

Asked if she knew whether the Servant of God had foreseen that the manuscript would be published, when she was writing it, Mother Agnes replied:

Certainly not when she was writing the first part of it; she wrote that under orders from me, when I was prioress. Nor did she have it in mind when she wrote the second part, which is addressed to her sister, Marie of the Sacred Heart. She did foresee the publication of chapters 9, 10 and the first pages of chapter 11, addressed to Mother Gonzague, but she certainly did not make any special effort because of that; she wrote in all simplicity, just as things came into her head.

Some days before her death, my sisters and I were busily taking care of her, when she suddenly said: "You are aware of course that you are nursing a little saint." And then, after a moment's silence: "Anyway, you're saints yourselves too."

Asked if the Servant of God raved or anything like that during her last illness, she answered:

She never lost her self-possession for one instant; in fact, the nearer her death approached, the calmer she became.

23. I noticed that even as a child she was regarded as exceptional. I was aware that this was not merely on account of her good looks, but rather because of something extremely pure and heavenly in her expression. I heard this remarked on several times. Victoire Pasquier, our maid, whom I met again in the parlour a few months ago, told me on that occasion: "It is true that Miss Thérèse was out of the ordinary; I was very fond of all of you, but Thérèse had something that none of the rest of you had. There was something angelic about her that struck me particularly." A venerable old lady who used to look after the Lady Chapel in St Peter's parish church in Lisieux and took charge of the children during processions said of her: "That little Thérèse is a real angel; I'll be surprised if she lives very long. But if she does, you'll see that she will be spoken of afterwards, because she'll be a saint."

In Carmel all the nuns, except one or two perhaps, were astonished and edified at how virtuous she was from the very first days of her novitiate. As the years went by, this favourable impression grew. Mother Marie de Gonzague, who was often very severe on her, once told the novice-mistress, by way of explaining her attitude: "Treating her like a child or being

C

afraid to humiliate her at every turn is no way to handle a person of this calibre." Before her profession Mother Prioress and the other sisters used to introduce her to their relatives when they came to visit them in the parlour, because they knew that the community's good name benefited as a result. Indeed, Mother Prioress herself was often praised as a result. The retreat masters and confessors who came to the convent spoke of her to Mother Prioress in terms that were worthy of an angel. The sacristan, who knew her from hearing her through the sacristy turn, esteemed her very highly. He said she was different from the other good sisters, and that when he came inside the enclosure to do some job he recognised her from the modesty of her bearing, even though she had her veil down.

Some nuns, however, saw her differently. One said it was not very difficult to be a saint when you had everything you wanted, like she had: she was with her family and held in high esteem. I feel obliged to point out that this nun, though a long time professed, was not possessed of very sound judgment. She eventually left the convent, and is now back in the world. During the Servant of God's illness, another said: "I wonder what Mother Prioress will find to say about Sister Thérèse of the Child Jesus. What can one say about a person who has always been pampered, and who has not had to acquire virtue at the cost of struggles and suffering like the rest of us? She is gentle and kind, of course, but she's that way by nature." I learned these words from Sister Thérèse herself; she overheard them. On the other hand, it must be noted that the lay-sister who said that (she is dead now) also said that Sister Thérèse was a saint.

24. Sister Thérèse of the Child Jesus died in the infirmary of the Lisieux convent on Thursday, 30 September, 1897, about seven o'clock in the evening, of pulmonary tuberculosis. About 1894 she had begun to suffer from little tumours in the throat. These were cauterised, and she continued her ordinary Carmelite life unchanged. Holy Thursday night, 1896, the haemorrhage described earlier took place, and the following day she had another. Still, to the very end of Lent 1897 she continued to attend all the exercises and practise all the penances that are customary in Carmel. She went on a meat diet only for a week or so after a particularly bad cough. At the end of Lent 1897 her condition became much worse: her temperature remained

Servant of God. I have no direct knowledge of her life, therefore, but I can speak from my own experience about her reputation for holiness and the favours obtained through her intercession after her death, especially where Great Britain and the
United States are concerned. I have collected a lot of information on this subject from what I have seen with my own eyes,
from correspondence, and from conversations.

9. I have a very great devotion to the Servant of God. It is
based on the virtues she displayed during her life, and on her
power of intercession, which I have experienced myself. I desire
with all my heart to see her Cause succeed, for the glory of God
and the salvation of souls by means of the way to holiness that
she teaches in her writings — what she calls her "little way of
trust". I have tried to make the Servant of God known, both by
distributing little pictures of her, and by helping her autobiography to reach a wider circle of readers, especially in Great
Britain, the Colonies, and the United States.

23. I have often had contact, both by letter and in conversation, with those nuns of the Lisieux Carmel who knew Sister
Thérèse. These were chiefly: Rev. Mother Marie de Gonzague,
the prioress; the Servant of God's own three sisters — Sisters Agnes
of Jesus, Marie of the Sacred Heart, and Genevieve of St Teresa;
and her cousin, Sister Marie of the Eucharist. On the occasion of
my "pilgrimages" they have several times told me what they
thought of the Servant of God's holy life. They stressed particularly her purity,[1] her untiring patience in the face of suffering,
her trust in God, and her devotion to frequent communion.

*Here the judge interrupted Fr Taylor to ask him if this
high opinion of Sister Thérèse's sanctity was shared equally by
all the above-named nuns, and especially whether Mother Marie
de Gonzague, who was not related to the Servant of God, concurred in this opinion, and spoke of her in the same way her
sisters did.*

I talked with Mother Gonzague in 1903, and I remember
thinking at the time how different she was from the Servant
of God's sisters. She was colder, less enthusiastic; her language
was entirely devoid of exclamations, and she seemed less femi-
nine than they were. I knew from the *Story of a Soul* that she
had been severe on the Servant of God during her novitiate. But,
in spite of that, her judgment about Sister Thérèse's virtue and

character was basically the same: she regarded the Servant of God as quite extraordinary in the matter of holiness.

26. Every time I come to Lisieux I make a pilgrimage to her grave, to ask favours for myself and a great many other people, and to thank her for favours already received. Except for the first time, I have always been accompanied on these occasions by many priests and religious who shared my devotion. The last time I was there I stayed about half an hour, during which time I noticed two priests, as well as many other people coming and going all the time. I was told for a fact by people in Lisieux that these pilgrimages to the grave are becoming more numerous daily. Many priests have been known to come, including several members of the Paris Foreign Missions Society.

27. In my own country the *Histoire d'une âme* was translated into English in 1901. The publication of this book marked the beginning of the Servant of God's reputation for sanctity in English-speaking countries, even in the United States. At first it spread slowly, perhaps because the book was expensive. But since 30 October, 1908, when a miracle took place at the Good Shepherd convent in London, which I took care to publicise, devotion to the Servant of God has visibly increased, especially in Scotland. From April, 1909, onwards the *Glasgow Observer*, a Catholic weekly, has been publishing acknowledgments of favours received. This list has appeared every week since then, but it eventually grew so long that the editor had to limit the amount of space allotted to it. At the moment, the number of inserts has dropped somewhat, but it has never ceased. During the last three months (April-July, 1910) I have counted 87 favours acknowledged in this way.

Among priests and religious the Servant of God's reputation for holiness is based chiefly on the heroism of her virtues, which they have come to appreciate by reading the *Story of a Soul*, but among the laity her reputation rests mainly on the wonders she works. People do not pray to her just for temporal favours, however; many do so to obtain the conversion of Protestants or fallen-away Catholics.

Asked whether this knowledge had been gleaned from the above-mentioned weekly, he answered:

I know it chiefly from reports I receive myself: I have a

very large correspondence on the subject, especially with several convents in Glasgow, but also with many more throughout England, Ireland and the United States — about twenty in all. The Little Sisters of the Poor are especially remarkable for their devotion to and faith in "Little Sister Thérèse", as they call her: they have recourse to her in every problem or difficulty that arises. I receive many letters every day from the above-mentioned countries, telling me of favours received, asking for relics or souvenirs, and expressing their devotion to the Servant of God in many different ways. Many of the letters are from superiors of religious houses.

28. I remember two incidents that are relevant to this question. The first concerns the Carmel of Blackrock in Dublin. When I spoke to the prioress of this convent about Sister Thérèse's life, she laughed heartily, and told me we might just as well canonise all the nuns in her convent. This was back about 1904, certainly prior to the great movement of devotion that developed later. That prioress is dead now, but I know for a fact that she changed her opinion before she died. I visit this Carmel every year, and the present prioress, who was sub-prioress about 1904, told me about this change herself. She said it was brought about by all the favours being obtained for people by the Servant of God.

The second occasion on which I heard some unfavourable remarks was on a visit to the Lourdes Carmel. I was talking to an Irish nun there a few days ago — I forget her name now, but she is the only Irish nun there. She told me that after reading the *Story of a Soul* she still had some misgivings. The chief reason for this was that when this nun was novice-mistress, she had a Spanish novice, who used to speak and write beautifully about the most sublime things. She was so impressive that the novice-mistress began to feel unworthy and incapable of directing her. The novice afterwards lost her fervour, and left the convent, so that this Irish Carmelite has been a bit suspicious of poetic nuns ever since.

When the tribunal re-convened after an adjournment, Fr Taylor had remembered a third case of this kind:

I had sent a petition to his Grace, Archbishop Bourne of Westminster, asking if he would grant an indulgence for reading the *Story of a Soul*, as several Portuguese bishops had done.

The priest who acted as my intermediary at first promised me a favourable reply, but when his Grace showed no signs of granting the request, I enquired from my friend the reason for the delay. He told me the archbishop had heard it said that this affair of Sister Thérèse was perhaps being rushed a little too much. He had also heard that the part played in it by members of her family would compromise her chances of success in Rome. Consequently, the archbishop deemed it prudent to wait a while.

Asked if he knew whether the archbishop's words "the part played by members of the family" was a reference to her sisters or to other relatives of hers, Fr Taylor replied:

I could not be sure about that, but my impression is that he was referring chiefly to the Servant of God's sisters.

The judge then asked him if he knew how the archbishop now felt about the Servant of God's reputation for holiness.

I was talking to his Grace quite recently (8 August), and when I brought this matter up with him, he admitted to a sincere respect for what he called "this extraordinary soul", and promised he would write the preface to the new edition of *Story of a Soul*, when he had read the manuscript.

The promoter of the Cause then asked him what he thought himself about this alleged pressure by the Lisieux Carmel in propagating her reputation for holiness.

I have never known the Servant of God, nor am I related to her. Yet I take a great interest in her Cause, and work hard to spread the knowledge of her life, virtues, and powerful intercession. So, it should not be so surprising to see her Carmelite sisters doing their best as well.

Asked whether this zeal of his was not perhaps the result of a certain "enthusiasm", and possibly guilty of some exaggeration, he answered:

My enthusiasm has lasted eight years; it is based chiefly on the evidence I have of numerous favours obtained through the Servant of God's intercession, and on my own convictions about her virtue as a result of reading and studying her life. During these eight years the Lisieux nuns have never tried to stimulate my activity. Three or four years ago I was a bit shocked when they started producing so many pictures and souvenirs, but I have since seen the tremendous demand there is for these things and the good that comes of making use of them, so I no longer feel that way about them. But whatever might be said about such active publicity, I think that in all of it there is not a single statement about the Servant of God's virtues or her power of intercession that is not faithfully borne out by the facts. Nothing is exaggerated; if anything, we have understated her case.

29. The favours, both spiritual and temporal, that have been obtained through Sister Thérèse in Great Britain are innumerable. . . The *Glasgow Observer* has published 550 since 24 April, 1909. I, too, have a large file of them from my own correspondence, and I shall now quote from two or three of these letters by way of example. The Mother Provincial of the Little Sisters of the Poor in Scotland and Ireland wrote: "I should like to testify to the numerous graces and favours granted to myself and to others. I try to make her powerful intercession known to everybody that I can do some good for. She has obtained the conversion of many old men (in our Homes) who had not fulfilled their religious duties for many years. But I find it impossible to enumerate all the marvellous graces of every sort obtained through her intercession."

Another person wrote to say that at the home run by the Little Sisters of the Poor they gave an old man a picture of Sister Thérèse, in an effort to reconcile him to dying. Sister Thérèse appeared to him in a dream, in which he saw himself all laid out and ready for burial, and, taking him by the hand, she assured him that the moment of death had not yet come. From that time onwards, he became very fervent and displayed an especially touching devotion to our Lady. "Don't you see that beautiful lady?" he said to the sister in charge the night before he died; and he died like a saint.

From another letter I quote this: "A poor worker was stricken by religious mania, and several doctors declared the case very difficult. After he had been ill for a year, and there were no signs of improvement, a novena was made to Sister Thérèse of the Child Jesus. At the end of the novena there was a marked improvement, and he has since been completely cured."

30. I would like to add a few details to complete and clarify my answer to question 27. I have been asked to specify the

religious houses where I knew that Sister Thérèse had a reputation for holiness. Here is a more precise list:

Houses of male religious

First of all the Major Seminary in Glasgow, especially the rector and his staff. Then the Redemptorist scholasticate in Perth (Scotland) and its rector. I also have it on reliable authority that Sister Thérèse is much loved in the Paris Foreign Missions Society, and by the Mill Hill Missionaries of London, founded by Cardinal Vaughan. The abbot of the Benedictine abbey of Ampleforth, near York, is also a devoted client of hers; in fact, two Benedictine monks and a postulant of theirs once came to Lisieux on pilgrimage with me. My brother, who is a member of the community at the Vincentian novitiate in England, informs me that the devotion has been established there too; many of the novices spread the devotion, and report that she is heartily loved in many convents and families.

Convents

The Mother Provincial of the Irish province of the Little Sisters of the Poor (which includes Scotland and part of England) has an extraordinary devotion to her. I can vouch personally for four of their twelve convents, but Thérèse has a wide circle of devotees among these simple and active sisters. Then there are the Sisters of Mercy in Glasgow: these have great devotion to her; the novena that led to the cure of Mrs Dorans from cancer was started by one of them. Strangely enough, the Reverend Mother would not allow the novices to read Sister Thérèse's life at first. But later she was in serious difficulties, and promised Thérèse that if she came to her aid she would hang a picture of her in the community room. A few days later her difficulties were all solved, and she kept her promise; she also gave permission to read the Story of a Soul. Devotees are also to be found among the Good Shepherd Sisters in Glasgow, Liverpool and London. She is loved, too, in the Scottish Carmel and in that of Blackrock in Dublin. Then there are the Franciscan convents, and that of Notre Dame, where devotion has increased since Mrs Dorans was cured. I know from my correspondence with the Loreto mother house in Dublin that Thérèse is loved and prayed to there. The same is true of the mother house of the Institute of the Blessed Virgin Mary at York. In the United States, she has friends at the novitiate of the Sisters of Charity in Emmetsburg, and at the Philadelphia Carmel. A letter from this Carmel speaks of "devotion to Sister Thérèse among rich and poor, priests and bishops". Her friends in the Carmels of Boston and San Francisco bring the list to an end.

3 Marie of the Sacred Heart, o.c.d.

Marie Martin, Thérèse's eldest sister, was born at Alençon on 22 February, 1860. She was a boarder at the Visitation convent at Le Mans from 1868 to 1875, and godmother at the baptism of the future saint on 4 January, 1873. From 15 November, 1877, she lived with her father at Lisieux, and after Pauline's entry into Carmel (1882) it was she who looked after Thérèse, especially during her mysterious illness.

She made a vow of chastity on 25 March, 1885, and entered the Lisieux Carmel on the following 15 October. She was clothed in the habit on 19 March, 1886, and made her profession on 22 May, 1888. Sister Thérèse had her as "angel" during her novitiate. She held the office of bursar in the community from 1894 to 1933. Already before her sister's canonisation she contracted rheumatoid arthritis, which grew steadily worse until she was at last confined to her bed or invalid chair. She died on 19 January, 1940.

Few perceived God's designs on Thérèse as clearly as Marie did. We are all greatly indebted to her because it was she who at the end of 1894 insisted that Mother Agnes order Thérèse to write the memories of her childhood (Manuscript A), and it was at her request that, in September 1896, Thérèse wrote her the magnificent letter which constitutes Manuscript B of her autobiography. Later, she committed all three manuscripts to memory.

It was she, too, who in May, 1897, asked Thérèse to put her thoughts on the Blessed Virgin in writing. This was the origin of the poem entitled "Why I Love You, Mary", of which the saint wrote shortly before her death: "My little song expresses all I think about the Blessed Virgin, all that I would preach about her if I were a priest."

Sister Marie testified from 6-13 September, 1910. On more

than one point, her contribution is among the most valuable,
particularly the subject of Thérèse's mysterious illness and sub-
sequent vision of our Lady. She brings light to bear on all the
humblest, simplest and deepest aspects of her sister's sanctity
in her balanced and concise testimony.

The testimony

8. Everything I have noted down for my evidence is the
outcome of my personal observations. I lived with the Servant
of God in my parents' house from the time of her birth until
I entered Carmel in 1886. The Servant of God was then thirteen
and a half years old. I was with her again from the time she
entered Carmel (1888) until her death. I read the manuscript
of her life just after she composed the first part for Mother
Agnes, and I read the third part, which she wrote to me. I did
not read the second part, that addressed to Mother Marie de
Gonzague, until after the Servant of God's death. I found she
had expressed her feelings and thoughts admirably in these
accounts, and I rediscovered there what I already knew from
having lived with her.

Asked about the origin and integrity of the manuscript, she
said:

One winter's evening after Matins, Sister Thérèse, Sister
Genevieve, Mother Agnes of Jesus, then prioress, and I were
warming ourselves together. Sister Thérèse related two or three
incidents from her childhood. I said to Mother Agnes: "Is it
possible that you should permit her to compose little poems to
please everybody, and that she should not write anything about
all the memories of her childhood? You'll see yet that she is an
angel who will not remain long on earth, and we shall have lost
all these detailed accounts that we find so interesting." Mother
Prioress hesitated at first; then, at our insistence, she told the
Servant of God that it would give her much pleasure if she
would give her an account of her childhood for her feastday.
Sister Thérèse obeyed, and this first part of the manuscript was
sent to our uncle, M. Guérin.

Later, Mother Agnes of Jesus, seeing that Sister Thérèse
was very ill, persuaded Mother Marie de Gonzague, the prioress
to order Sister Thérèse to write the story of her religious life,
which forms the second part of the manuscript.

Finally, I asked her myself during her last retreat (1896) to write down for me what I described as her little way. She did so, and these pages were added to form the third part when the *Story of a Soul* was published. I am convinced that this manuscript is absolutely reliable for an understanding of the thoughts and feelings of the Servant of God. She wrote it quite simply, just as it occurred to her.

When it was time to publish the manuscript, the prioress, Mother Marie de Gonzague, wished the entire manuscript to appear as if it had been addressed to her personally. For this reason a few names and intimate details concerning our family life were erased. But this did not really alter the narrative. Besides, the original text was restored after Mother Marie de Gonzague's death.

9. Obviously; I wonder how you can even ask me that question. I love her because one naturally loves one's own sister, and also because I looked on her as an angel. I desire very much to see her beatified, because then we shall see what she wanted us to see: that one must have confidence in the infinite mercy of God, and that holiness is accessible to all kinds of people. That does not express my thinking fully, but I do not know how to put it into words. I also desire her beatification because it will give people more confidence in her, and she will thus be better able to fulfil her desire to do good on earth.

11. Our parents had the reputation of being extraordinarily devout. Mother observed Lent without availing herself of any lawful mitigations, and both of them attended 5.30 Mass every morning, because, they said, it was the poor people's Mass. They received communion frequently, more than once a week, which was rather exceptional at that time. At Lisieux, my father received communion four or five times a week. My mother had a great abhorrence of worldliness, and wanted nothing luxurious in the house. One day, whilst reading the life of Madame Acarie (Blessed Mary of the Incarnation), mother said: "How blest she was to have given three daughters to God!" Mother was very energetic and lively, but without any harshness, and she had a very sensitive and generous heart. Above all, she had the spirit of self-denial, which made her forgetful of herself, and she worked with great fortitude so as to have the means of giving us a good Christian upbringing. In sorrow, too, for example at

the death of my brothers and sisters, she showed wonderful strength of soul. One could see from her letters that she was brokenhearted, but her faith helped her to rise above it all.

Father's outstanding characteristic was his very great honesty. He set himself the task of declaring his faith even before unbelievers. When the priest came to bring Holy Viaticum to our dying mother, he offered to escort the Blessed Sacrament as far as the church, with a candle in his hand. He was very charitable, and so devoted to his neighbour that he would never allow anyone to speak ill of him. His whole character gave an impression of kindness. One also observed in him a great purity of life, which was reflected in his whole person. He took the utmost care to remove from us anything which he thought might be an occasion of temptation.

13. Our parents reared all of us in a spirit of detachment from the good things of this world. This seems to me to have been the characteristic note of our upbringing. They frequently reminded us of eternity. Our family upbringing was very affectionate, but by no means soft. It is very true that father loved our little sister especially, but he did not spoil her for all that. When, after mother's death, we used to give her lessons, father always respected the punishment we meted out for her little faults.

14. When my sister Léonie left the Benedictine Abbey in Lisieux, where she was educated, Thérèse was sent there to take her place. She was then eight and a half years old, and she remained there until she was twelve and a half, returning home every evening. It was there that she made her first communion on 8 May, 1884, and that she was confirmed on the following 14 June.

Regarding the character and virtues of the Servant of God during this early part of her life I have this to say: from the age of two, one noticed in her an intelligence far in advance of her age. She was a deep and thoughtful person; in fact, I found her too serious and too advanced for her age. At the time of her mother's death, the ceremony of Extreme Unction impressed her deeply. As she wrote herself: "I did not mention to anyone the feelings that filled my heart. I looked on and listened in silence."[1] Indeed, at the time of my mother's death I thought her quite exceptional. We had no time to look after her, nor did she attempt to attract attention. But I took great care not to ask her what she was thinking, so as not to develop further the profound feelings of which she spoke.

It was not necessary to scold her when she was at fault: it was enough to say that such a thing was not right or that it displeased God, and she never did it again. She had herself already well under control. Whilst still small she attended the lessons I was giving to her sister Céline, and she controlled herself sufficiently not to utter a single word during the lesson, which lasted two hours.

She was also exceptionally open. Of this my mother wrote: "The little one would not tell a lie for all the gold in the world."[2] She wanted to accuse herself of the least faults: as soon as she committed them, she went to tell them to her mother. One day, when she was about five and a half, the domestic was telling her some little untruths in order to amuse her. "Victoire!" said Thérèse, "you know well that that offends the good God." At four, she began to count her little acts of virtue and her sacrifices on a string of beads made especially for the purpose. She called these her "practices". In her games with her sisters these "practices" occurred constantly, and greatly puzzled one of our neighbours. Many a time, her practices consisted in giving way to her sister. She exerted herself to the utmost to do this, because at that time she was very obstinate.

She was very devout. Mother told us: "Thérèse always has a smile on her lips; she has the face of one of the elect. She likes to speak only of God, and she would not miss saying her prayers for anything."[3]

When she was about ten, the Servant of God was stricken with a strange illness, an illness which certainly came from the devil, who, as she says herself in her autobiography, had been given an external power over her. She says that during this illness she never for a moment lost the use of her reason. Indeed, I have never heard her utter a senseless word, and she was never delirious for one instant. But she had terrifying dreams that depressed all who heard her cries of distress. Some nails fixed in the wall of the room suddenly became as thick, charred fingers to her, and she cried out: "I'm afraid, I'm afraid!" Her eyes, usually so calm and so kindly, had a terror-stricken expression that is impossible to describe. Another time, when my father came to sit by her, he happened to have his hat in his hand. Thérèse looked at him without saying a single word, as she spoke very little during her illness. Then, suddenly, as always, her expression changed. Staring at the hat, she wailed: "Oh! The great black beast!" Her cries had something supernatural about them: one should have heard them to have any idea of them. One day the doctor was present during one of these attacks, and he said to my father: "Science is powerless before these phenomena; there is nothing to be done."

I can say that the devil even tried to kill our little sister. Her bed was in a big alcove, and there was a space between wall and bed at both ends; she used to try and throw herself into this space. Several times she succeeded, and I wonder how she did not split her head on the paving-stones; but she never had even a scratch. At other times she would bang her head against the wood of the bedstead. And there were times when she tried to speak to me, but no sound could be heard.

The most severe attack, however, was the one she has described in her autobiography. I thought she was going to die from it. Seeing her exhausted by this painful struggle, I wanted to give her a drink, but she cried out in terror: "They want to poison me." Then I knelt with my sisters at the foot of the statue of the Blessed Virgin. Three times I repeated the same prayer. At the third time, I saw Thérèse fix her gaze on the statue, radiantly, like one in ecstasy. She confided to me that she had seen the Blessed Virgin herself. This vision lasted four or five minutes, and then her gaze shifted lovingly to me. From that moment there was no further trace of her illness. Next day, she resumed her usual life, and, apart from one or two falls that occurred without apparent reason as she was walking in the garden during her first week up, we saw no further incident of this kind throughout the rest of her life.

Thérèse made her first communion on 8 May, 1884, at the age of eleven years and four months. The period of waiting that was imposed on her caused her a great deal of suffering. She could not understand this law by which she was put back a year, because, as she said herself, she was born two days too late. It seemed so severe to her. One day we met Mgr Hugonin going to the station. "Oh, Marie!" she said, "would you like me to run and ask him for permission to make my first holy communion?" I had a hard job to hold her back. When I told her that in early Christian times very small children received the Holy Eucharist after their baptism, she was amazed and asked: "Why, then, is this no longer the case now?" At Christmas time, when she saw us go off to midnight Mass whilst she had to remain at home because she was too young, she said to me: "If you will take me with you, I, too, will go to communion. I could slip in among the others, and no one would take any notice. Could I do that?" She was very sad when I told her that that was impossible.

She prepared herself for her first communion with extra-ordinary fervour: she performed innumerable acts of virtue each day, and wrote them all down in a special little notebook. She also loved to meditate on a little leaflet I had given her about self-denial. We felt that her soul aspired with all its strength to be united to Jesus. On the day of her first communion, too, I thought I was looking at an angel rather than a mortal creature.

During the retreat that preceded her second holy communion, Thérèse fell a prey to scruples. It was especially on the eve of her confessions that they recurred. She came to tell me all her so-called sins. I tried to cure her by telling her that I took her sins upon myself (they were not even imperfections) and by allowing her to confess only two or three of them, which I indicated to her myself. She was so obedient that she followed my advice to the letter. Here is what she wrote about this matter: "Marie was indispensable to me, so to speak. I spoke only to her of my scruples, and I was so obedient that my confessor never knew about my wretched malady. I told him just the number of sins, and not one more, that Marie had allowed me to confess. I could have passed for the least scrupulous of people in spite of being extremely so."[4] She was released from her troubles through prayer: she addressed herself to her brothers and sisters who had preceded her into heaven, and very soon peace once more pervaded her soul.

14. At the boarding-school run by the Benedictine nuns she had to suffer on many occasions. We had educated her at home, and she was very advanced for her age. For this reason, she found herself in a class where the pupils were much older than she — Thérèse was eight, while her companions were

thirteen and fourteen. As she always came first in the class, one of her companions became jealous of her and made her go through a minor persecution, a fact which caused her a great deal of suffering. But, in accordance with her own principle of never complaining, she never complained. It was only later, in Carmel, that we learned the cause of her sadness at that time.

15. The Servant of God was withdrawn from the boarding-school about January, 1886. Her sister Céline, who had previously been with her there, had completed her studies in August, 1885. Our little sister returned to the Abbey by herself in October. This isolation, in a house where she had already met with her share of suffering, seemed to endanger her health. And besides, she was suffering from scruples. So father thought it would be better to keep her at home and let her finish her studies there. I was acting as mother to her, and I agreed.

Asked if she knew what the teachers at the school thought of Thérèse, she continued:

They considered her a very intelligent and very devout pupil, but a little timid. They had a great affection for her, and took great care of her. They noticed that as she was used to the intimacy of family life, she adapted herself with difficulty to the very different atmosphere of the boarding-school.

The judge asked how she behaved in the family.

She received communion four or five times a week. She would have liked to do so daily, but she waited for her confessor to suggest it to her, not daring to take upon herself the initiative of asking him. Later on she wrote: "I had not the audacity then that I would have now. Jesus did not become a victim to remain in his golden ciborium; he wanted to make our hearts, where he likes to be, his ciborium."[5] Such was her desire to be a member of the Association of the Children of Mary, established at the Benedictine Abbey, that in spite of her repugnance, she returned twice a week for several months to the boarding-school which she had left. Meanwhile, I entered Carmel (October, 1886) and the Servant of God remained at home with my father and her sisters Léonie and Céline.

16. Ever since she was two years old, the Servant of God showed a desire for the religious life. When she was about fourteen, this call became so vehemently directed towards Carmel that she no longer doubted that it was her duty to embrace it.

No doubt our parents were glad to give their children to God, and even wished that this would happen; but they never exerted any pressure on us in this direction. My sister Pauline (Mother Agnes of Jesus) put forward some objections to the wishes confided to her by our young sister, so as to test her vocation. But I opposed her much more strongly and stubbornly. The chief reasons for my opposition were our sister's tender age and the fear I had of the great sorrow which our father would endure, for Thérèse was the real ray of sunshine in his life. Despite these obstacles, the Servant of God persevered in her efforts to enter Carmel. I only knew from the account she gave me of it in the parlour what obstacles she met with from superiors and the means by which she overcame them, going even to Rome to beg the Holy Father Leo XIII for permission to enter Carmel at the age of fifteen. Anyway, she has told all this in her autobiography.

17. She entered the Lisieux Carmel on 9 April, 1888, and took the habit on 10 January, 1889. She had waited longer than others for this, on account of her tender age. She made her vows on 8 September, 1890; she should have made them in January, but she was again kept back. It was the superiors who caused the delay, again because of her youthfulness.

Asked if she knew whether the superiors had had any other motives, she said:

There was no other reason. Where her dispositions were concerned, Mother Prioress and all the sisters said of her that she was a very fervent novice and that she had never been seen to infringe the rule even in the smallest detail. She never asked to be dispensed from anything.

18. She carried out successively various ordinary duties in the community, such as in the sacristy, in the linen-room, at the "turn", in the refectory, etc. In all these offices we saw her always ready to practise charity and to fulfil her task in a spirit of deep faith and constant attention to the presence of God.

When Mother Agnes was elected prioress (1893), she secretly entrusted the care of the novices to Sister Thérèse, though she had to appear to leave it to the outgoing prioress. So she carried out this task during the three years that Mother Agnes was prioress. When, in 1896, Mother Marie de Gonzague was re-elected prioress, she did not appoint a regular mistress of novices, but ordered Sister Thérèse to look after them under her own direction. Sister Thérèse executed this delicate and difficult task with great wisdom and good sense. She faced it with great courage, and was not afraid to do her duty even when it brought some unpleasantness on herself.

19. Besides the manuscript on her life, of which I have already spoken, she wrote quite a number of letters to members of her family, as well as poems on pious subjects, and some dialogues which we call "pious recreations". The manuscript containing her life has been published, and in the complete edition a selection of her letters and poems has been added.

20. I regard the life of the Servant of God as a marvel of perfection in everything, whether in the great trials she had to endure or in the minutiae of religious practices. Indeed, it is not usual to see always the same equanimity, the same smile on the lips, in the midst of the trials and troubles of daily life. There seemed to be nothing but joy in her life, even during the time of her severest trials, to such an extent that I knew nothing of her sufferings. I did not know, for instance, what she had gone through in her temptations against the faith, until I read her manuscript after her death. As she was constantly affable, she always appeared active and dedicated in God's service, even, and above all, in the time of trial.

21. Sister Thérèse had an ardent faith, which found expression even from her childhood in her love for the Holy Eucharist. After her first communion, she lived only for the moment when she could receive our Lord a second time. Her faith showed itself throughout her trials too. At the time of her father's illness, she wrote to me: "Jesus has come to visit us: he has found us worthy of passing through the crucible of suffering. It is our Lord who has done this; it is our duty to thank him."[6] She said father was undergoing his purgatory, and, with Mother Prioress's permission, she spent all the savings of her youth to have the sacrifice of the Mass offered for him. She numbered this big ordeal of our father's cerebral paralysis among the days of grace in her life; she marked the exact date on the back of a holy picture, and emphasised it with the words: "Our great wealth."

She brought the same faith to bear on her own interior trials, which she always looked at from a supernatural standpoint. In 1890 she wrote to me: "You may be inclined to think that your little sister is grieving over her dryness and dark-ness. But no; on the contrary, she is happy to follow her spouse out of love for himself alone, and not on account of his gifts."[7]

She also showed great faith in dealing with her superiors. One or two months before her death she underwent a most painful crisis in her illness. As the community doctor was away on holiday, we asked Mother Prioress to fetch Doctor La Néelle, a relative of ours, but she refused. For a whole month Sister Thérèse was in terrible agony. When we complained about such behaviour, this angel of peace told us: "My dear sisters, one must not murmur against the will of God. It is he who does not allow Mother to give me any relief."

I asked her to write out for me what I called her "little way of confidence and love". Having asked our Mother's per-mission, she did so during her last retreat, in September, 1896. This letter is now chapter 11 of the published Life. When I had read those glowing pages, I told her it was impossible for me to reach such lofty heights. It was then that she wrote me the letter of 17 September, 1896,[8] in which, among other things, she told me: "How can you ask me if it is possible for you to love God as I love him? My desire for martyrdom is nothing. . . . I know well that it is not that at all that God finds pleasing in my soul. What does please him is to see me love my little-ness, my poverty, and to see the blind trust which I have in his mercy. . . . That is my sole treasure."

One day, when she had asked for a *double portion* of the love of the angels and saints, as Elisha had done in the case of the spirit of Elijah (*cf. 2 Kings 2:9*), she added: "Jesus, I cannot go more deeply into what I am asking: I should fear to be crushed by the sheer weight of its audacity. My excuse is that I am only a child, and children do not reflect on the full implications of what they say. Yet, if their parents were to mount a throne and inherit vast wealth, they would not hesitate to grant the desires of their little ones, whom they cherish as much as themselves. To please them they would spend most lavishly, even to the point of weakness. Well, then, I am a child of the Church, and the Church is a queen because she is your spouse, O divine King of Kings. . . . Dear Jesus, how I wish I could explain to all those who are conscious of their own littleness how great your condescension is! I feel that if, by some impossible chance, you could find someone weaker and more insignificant than me, you would overwhelm her with still greater graces, provided she gave herself up with entire confidence to your infinite mercy."[9]

Sister Thérèse loved God ardently and never ceased to think of him. One day I asked her: "What do you do in order to think of God always?"

"It is not difficult," she replied; "we naturally think of someone we love."

"Do you never lose his presence, then?" I asked.

" Oh, no; I doubt if I have ever been three minutes without thinking of him."

A few weeks before she died, she confided this secret to me: "If God were to tell me that I would have a very great reputation were I to die immediately, but that if I died at the age of twenty-four my reputation would be less and his pleasure much greater, then I would not hesitate to reply: 'My God, I wish to die when I am twenty-four, because I am not seeking my reputation but your pleasure.' "

Recalling the time when she was only five or six, she said: "I loved God more and more as I grew up. . . . I made great efforts to please Jesus in all my actions, and I took great care never to offend him."

I would like to call attention, too, to this other passage from the letter of 17 September, 1896, which I quoted from above: "But above all, I want to shed my blood to the last drop for you, my beloved Saviour. Martyrdom was the dream of my youth, a dream that has grown in intensity in the cloisters of Carmel. Yet here, too, I realise that my dream is an extravagant one: no one form of martyrdom would ever be enough for me; I should want to experience them all."

Even when she was still very young, Thérèse loved to give alms to the poor. She did it with a compassionate and respectful expression on her face as if it was our Lord himself she saw in his suffering members. When she was ten, she asked if she could go and look after a poor woman who was dying and had no one to help her. She wanted to take some food and clothing to another woman, who inspired her with particular compassion because she was burdened with several children.

Whenever she was unable to help people in a practical

way, she gave them her prayers by way of alms. One day whilst out walking with father, she met an old cripple. She approached him to give him her small coin, but he did not consider himself poor enough to receive alms, so he refused it. Thérèse, very sorry to have humiliated someone she had wanted to help, consoled herself with the thought that she would pray for him on the day of her first communion. Five years later, she faithfully kept that resolution.

At recreation in Carmel, she always showed a preference for the company of those who seemed most forlorn. As a novice, she had as her companion a young lay-sister who had a very difficult temperament, but she did not stand aloof from her because of that; rather, she went to sit by her as often as possible and treated her so gently and kindly that she won her companion's affection and had a very great influence on her.

Her charity induced her to want to help a sister in the linen-room whose temperament was such that no one wanted to be in her company. This sister was subject to the blackest moods, and did scarcely any work. I saw her, when Sister Thérèse was already an invalid, come to her to call for the week's linen, which she had given her to repair, and because Sister Thérèse had not been able to complete her task, this sister reproached her severely instead of thanking her for what she had done in spite of being so ill. Sister Thérèse took the reproaches as if they were so much praise.

This poor, unfortunate sister became the object of Sister Thérèse's tenderest compassion. One day, when I had confided to her how much trouble that sister gave me, the Servant of God said: "Ah! If you only knew how necessary it is to forgive her, how much she is to be pitied! It is not her fault if she is so poorly gifted; she is like an old clock that has to be re-wound every quarter of an hour. Yes, it is as bad as that. Well, wouldn't you have pity on it? Oh, how necessary it is to practise charity towards one's neighbour!"

There was a sister in the infirmary who tried everyone's patience with her various manias. When we showed a certain reluctance to keep her company, Sister Thérèse said: "How happy I would be to have been asked to do that! Perhaps it would have cost my nature very much, but I think I would have done it very lovingly, because I remember our Lord's words: 'I was sick and you comforted me.' "

She practised really heroic charity towards the sister she speaks of in Chapter X of her autobiography.[10] This poor sister was very abrupt and bad-mannered. She bristled with impatience if one even touched her. When I saw Sister Thérèse being disturbed from her prayer every day during her novitiate, in order to take her to the refectory, I admired her virtue, for she must have had real courage to continually show her such delicate and tender-hearted charity.

I often spent my recreations in the infirmary, sitting by the Servant of God's bed of pain. One day I told her that with another sick person I would have found it irksome to be deprived of recreation, but that with her it was a great comfort to me. She immediately retorted: "I, on the other hand, would have been very happy to do so. Since we are on earth to suffer, the more we suffer, the happier we are. We practise charity better with a person who is less congenial. Unfortunately, we manage our affairs here on earth rather badly."

Her charity made her forget herself on every occasion. During the last three months of her life, which she spent in the infirmary, she would not allow anyone to stay up with her, even for one single night. Even the night before she died, she begged to be left alone so as not to be the cause of anyone's being tired.

Her charity also made her wish to do good after her death. This thought engrossed her. After making a novena to St Francis Xavier (4-12 March, 1896), she said to me: "I have asked for the grace to do good after my death, and now I am certain of being granted it, for through this novena one obtains all that one wants."

I was reading in the refectory a passage from the life of St Aloysius Gonzaga, which told how a certain sick man saw a shower of roses fall on his bed as a sign that his prayer for a cure would be answered. At recreation afterwards she said: "I, too, will let fall a shower of roses after my death."

I am bound to say that during the years that Sister Thérèse spent in the Lisieux Carmel, the community suffered some rather deplorable disturbances: factions and personality clashes arising chiefly from the vexatious temperament of Mother Marie de Gonzague, who was prioress at various times for more than twenty years. In this very troubled atmosphere, the Servant of God's prudence and virtue shone forth all the more remarkably. In the midst of all the disturbance she was able to avoid every kind of conflict, and never deviated from her union with God, from her concern for her own perfection, from the love of all her sisters, or from the most devoted respect for authority.

Love for the Holy Eucharist was one of the chief characteristics of her piety. In Carmel, her main source of suffering was her inability to receive communion daily. Some time before her death, she told Mother Marie de Gonzague, who was afraid of daily communion: "Mother, when I get to heaven, I will make you change your opinion." And that is exactly what happened. After the Servant of God's death, our chaplain gave us holy communion every day, and Mother Marie de Gonzague, far from being indignant as before, was very happy about it.

About the time of her first communion, the Servant of God asked my permission to make half an hour's prayer every day. I would not grant it. Then she asked for just a quarter of an hour, but I did not permit this either. I found her so devout, and possessed of such an understanding of supernatural things that it made me afraid, so to speak: my fear was that God would take her to himself too soon.

She had a tender love for the Blessed Virgin. When she was very young, and not yet able to go to the May devotions, she made a little altar, before which she used to pray with great devotion. During the illness she had when she was about ten, her favourite pastime was to plait garlands of daisies and forget-me-nots for the Queen of Heaven.

In Carmel, the last flowers we gave Sister Thérèse were some cornflowers. She made two wreaths out of them, which she asked us to put in our Lady's hands; they remained there until her death. It was at the shrine of Our Lady of Victories in Paris that she felt her interior trials had ceased. Of this she wrote: "I can't describe what I felt, kneeling in front of the statue. . . . I knew then that she was really watching over me, that I was *her* child. I could no longer call her anything but 'Mamma'; 'Mother' did not seem affectionate enough."[11]

"When we pray to the saints," she once said, "they keep us waiting awhile: one feels that they have to go and present their request. But when I ask the Blessed Virgin for a favour.

PRAYER TO ST. JOSEPH

ST. JOSEPH, just and gentle servant, you were unfailingly obedient to the will of God. Obtain for us courage to embrace God's will as revealed to us in the depths of our hearts and in the events of our lives.

JOSEPH, loving husband and father, you knew the fear of fleeing your country, seeking safety and shelter for your family. Help today's immigrants and refugees, the poor and the starving. Guide us that we may seek paths of peace, truth and hospitality.

JOSEPH, man of faith and prayer, deepen in us respect for God's gift of life in the wonders of all creation. With confidence in your powerful intercession, we entrust these and all our needs into your care. We ask this through Christ our Lord. AMEN.

Discalced Carmelite Nuns
89 Hiddenbrooke Drive • Beacon, NY 12508
www.carmelitesbeacon.org

I receive help immediately. Haven't you ever noticed that? Try it and you'll see." Then I asked her to write out her thoughts about the Blessed Virgin for me, and in May, 1897, she wrote her last poem in her honour. "My little song," she told us, "expresses all that I think and all that I would preach about the Blessed Virgin if I were a priest." That was the poem entitled "Why I love you, Mary"; it is printed in the *Story of a Soul*.[12] She had always had a very special devotion to the Child Jesus and to the Holy Face; but it was the latter which developed more in Carmel.

Her fortitude showed itself right from her early years. When she was reprimanded, she never made excuses. One day she received a severe scolding from my father for something which was not her fault, but she did not utter a word in self-defence. The day my father decided that Céline should take painting lessons, he asked Thérèse, who was barely ten years old, "And you, my little Queen, would you like to learn to draw too? Would that please you?" Not realising that I was going to be the cause of her making a great sacrifice, I intervened and said sharply: "That would be a waste of money; Thérèse has not got the same aptitude as Céline." She said nothing, so the matter stopped there, and she did not learn to draw. When she was in Carmel, she confided to us what a sacrifice this had been for her. When I told her she need have only expressed her wish to do so, she replied: "Yes, but I did not want to refuse God anything."

At the time of our father's illness, it was Sister Thérèse who kept our spirits up. Seeing her so vigorous, we never thought of worrying about her. She showed great fortitude too in the mortifications that came her way daily. For example, on the days when there were beans for dinner, no one knew that they did not agree with her, so she was given a large portion every time. And since Mother Prioress had urged her to eat all that was set before her, she was very ill each time. But she said nothing about it then; it was only when she was in the infirmary that she told us her secret.

Her fortitude manifested itself too in her relations with a certain sister for whom she felt a great aversion.[13] She hid her aversion so well that I thought she loved this sister very much, and I felt jealous. One day I said to her: "I cannot help telling

D

you in confidence about something that is annoying me. . . . I think you love Sister — more than me, and I don't think it's fair. After all, God made family ties. You always seem so pleased to see her that I cannot think otherwise, since you have never shown such happiness about being with me." She laughed heartily at this, but she gave me no idea of the aversion she felt for this religious.

She knew how to constrain herself in everything, and had extraordinary courage. During the night of Maundy Thursday and Good Friday 1896 she experienced her first spitting of blood. I met her the following morning, pale and exhausted, and tiring herself with housework. I asked her what was the matter, as she appeared to be ill, and I offered to help her. But she just thanked me, and said nothing about the mishap she had experienced.

During recreation she could often have found a place near us (her own sisters), but she sought in preference the company of those who tested her charity the most. She did not lose her temper if one said a sarcastic word to her. One day, when she was doing her best to arrange some bunches of flowers that had been sent to be placed around Mother Genevieve's coffin, a lay-sister said to her: "Obviously, these bunches of flowers have come from your family; you are putting them well in front and disregarding those of the poor." I was wondering what Sister Thérèse was going to say to such unfair comment, but she just looked affectionately at the sister and hastened to satisfy her wishes by bringing the less beautiful flowers to the fore.

When she was in charge of the novitiate, one day I saw a young novice heaping abuse on her and saying some very unkind things. Sister Thérèse kept perfectly calm, but I could see what an effort she was making to bear those very biting words so calmly.

Sister Thérèse practised poverty constantly and without complaint. From the moment she entered Carmel, although she was only fifteen, she was treated unsparingly and was served with the most tainted remainders of meals. In the kitchen they said: "No one will eat that; let's give it to Sister Thérèse, she never refuses anything." We also saw some omelette or herring that had been cooked on Sunday re-appear on her plate throughout the week. She had to share with the sister sitting next to her at table a little jug of cider which contained barely enough for two glasses. She never drank any of it, so as not to deprive her neighbour. She could have helped herself to water from the jar, but she refrained so that her mortification and act of charity would not be noticed.

Three days before her death, when she was tormented by fever, she refrained from asking for some iced water; nor would she ask for some grapes, when someone had forgotten to leave them within her reach. I noticed her mortification when I saw her looking at her glass, and I said: "Would you like some iced water?"

"I would, very much," she replied.

"But," I pressed on, "Mother Prioress has obliged you to ask for all you need; do so, then, out of obedience."

"I ask for all I need," she said, "but not for what gives me pleasure. I would not ask for grapes either, if they were not there."

In a spirit of poverty, she never asked for anything back if someone took it; nothing belonged to her, she said. She let the intellectual gifts which God had given her in abundance be stolen from her, so to speak, for at recreation, if another profited from her witty retorts by repeating them as their own, she willingly gave her the honour of amusing the others, without making known their origin.

Sister Thérèse had the purity of an angel. During the illness she had at the age of ten, the doctor prescribed showers. This distressed her so much that she begged me to discontinue this treatment. And concerning her journey to Rome she wrote: "I asked Our Lady of Victories to remove from my path anything that might tarnish the purity of my mind. I realised that on a long journey like this I might come across things that were apt to shock me. I was unacquainted with evil, and afraid to discover it."[14] She was so pure, and yet so simple, that one could confide to her any temptation of this kind. One felt that she would not be disturbed by it.

I never saw Sister Thérèse commit the slightest act of disobedience. As a child she carried out every command to the letter. She loved to read, but she stopped in the middle of even the most absorbing passage when it was time to do so. In Carmel she was obedient to the smallest details of the rule. It was forbidden, for instance, to read books or magazines which were not for our own use, even if it was a matter of only a few words. During a preached retreat she told me that she had accused herself of glancing at a page of a fashion magazine. When I pointed out that it was not forbidden to look at pictures, she replied: "That's true, but father told me it was more perfect to deprive oneself of them. Anyway, looking at the vanity of the world only served to raise my soul to God. When I come across these illustrations now, I no longer look at them. Will you do the same?"

She told me in confidence that when Mother Prioress gave Mother Agnes permission to come and talk with her sometimes, it became an occasion of great sacrifice for her, because she had not received permission herself to reveal *her* most secret thoughts to Mother Agnes; she had to confine herself to listening to the secrets of her whom she called her "little mother", without being able to return her confidence. And yet, she had only to say one word and permission would straightaway have been granted her. "But," she said, "one should not get used to being granted permissions which could soften the martyrdom of religious life, for then it would be a natural life and have no merit."

Whenever she was busy writing and the bell rang, she stopped without completing the word she had started. Once, for instance (it was during the last weeks of her life), I wanted to finish writing down something she had just told me, because I was afraid I would forget it otherwise. "It would be much better to lose it, and be observant," she said, and added: "If only people knew what that was!"

During the last days of her life, when she was burning with fever, I wanted to remove the sheet from her feet so as to cool her, but she said: "Perhaps that is not allowed." Mother Marie de Gonzague had in fact once told us that even in summer it was better to keep on the woollen blanket, and Sister Thérèse did not consider herself dispensed by illness from practising obedience and mortification to an heroic degree. She had only to say a word to have this relief, which those who are ill take anyway without even thinking that permission for it might be necessary.

Throughout her life, Sister Thérèse strove to pass unnoticed. On the eve of my profession (1888) she wrote to me: "Pray for the feeble little reed that is at the bottom of the valley. Ask that your little daughter may always remain as a tiny grain of sand, unnoticed and hidden from everyone's eyes so that Jesus alone can see it, that it may become smaller and smaller until it is reduced to nothing."[15] In 1896 she wrote this to me: "Oh! If only all those who are weak and imperfect could feel the same way about it as the least of them all—your little Thérèse—does, not one of them would despair of reaching the summit of the mountain of love."[16]

Her humility did not prevent her from acknowledging the spiritual privileges God had given her, but she always knew how to refer them all to him. On the evening of 25 July, 1897, during her illness, she told me: "When I leaned over a little, I saw through the window the setting sun casting its last fiery rays over nature, and the tops of the trees seemed gilded. Then I thought: what a difference it makes whether you remain in the shade or expose yourself to the sun of Love; in the latter case one becomes golden all over. That is why I look all gilded, whereas in reality I am not, and I would immediately cease to appear so if I estranged myself from love."

22. When she was about six years old, Thérèse had a prophetic vision in which she saw the ordeal that was in store for our good father. I was in the room next to hers, when I heard her call out in a trembling voice: "Papa, papa!" I understood that something extraordinary was happening, because my father was away for several days. She herself relates this strange happening in the *Story of a Soul*.[17] She had seen father walking in the garden, but as if bent with age, and wearing a kind of veil over his head. It was only later, in Carmel, that God fully enlightened us concerning this vision: when our father was subjected in the last years of his life to a grievous and humiliating ordeal brought about by cerebral paralysis. It must be pointed out that right from the first attack of this malady, our poor father used to cover his head with a handkerchief, just as the Servant of God had seen in the vision of 1879, ten years before the event.

Asked if the Servant of God had spoken in any way of the meaning of the vision before the event, she continued:

She did not know the exact meaning of it, but she considered this vision to be certainly prophetic, and she was confident that its meaning would be disclosed to her one day.

Thérèse's strange childhood illness ended with an apparition of the Blessed Virgin. As soon as I saw her posture and the ecstatic look in her eyes, I knew that it was the Blessed Virgin herself that she saw. It lasted four or five minutes; then two big tears fell silently from her eyes, and she turned her gentle gaze affectionately on me. When I was alone with her, I asked her why she had cried. She hesitated to tell me her secret, but as I insisted, she finally said: "It was because I saw her no more."

Four years later, when she was praying to Our Lady of Victories in Paris, on her journey to Rome, she had a kind of confirmation of the reality of this vision. As she says herself: "It was there that my Mother, the Virgin Mary, made me feel that it was really she who had smiled at me and cured me."[18]

Finally, on the very day Sister Thérèse was taken to the infirmary, where she was to die, this same statue of our Lady was placed there. She looked lovingly at it, and said: "Never has she looked so beautiful, but today it is only the statue; that other time, as you know well, it was not the statue."

One day during her last illness, I felt a sorrow bordering on despair at the thought of having to watch her die, but I wept silently and took care not to let her see how I felt. Later that same day, as I entered the infirmary without any sign of emotion, she welcomed me with these words, uttered in a tone of gentle reproach: "You must not cry like those who have no hope."

A little robin used to pay her a visit from time to time, and, indeed, she had always protected the birds in the garden. One day I wanted to set traps for the blackbirds, because they were eating our strawberries. "Don't do them any harm," she said; "they have only this life to enjoy. I promise that when I get to heaven I will send you fruit, if you do not kill these little birds." And, in fact, the following year a box of pears and a basket of strawberries arrived for us. It was the superior of the hospital at Brest, whom we did not know at all, who sent them to us; she said she thought it would please Sister Thérèse. Ever since, we receive some each year.

One day I said to her: "I wish I were the only one to suffer by your death, but how will I be able to console Mother Agnes?"

"Don't worry about it," she replied; "Mother Agnes will not have time to think of her sorrow, because she will be so busy with me right to the end of her life that she won't even be able to cope with it all."

During the last days of her life, she had a strange premonition of what is happening now with regard to her. She spoke to us (her three Carmelite sisters) about these future events, which are a reality today, with that childlike simplicity and sincere humility with which she always spoke of the favours she received from God. She told us, among other things, that we must treasure the rose-petals which she had placed round her crucifix: "Later," she said, "you will find all these things useful." She alluded also to the great flood of letters we would receive about her after her death, and to the joys these letters would bring us. One day, she even told us half playfully: "My dear sisters, you know, of course, that you are looking after a little saint."

23. Generally speaking, the Servant of God did not attract any attention during her lifetime. Her virtue consisted principally in doing the ordinary things extraordinarily well. Those who observed her more closely, however, noticed an absolutely rare degree of perfection in her. When she was still very young, people said of her: "There is something heavenly about that child's eyes." In Carmel, her extraordinary observance appeared to some religious as a silent reproach, and they sometimes expressed annoyance and jealousy about it. But there were others, and these were more numerous, who did her fervour justice: some said openly that this constancy in virtue was out of the ordinary. One of them, noticing how particular she was to obey even the least important of counsels, said: "Sister Thérèse is a saint." Another, seeing the meekness with which she took a hurtful reproach, considered her an exceptionally virtuous person from that day on. And, finally, Mother Marie de Gonzague, our prioress, who was not given to flattering her, said: "A soul of such mettle ought not to be treated like a child."

24. During the last three months of her life, she suffered intense pain, but always calmly and even joyfully. Mother Agnes once said to her: "Perhaps you will suffer more before you die."

"Oh!" she replied. "Don't worry about that; I have such a great desire for it."

On another occasion, I remarked: "So this is how God has answered my prayer that you would not suffer much!"

"I asked God," she replied, "not to listen to prayers that could be obstacles to the fulfilment of his designs for me."

On 13 July, 1897, she told me: "If you only knew the plans I make, and the things I am going to do once I get to heaven!"

"Well, what *are* your plans?" I asked.

"I will commence my mission. . . . I will go down there to help missionaries, and prevent little pagans from dying without being baptised."

One day, when she was in great pain, a novice tired her out complaining about her companions. Sister Thérèse strove in vain to reason with her, and in the end was obliged to reproach her for it. When the novice had gone, I remarked: "What a tiresome novice; you must dread to see her coming."

"A good soldier does not fear battle," she replied, "and haven't I said that I will die fighting?"

A few weeks before she died, I was thinking of the suffering that still lay in store for her, and I said: "What hurts me is the thought that you are going to suffer still more."

"It doesn't worry me," she replied. "God will give me the strength to endure it."

On another occasion she showed what a degree of detachment she had reached. Alluding to the fact that at the hour of her death her sister Pauline (Mother Agnes) would no longer be prioress, she said: "Yes, I can say in all honesty that I will be happy to die in the arms of Mother Marie de Gonzague, because she is God's representative. With you, little mother, there would have been a human element, and I prefer it to be only divine."

One day I said to her: "You don't fear death at all, then?" She became serious and replied: "No, not yet . . . but I could well be afraid of it like everybody else, since it is a rather notorious moment . . . but I leave myself wholly in God's hands."

My sister Genevieve said to her one day: "The angels will come to fetch you, and we, too, would like to see them."

"I don't think you will see them," she replied, "but that won't stop them from being there. Nevertheless, I would like to have a beautiful death, so as to please you. I've asked the Blessed Virgin for it. I did not ask God, because I wish to let him do whatever he likes. Asking the Blessed Virgin is not the same thing: she knows how to deal with my little desires; whether she passes them on or not is up to her, so as not to oblige God to grant them."

On 22 August, she was told that several people were praying for her. Apropos of this she made the following remarks: "I was pleased to think that people were praying for me, but then I told God that I wished it was sinners they were praying for."

"You don't want them praying for your relief, then?"

"No," she replied.

She had become extremely emaciated during her last illness, but strange to say, and to the astonishment of many doctors, her face did not seem changed by illness right up to the time of death. One day, when she was looking at her skinny hands, she said: "What joy I feel to see myself fading away! I'm becoming a skeleton, and I'm glad." My sister and I told her how happy we would be if her body was preserved, but she said: "All you'll find of me is a little skeleton; that is all they found of St Aloysius Gonzaga."

After she had received Extreme Unction joyfully and peacefully, she expressed particular happiness at the fact that the priest had told her that her soul now resembled that of a newly-baptised child.

Her last day on earth was one of great suffering. She was so breathless and in such pain that we dared not leave her. "If that's the agony," she said, "what's death like?" She seemed forsaken by heaven and earth; it reminded us of our Lord's own abandonment on the Cross. "Oh, poor little Mother," she said, "I assure you the chalice is full to the brim. Yes, God, as much as you wish, but have pity on me! . . . I could never have believed that it was possible to suffer so much. Oh! It is sheer agony; there are no consolations, not even one! . . . It is because of my desire to save souls." That evening she said: "Mother, prepare me to die well!"

A few moments before she died, Sister Thérèse clasped her crucifix to her and with great difficulty uttered these words: "Oh! I love him . . . My God . . . I love you." These were her last words. Then she was enraptured by a heavenly vision similar to the one I had witnessed when, at the age of ten, she was cured by the apparition of the Blessed Virgin. During this ecstasy, a sister held a candle near her eyes, but her gaze remained fixed with inexpressible peace upon the object which enraptured her. This ecstasy lasted several minutes. Then she lowered her eyes and breathed her last.

25. She was buried on 4 October in the part of the public cemetery in Lisieux reserved for Carmelites. There is nothing extraordinary to draw attention to about her burial. I have learned, and besides it is well known, that on 6 September of this year (1910) Sister Thérèse's remains were exhumed by order and under the presidency of the bishop. They were placed in a leaden coffin, and re-interred a short distance away from the original place.

26. The crowds of people visiting the Servant of God's grave continue to grow. Although we never leave the enclosure, we know this only too well by the great number of pilgrims who also come to the parlour and persist in asking the out-sisters if they can meet one or other of the Servant of God's own sisters, which we obviously refuse to permit. Among the pilgrims there is a large number of priests, many of whom ask to say Mass in the convent chapel. Anyway, this concourse of people is a well-known fact, and the general public can testify to it.

27. About this I know only what everybody knows: namely, that the Servant of God's reputation for holiness has spread throughout the entire world. As proof, I have the letters that arrive here in ever-increasing numbers every day, asking for prayers and giving thanks for favours received. These letters come from every country, some from simple and uneducated people, others from persons who are distinguished for their learning or for their rank in society. At present the letters are in the order of sixty a day.

It is not correct to say that the Carmel has engaged in publicity to spread this reputation for holiness. Hardly had the first edition of the *Story of a Soul* been given to the public than we were literally inundated with requests for pictures, souvenirs, etc. It was to meet these demands that we have produced the publications available today.

29. We have boxes full of letters that tell of favours received and ascribe more or less wonderful happenings to the intercession of the Servant of God. Part of this correspondence

has been published at the end of the *Story of a Soul*.[19] I consider several of these events to be quite remarkable (cures, etc.), but the persons who have received these favours are better qualified than me to speak of them.

Several wonderful events have, to my knowledge, taken place even here in the convent. On the evening of Friday, 1 October, the day after her death, Sister Mary of St Joseph towards whom Sister Thérèse had exercised great charity during her lifetime, found her cell so scented with the perfume of violets that she thought someone had placed a bunch of them in her cell, and looked everywhere for it. In fact, nearly all the nuns in this community have smelt this mysterious perfume; I experienced it four or five times myself. We all experienced it when we least expected it. Anyway, I paid no heed to these phenomena; I consider them less important than an interior grace.

In conclusion, she describes the miracle of the cauldron, better told by other witnesses.

4 Genevieve of Saint Teresa, o.c.d.

Céline Martin was born in Alençon on 28 April, 1869. She was educated at the Benedictine Abbey in Lisieux, finishing there in 1885. In May, 1887, her father experienced the first onset of the cerebral paralysis that made one long martyrdom of his last years on earth. After Thérèse entered Carmel in April, 1888, Céline remained at home alone, taking care of her father. In 1889, she made a vow of chastity, which she renewed every year in the hope of being able to enter Carmel herself one day. She eventually did so on 14 September, 1894, less than two months after her father's death.

She took the habit as Sister Genevieve of St Teresa on 5 February, 1895, and did her novitiate under the firm guidance of her sister Thérèse. She made her profession on 24 February, 1896. Shortly afterwards, Sister Thérèse was laid low by the illness that was to take her from this life, and Mother Marie de Gonzague appointed Sister Genevieve assistant infirmarian to help nurse her. She thus became a privileged witness to the Saint's last months on earth.

Fortunately, Céline took her camera with her when she entered Carmel; thanks to her, we possess more authentic photos of St Thérèse than of any other saint.

It was Céline who wrote Appel aux petites âmes, *the first ever biographical sketch of St Thérèse, and it met with extraordinary success. With some help from Mother Agnes, she also composed* The Little Catechism of the Act of Offering to Merciful Love. *Later, after years of study, she published* L'Esprit de la bienheureuse Thérèse de l'Enfant Jésus d'après ses écrits et les témoins oculaires de sa vie *(Lisieux, 1923). This went into several editions, and was translated into all the principal languages.[1] She published a revised edition of this in 1946. In 1952 she published* Conseils et Souvenirs, *known in English as A* memoir of My Sister, St Thérèse (*Gill, Dublin, 1959*). *In 1955 and 1957 she wrote little biographies of her father and mother respectively; these were translated into English by Fr Michael Collins, s.m.a., and published by Gill in the same years.*

She also helped Mgr Combes prepare his edition of St Thérèse's letters, published 1948, though here she was hampered by her prejudice against some of the demands of textual criticism. Shortly before her own death, Mother Agnes commissioned her to accede to the oft-expressed desire of the saint's friends to have the original text of her autobiography. This painstaking work was accomplished in 1956 by the late P. François de Sainte Marie, o.c.d., when he published a definitive photographic edition of the manuscripts.

Céline was a first-hand source for much of Fr Piat's Story of a Family *(Gill, 1947), and in 1957 she had the joy of being able to testify in the process of beatification of both her parents.*

She died in full possession of her faculties on 25 February, 1959, after a long and painful illness.

Her testimony, one of the longest and richest in detail, is the fourth of the series; it was presented from 14-28 September, 1910.

The testimony

7. I love my little sister very much, but I testify freely, and I feel I would say the same things if she was not my sister. My sole intention in coming to give evidence is to obey the Church, which asked me to do so.

8. I was separated from her for only six years, i.e. from the time she entered Carmel (1888) until I did so myself (September, 1894). Apart from this interval, I lived with her, at home during her childhood, and in Carmel from 1894 till her death.

During our childhood days Thérèse and I were inseparable. We looked on our elder sisters (Marie and Pauline) more as mothers, but we were much younger and regarded one another as sisters. What I have to say here will be chiefly the result of personal observation. I have read the *Story of a Soul*, of course, but I have not really learnt anything new from it; at most, it has reminded me of some details I had forgotten.

9. I wish this cause to be successful, because I think it desirable to see raised to the altars a person who was sanctified

in an ordinary way, without anything unusual or wonderful, and because I foresee the good that can come from her example and teaching becoming more widely known. I don't think family affection is influencing me in this. I believe she has deserved this honour, and it is for this reason that I desire these proceedings to be a success. That, of course, does not alter the fact that I am very happy to be the Servant of God's sister.

10. *After family details with which we are already familiar, Sister Genevieve has this additional information:*

For several weeks (after her birth) Thérèse was breast-fed by my mother, but a most serious decline in health put her life in danger; so, after two months, mother was obliged to entrust her to the care of a more robust wet-nurse, a very good woman with whom she stayed for one year. Mother took her back in March, 1874.

11. What impressed me most about my parents was their detachment from the things of this world. Life at home was simple and patriarchal; we shunned the disturbance of worldly acquaintances, and tended to keep to ourselves.

Eternal life was the dominant concern of my parents. My mother once wrote to Pauline (4 March, 1877): "I wanted to have many children, so as to rear them for heaven." Whenever one of my little brothers or sisters died, her spirit of faith gave her such energy and she was so consoled by the thought that these little angels were in heaven, that people around her said: "It is not worth commiserating with Mme Martin; she does not grieve over the death of her children."

Both my parents went to early Mass every day, and received communion as often as they could. Both fasted and abstained throughout the whole of Lent, and said that the mitigations that had just been introduced were not made for good Chris-tians.

My father was wonderfully kind to his neighbours, and never spoke the least evil of them. He made excuses for all their faults and allowed no criticism of them. Above all, he had great esteem for priests. People spoke of him as a saint.

12. The Servant of God was baptised at Alençon, in the Church of Our Lady, on 4 January, 1873, thirty-six hours after she was born. Although this delay was not very long, it troubled our mother. Our eldest sister, Marie, was godmother.

13. The Servant of God was brought up by our mother until she was four and a half years old. Then mother died, and our elder sisters, Marie, who was seventeen, and Pauline, who was sixteen, found themselves entrusted with the duty of bringing us up. Father left Alençon at this time, and brought the family to Lisieux, where my mother's brother, M. Guérin, lived. Mme Guérin and her two daughters provided us with a family milieu.

Our father loved his children very much; he had an almost maternal love for us. We, for our part, had an affectionate reverence for him that almost amounted to worship. He was especially fond of Thérèse, whom he called his "little queen", but we found that quite natural, and were not at all jealous. Besides, we were conscious of the fact that at heart he loved us all equally. Nor did Thérèse take advantage of this affection for her own ends.

14. Before my mother's death, Thérèse was high-spirited, lively, demonstrative, naturally proud and stubborn. As long as there was no question of displeasing the Child Jesus, that is; for even then, as she admits herself, she took great care to please him in all her actions and never to offend him. A temperament such as hers, had it not been restrained, could have exposed her to eternal damnation, as she said herself, but her love of what was right, together with extraordinary will-power, sufficed to preserve her from evil. Even at that tender age, I saw her practise acts of heroic virtue. She knew how to master herself perfectly, and had already acquired absolute control over all her actions.

After mother's death, Thérèse's happy disposition changed. She was cheerful only in the family circle at Les Buissonets (our house in Lisieux). Everywhere else she was extremely timid, and other girls, finding her ill-adapted to their games, disregarded her. She did try, but she never succeeded in pleasing them. So, she suffered a lot from the rude treatment that was meted out to her. From then on, she liked to keep away and not be seen, sincerely believing herself to be inferior to the others.

At first, she studied at home under the direction of Pauline, whom she used to call her "little mother". When she was eight and a half, she went as a day pupil to the school run by the Benedictine nuns in Lisieux; I was there myself already at this time. The change was very hard on her, especially as she found herself among children who had neither the same tastes nor the same ambitions as herself.

She was very successful at her studies, for although she did not learn things by heart very easily, she retained the meaning of things very well. She was in a class of pupils much older than herself, yet she won all the prizes. This caused some jealousy: one of the girls, a fourteen year old who was not very bright, made her pay for her successes with all kinds of nasty tricks. As I was in a different class, I did not witness these annoyances. Thérèse was content to cry in silence over them, and never reported them to me, because she knew well that I would soon put things to rights. She preferred to suffer in silence, firstly for the love of God, and, secondly, to avoid causing trouble to others. She only confided this to me some time later; then I understood why her stay there had been so painful.

14. She was very fond of studying, mainly scripture and Church history; she would have liked the catechism too, because this book speaks of God, but the way she had to repeat it word for word cost her heroic efforts. However, she did extremely well in it. Her marks were always very good. Just the odd time she would have a lower mark, and then the poor little mite was inconsolable, for at that time she was not at all settled in herself, and made much ado about everything. On such an occasion she could not bear the thought that her father would have less pleasure in listening to her marks. In the religious knowledge class she never failed to give an answer, so that Fr Domin, the school chaplain, used to call her his "little doctor". Indeed, she answered the most difficult questions with great accuracy for a child of her age. Her reasoning and judgment never deceived her, and the precociousness we had noticed in her early years grew more marked, above all where heaven was concerned.

When she was about ten and a half, she suffered a strange illness which ended with an apparition of the Blessed Virgin and a miraculous cure. As the tribunal has requested, I will take up the detailed account of this event later. If Thérèse did well at her studies, she topped the class as well for good conduct. She belonged to the Association of the Holy Angels, to which only exemplary children were admitted.

She took great care with her preparation for her first communion, offering Jesus a bouquet of sacrifices every day. Marie, our eldest sister, gave her private lessons every evening, and in this school her heart was opened to the love of suffering. She made her first communion on 8 May, 1884. As she returned from the holy table, I saw her in tears: her face and whole appearance reflected peace and a very intimate union with Jesus.

She received the sacrament of Confirmation on 14 June of the same year. The few days that preceded it have remained particularly engraved on my memory. Thérèse was no longer her customary calm self: there was a kind of enthusiasm and excitement about her. One day during her preparatory retreat, when I told her how astonished I was to see her like this, she explained to me what she understood of the power of this sacrament: how the Spirit of love was going to take possession of her whole being. There was such vehemence in her speech and such fire in her eyes that I left her deeply moved and completely affected by something entirely supernatural. This episode stuck in my mind so much that I still see her gestures, her attitude, and the place she occupied; this memory will never be blotted out of my mind.

15. During the retreat for her second communion (May, 1885) the Servant of God was assailed by a severe attack of scruples: she suffered from it to such a degree that she was obliged to leave school at the age of thirteen. Moreover, I had just left the Abbey, having completed my studies, and being compelled to live alone in an environment which was not her own, together with her interior trials, gave us grounds for being seriously worried about her health.

After that, she continued her studies at home, taking lessons from a governess. It was at this time that she made the big sacrifice of asking to return to the Abbey twice a week, so that she could be received into the Children of Mary sodality. This resolution cost her a lot; as she said herself, she had never been happy at school because of having to "associate with pupils who were worldly and unwilling to obey the rules",[2] and that, she admitted, made her very unhappy. "Indeed, it was only for our Lady's sake that I went to the Abbey," she wrote, " and sometimes I felt very lonely there, as I did when I was at school there."[3]

Eighteen months before Thérèse's first communion, Pauline, whom she called her "little mother", left us to enter Carmel. This was a heart-rending ordeal for Thérèse. Four years later, a further trial was added to the anxieties that were causing her scruples: our eldest sister Marie, too, left us to enter Carmel (October, 1886). Ever since Pauline's departure, Marie had become Thérèse's indispensable confidante, so that this new separation crowned her sorrows. No longer knowing where to look for help on this earth, she now confidently appealed to our little brothers and sisters who had gone to heaven before us, and she found herself suddenly and completely freed from her interior trials. She told me this in confidence, in order to prompt me, in my turn, to pray to them in difficult circumstances.

At Christmas 1886 a notable change occurred in the state of her soul. But, in order to understand her character and dispositions properly, it is important that we consider them, by way of contrast, before and after this date.

Before Christmas 1886

From the time she was four and a half, i.e. from the time her mother died, until Christmas 1886, when she was fourteen, Thérèse passed through a period of darkness. It was as if a veil had been drawn over all the fine qualities which the Lord had bestowed on her. Her school-mistresses recognised her intelligence, but in the world she was considered incompetent and stupid. This opinion was caused chiefly by her excessive shyness: it made her indecisive and had a paralysing effect on her in everything. My uncle, M. Guérin, said that her instruction had been curtailed and her education incomplete. It is true that she laid herself open to being misunderstood, by not saying much and always allowing others to do the talking. Contrary to appearances, her life was strewn with trials from childhood. She suffered a real martyrdom in both soul and body. She had almost unceasing headaches, but the extreme sensitiveness of her heart and the refinement of her feelings were a still greater source of her sufferings. She bore all that without complaining, but it depressed her.

It is important to notice that even at that stage in her life she was, on the whole, quite a strong character, notwithstanding the apparent lack of energy which her extreme sensitiveness was the cause of in her. I could see this remarkable strength, for example, in the fact that her distress was never allowed to cause the slightest deviation from duty. Even during this period, I was never able to detect a change of character, a harsh word, or a failing in virtue in her; her mortification was unceasing and extended to even the tiniest things in her life. I don't think she let slip any opportunity to make sacrifices to God. I know she would agree with me about this fidelity in the midst of trials, for she said to me one day, to give me a bit of encouragement during my novitiate, that until the age of fourteen she had practised virtue without feeling the sweetness of it. And on her deathbed she told us: "I have never refused God anything since I was three." She looked on the trials of this period of her life as God's particular way of training her in humility: "I had needed this strict training all the more," she wrote, "because I was not insensitive to praise."[4]

The Servant of God's most noticeable fault at this time was her hyper-sensitiveness: she cried over the least bit of trouble, and then, when she had been comforted, she cried for having cried. She admits herself that this state was a great weakness on her part, and calls the sudden change she underwent on Christmas Eve 1886 her "conversion"; it was a change that made her look extraordinarily self-possessed and courageous from then on. As she says herself: "Jesus made me strong, and from that blessed night onwards I was never again overcome in battle. . . . On the contrary, I began to 'rejoice like a champion to run my course'."[5]

After Christmas 1886

Thérèse herself gives a detailed account of the circumstances surrounding the change that took place in her on that Christmas Eve.[6] I witnessed the sudden change myself, and I thought I was dreaming when, for the first time, I saw her completely control herself in a disappointment that would previously have left her desolate, and then go and cheer my father up so charmingly. The change was permanent; never afterwards was she dominated by the dictates of her sensitiveness. Nor was this transformation limited to her self-possession; she blossomed forth and took an interest in practical expressions of zeal and charity. She longed for the salvation of souls, and dedicated herself generously and fervently to the conversion of sinners. In a short time God had brought her out of the narrow circle she had been living in.

No longer fettered by scruples, or her hyper-sensitivity, she matured spiritually, and became extremely hungry for knowledge. These latter desires, however, did not monopolise her attention, because her heart was already given up to God. Spiritual books were her daily nourishment; she knew the *Imitation of Christ* by heart. Communion and daily Mass were her greatest delight. Jesus was her spiritual director. Our two elder sisters, Marie and Pauline, were in Carmel now, so Thérèse and I became more and more intimate. Each evening, at the window of the summer-house, we exchanged thoughts and chatted about eternity. The words of St John of the Cross— "Lord, to suffer and be despised"—returned constantly to our lips and set our hearts aflame. We thought contempt the only attractive thing on this earth, and suffering the only thing worth desiring.

16. I had become Thérèse's sole confidante, so she could not hide from me the desire she had to enter Carmel. Her attraction to the religious life was something that went back to early childhood. Not only did she often say that she would like to be a nun, she also had a longing for the hermitical life and would sometimes isolate herself in a corner of her room, behind the curtains of her bed, and talk with God there. She was then seven or eight years old.

Later, at fourteen, after her "conversion" (as she called it), she thought of religious life chiefly as a means of saving souls. For that reason she toyed with the idea of joining a congregation of missionary sisters, but the hope of saving more souls through mortification and self-sacrifice made her decide to shut herself up in Carmel. She told me the reason for this decision herself: it was in order to suffer more, and in that way win more souls for Jesus. She considered it harder for human nature to work without ever seeing the fruit of one's labours, to toil on without encouragement or any kind of relief. She said the hardest work of all was to work on oneself in order to gain self-mastery. So it was this living death, which was more lucrative in souls won, that she decided to embrace, wishing, as she said herself, "to become a prisoner as soon as possible, in order to bring people the beauties of heaven."[7]

Finally, when she entered Carmel, she had as her very special purpose to pray for priests and to offer herself for the needs of the Church. She called this kind of apostolate "bulk buying", because if she got the head, she would get the members too. Here is how she declared her intentions in the canonical examination that preceded her profession: "I have come to save souls, and especially to pray for priests." This answer was her own, as everyone answers as they wish on that occasion.

Asked whether the Servant of God had been attracted to Carmel under the influence of her sisters who were already there, she said:

That thought had never occurred to me. God could have used that circumstance to bring us where he wanted us to be, but Thérèse's decision, like my own later, was entirely spontaneous. And, while we're on the subject, it is worth noting that if Mother Agnes (Pauline) was quite favourable to the idea, our eldest sister, Marie, was very much opposed to it.

Asked if she knew what influence Thérèse's spiritual director might have had in this decision, she answered:

Strictly speaking, she had no spiritual director. She saw what she had to do so clearly that she never felt the need to ask. Putting her plan into effect was not accomplished without great difficulties. As we were both of the same mind, I promised to help her as much as I could. The first step was to tell father of her plan. It cost her a great deal to do this; at her request, I joined my prayers to hers all day for the successful outcome of the discussion. She was entirely successful with father, but not so with our uncle, M. Guérin; he refused his support: a child of fifteen entering Carmel would be unique in the whole of France, he said, and a public scandal. But after some weeks of anxiety, Thérèse, through her prayers and sufferings, succeeded in having her uncle suddenly change his mind and give his consent. Thérèse saw this success as a compensation on God's part for the three days of anguish during which, she says: "I felt alone, with no consolation on earth or coming from heaven; it looked as if God had abandoned me."[8]

The opposition of Fr Delatroëtte, the superior of the Lisieux Carmel, was more difficult to overcome; so difficult, in fact, that

she had to enter the convent without having succeeded in overcoming it. But she tried, and father and I went with her to
visit him. I admired the way Thérèse, who was so shy by nature,
dared to explain herself and put forward her reasons for wanting
to enter Carmel immediately. But she had to leave with a very
definite "No". Father then brought her to Bayeux, and she
describes this new attempt in her autobiography.[9] As the
bishop's reply was evasive and dependent on Fr Delatroëtte's
consent, Thérèse thought her cause was lost. So she decided to
avail of her forthcoming journey to Rome, to ask the Holy
Father for the desired permission. During the whole of this
journey she never lost sight of what had now become her main
objective. When on Sunday, 20 November, 1887, she was received
in audience, together with pilgrims from the dioceses of Cou-
tances, Bayeux and Nantes, she overcame her shyness and made
her request. The Holy Father told her that she would enter
Carmel if that was God's will. Thérèse was very disappointed
at the evasive element in this answer, but she bore it with calm
resignation, because she knew she had done all in her power
to respond to her Divine Master's call.

As soon as she got back to Lisieux, she tried the bishop
again, and on 28 December, 1887, he finally gave his consent.
She would have liked to enter Carmel without delay, now that
she had this authorisation, but she was obliged to wait until
after Lent 1888. The chief reason for this delay was, no doubt,
to humour Fr Delatroëtte, who was still opposed to the idea. This
last period of waiting was particularly distressing for the Servant
of God: the devil, who no doubt wanted to discourage her, suggested some relaxation in her spiritual life. Far from listening
to him, the Servant of God led a strict and mortified life during
these months. Her mortifications were: to do little acts of kindness without attaching any importance to them, repressing a
rejoinder, or thwarting her self-will. These practices, she says,
made her grow in surrender to the divine will, humility and
other virtues. I witnessed them myself, and I was very edified.

Thérèse entered Carmel on 9 April, 1888, and left me alone
with my father. This separation was a great sacrifice for everybody concerned, for she loved her father more than anyone on
earth. However, she parted from us without shedding a tear. At
the moment of separation, Fr Delatroëtte said: "You can now

sing your *Te Deum*. I am only the bishop's delegate in this matter; so if you are disappointed, don't blame me."

17. I have hardly any personal observations to make on the period from her entry until my own (September, 1894), because we were separated during this time. But I saw her and my other Carmelite sisters in the parlour every week. On these visits I learned that our little sister had a lot to suffer during her novitiate. Pauline especially spoke to me of her annoyance at seeing our little sister badly cared for, exposed to the opposition of several of the nuns, and scolded right and left. On such occasions, Thérèse comforted her and assured her that she was happy and had quite enough to live on. I can still see her pale face and its expression of holy joy at having to suffer for God. From our conversations in the parlour I gathered that the chief causes of her trials were: 1, an almost uninterrupted dryness in prayer; 2, the indiscretion of some nuns, who took advantage of her heroic patience: seeing her so meek and uncomplaining, they gave her left-overs to eat when they should be building her up; several times she had nothing on her plate but some herring heads or other rubbish reheated several days in a row; 3, the unsatisfactory government of the community by Mother Marie de Gonzague, whose unstable and eccentric temperament inflicted a lot of suffering on the nuns. Everything depended on her latest fancy; anything good never lasted for long, and it was only by dint of diplomacy and tact that stability could be achieved even for a few weeks.

The information I have given was confirmed to me by other nuns, when I entered Carmel myself. Thérèse made her profession on 8 September, 1890; I was present when she took the black veil on 24 September of the same year.

18. When I entered Carmel (14 September, 1894) after my father's death in July, I found the Servant of God still among the professed novices, in spite of her six years in religious life. Out of humility, and in order not to leave the stricter atmosphere of the novitiate, she had asked to be left there. Mother Agnes was prioress at the time, and she had given her to the novices as a kind of prefect, with all the rights of a novice-mistress. But this status was not official; it would not do to infringe on the domain of Mother Marie de Gonzague, who was the official novice-mistress. When Mother Marie de Gonzague was re-elected

prioress in 1896, she kept the full authority of novice-mistress for herself as well. But when she found herself too busy, she appointed the Servant of God to assist her and substitute for her as the need arose. Strictly speaking, one cannot say that Sister Thérèse was ever novice-mistress. Because of the prioress's fickleness, Sister Thérèse hadn't a moment's security in this so-called office, which was taken from her and given back again every two weeks or so. In this situation, any peace the novices enjoyed was due solely to the Servant of God's prudence. If Sister Thérèse's influence was too strong, Mother Prioress was offended and said she had no right to be giving us advice, that she was overstepping her instructions. We novices had to be crafty to avoid conflict, and we had recourse to a thousand stratagems.

Meanwhile, in the midst of these difficulties, God's work was being done, if not by the novices, at least by Sister Thérèse. I say that because Sister Thérèse was not very particular in her choice of novices; they were far from being well on the way to perfection like those whom her intercession sends us today. One of them was really uncouth and sullen, and ignored her counsels; another, who was rather stupid and had no vocation to Carmel, exhausted the Servant of God's zeal and energy, apparently in vain; a third was so difficult to train that if she remained in Carmel it was due only to our young mistress's patience. This was the difficult kind of ground she had to cultivate. Her guidance was sound; she had an answer to everything. She never shirked her duty, and was not afraid to do battle with the defects of the novices; but she was also very gentle and compassionate when that was what was called for. She could not bear people to attach importance to childish ailments. Though not everybody admitted it, all went to her for guidance at one time or another; she was not soft or easy-going, but people turned to her out of a natural need for the truth. Some of the older nuns went to her secretly, like Nicodemus, when they needed advice for themselves.

The Servant of God once told me in confidence that she had asked God never to be loved in a human way, and that was how it was, because although the novices had a deep love for her, their affection was never a natural attachment. Our young mistress's whole strength lay in her detachment from herself:

she forgot herself completely and was always careful to mortify herself. She never asked a question to satisfy her curiosity, because a maxim of hers was that no good could ever come of self-seeking.

On the subject of offices in the community, I should point out that neither Sister Thérèse nor I ever had a vote in the chapter, because our constitutions forbid us to have more than two sisters in a chapter at one time.

19. The Servant of God "published" nothing; she composed some writings which were published after her death. They are: the manuscript of her life; letters, mostly addressed to her sisters; poems on religious subjects; some dialogues or "pious recreations", composed for our community feasts.

Her chief work is the *Story of a Soul*. She composed it by order of Mother Agnes, when she was prioress. She had no ulterior motive when she started writing; she just wrote it out of obedience, and tried to tell certain facts about each member of the family, so as to please them all with this account of childhood memories. The manuscript was really a family souvenir, and meant only for her sisters. That explains its easy familiarity and the inclusion of certain details of her childhood that she might have baulked at, if she had foreseen that the manuscript would leave the family circle. She only wrote off and on, in the rare moments of leisure allowed her by the rule and her work with the novices. She wrote as it came to her, without any rough draft, and yet her manuscript contains no erasures.

When the Servant of God had finished her account of her childhood she gave it to Mother Agnes, then prioress. Mother Agnes put it casually aside, without bothering to read it, for she looked on it as a family souvenir that would be nice later.

The second part of the manuscript was written when Mother Marie de Gonzague was prioress, and Sister Thérèse herself already very ill (1897). By this time, the Servant of God foresaw that her composition would be a means of apostolate, so, with its publication in view, she instructed Mother Agnes to delete or add to it as she would see fit for the glory of God. In fact, Mother Agnes did not make any substantial changes in this part.

The third part was a souvenir of her last retreat (1896), and is addressed to Sister Marie of the Sacred Heart.

The Servant of God wrote the *Story of a Soul* to three different people, therefore, and at different times. After her death, the manuscript was submitted to the Norbertine Fathers at Mondaye Abbey (Frs Godefroy Madelaine and Norbert). They strongly urged us to publish it, and obtained the necessary *imprimatur* for that purpose from the Bishop of Bayeux. Mother Agnes then undertook to publish it, convinced that in this she was working for the glory of God. Her aim was to make it available to the convents of the Order in place of the customary circular that was sent out after the death of each sister. To get Mother Marie de Gonzague's permission for this, she had to make some changes, so as to make it appear that all three parts were addressed to Mother Gonzague herself, who then signed it. The material thus suppressed, however, has been carefully restored to its original position in the text by Sister Marie of the Sacred Heart.

20. The Servant of God always practised the virtues heroically; she was distinguishable from even the best nuns both by the degree of perfection and the continuity of her practice of all the virtues. Her courage never failed. She did not practise virtue occasionally, or for a day or a month; she did so throughout her life without fail. I have never seen that in anybody else to so high a degree; no matter how resolute people are, they let themselves down once in a while. That is why I had grouped all her virtues under fortitude before I saw the headings under which the vice-postulator had classified them. The Servant of God really lived what she wrote and what she taught me. Yes, I have seen her prove her love for God by "not missing any opportunity of making some small sacrifice, controlling every look and every word, profiting by the least actions and doing them for love."[10]

21. The Servant of God nourished her soul on the Sacred Scriptures. From childhood she also liked the *Imitation* very much, and knew it by heart. But what she used most of all in prayer was the Holy Gospel. She even carried this sacred book around next to her heart, and used to go to considerable trouble to find editions of the individual gospels, which she then bound together so that others could do as she did. She studied the Bible "in order to find out what God was like". The differences between the various translations bothered her: "If I had been a priest," she used to say, "I would have studied Hebrew and

Greek real well in order to know the divine thinking exactly as God deigned to express it in human language."[11]

Faith

Everything, no matter how ordinary, helped to increase her faith, and purely secular things were for her an occasion of calling religious thoughts to mind. For instance, when our cousin, Jeanne Guérin, was getting married (which happened a week after she took the veil herself), she was impressed by all the little attentions she lavished on her fiancé, and immediately drew from it the lesson that she must be just as assiduous in her attentions to Jesus. Imitating Jeanne's wedding invitation, she even sent me an invitation to her own spiritual nuptials.

Nature and artistic masterpieces raised her mind to God too. Particularly on her journey to Rome, she hardly knew how to express the beauty of the countryside, the splendour of the buildings, the fineness of the paintings and sculpture, or the melodiousness of the language. As she wrote to her cousin Marie Guérin: "Italy is beautiful. I could never have imagined that we would see such beautiful things."[12] In her autobiography she adds: "The sight of so much beauty set me thinking deeply; I felt I already understood the grandeur of God and the wonders of heaven."[13]

The faith by which she lived was subjected to the hard test of temptation. She describes this herself in the *Story of a Soul*.[14] These temptations concerned the existence of heaven, in particular. She spoke to nobody about it, for fear she would pass her own indescribable torment on to them. But from time to time in our intimate chats she would let slip something like: "If you only knew! If you only had these trials of mine for just five minutes!" She discussed this temptation with the confessors she was allowed to consult. One of them made matters worse by telling her she was in a very dangerous state. On the advice of a more enlightened director, she copied the Creed and carried it around with her; she was prepared to write it with her blood. She told me she had made many acts of faith in an effort to combat this temptation. This trial lasted till her death.

The Servant of God's spirit of faith made her see God's will in all her trials, and thus rendered them dear to her. On the occasion of our father's illness, she wrote to me (26 April,

1891): "Jesus has given us a loving look, a tear-veiled look, and this look has become for us an ocean of suffering, but also an ocean of grace and love."[15]

This spirit of faith made her see God's hand even in the most human situations. As she wrote to me: "God alone orders the events of this life of ours in exile. But we don't see him; he hides himself and we see only creatures. . . . Creatures are steps, or instruments, but it is the hand of Jesus that guides everything. We must see only him in everything."[16] And whatever Sister Thérèse taught me she practised it herself.

She was very sorry that, contrary to our hopes, father was unable to be present when she took the veil. About this she wrote to me (23 September, 1890): "You know how much I wanted to see our beloved father again this morning. Well, now I see clearly that it was not God's will that he should be there. He allowed that just to test our love. . . . Jesus wants me to be an orphan, he wants me to be alone with him alone. . . . This was Jesus's doing and nobody else's; it was he, and I recognised his loving touch."[17]

Hope

The Servant of God always had a holy ambition for the good things of heaven and for the attainment of holiness. Nothing could lessen this desire of hers or her confidence in the realisation of her desires. But it was not on account of her merits that she hoped to attain to sanctity, for she never claimed to have any, but through the infinite merits of Jesus, which, she said, were " her property". She once confided her ambitions for great sanctity to a retreat master. He considered her very rash, and tried to discourage her pretensions. The moment had not yet come when another director "would launch her with full sails on the waters of trust and love".[18] She persisted, nevertheless, in her hopes and desires. In May, 1890 (when she was seventeen) she wrote to me: "For my part, I am not telling you to strive after the seraphic sanctity of St Teresa, but just 'to be perfect as your Father in heaven is perfect' (Mt 5:48). Oh! Céline, though our desires border on the infinite, they are not dreams or hallucinations, for it was Jesus himself who gave us that commandment."[19] In the same way, she hoped to see all her sins blotted out by the infinite merits of Jesus. On one of the last days on which she was still able to recite the divine office alone, I was with her and I saw her expression suddenly soften. She pointed to one of the readings for Matins, and said: "Look at what St John says: 'My little children, I have written this for you so that you will not sin. But should you sin, remember that you have a Mediator who is Jesus' *(1 John 2:1)."* There were tears in her eyes as she read out those last words.

Another thing she looked forward to was the Communion of Saints. Seeing how perfectly and faithfully she sought God's glory in everything, I said to her one day: "What I envy about you are your good works. I, too, would like to do good, write nice things and paint nice pictures that would make God loved more." "Ah!" she answered. "You mustn't set any store on that. We must concentrate on loving, and not allow ourselves to be upset by our impotence. . . . However, if our wretchedness causes us too much suffering, we must offer God other people's good works: that's one of the benefits of the Communion of Saints. Tauler says: 'If I love the good that is in my neighbour as much as he loves it himself, that good is as much mine as it is his.' Through this communion I can enrich myself with all the good there is in heaven and on earth, in the angels, in the saints and in all those who love God. You'll see; you'll do just as much good as me and more, when you perform the tiniest action out of love, even a slight favour, when it costs you something." She believed it was wrong to be afraid of desiring too much or asking God for too much: "We must say to God: I know I'll never deserve what I am hoping for, but I stretch out my hand to you like a little beggar, and I am sure you will hear me fully, because you are so good."

For the Servant of God these hopes of eternal life and sanctity were a great source of detachment from created things. As she once wrote to me: "It struck me the other day that we must not become attached to what surrounds us, since we might easily be in a different place from where we are."[20] One day I told her I wished others would take my efforts into account and would remark on my progress. She said: "What vanity it is to want to be appreciated by twenty people living with us. I want to be loved only in heaven, for it is only there that everything will be perfect."

Her hope was invincible, too, in the difficulties of daily life.

The way she looked at it was, that if she did all in her power to respond to the Lord's call, God would bless her efforts. During our father's illness she kept our courage up by her words and example. At that time, she said to me: "Life is but a dream; we shall soon wake up, and what a joy that will be! The greater our sufferings, the more infinite will our glory be."

She was never discouraged. She sometimes felt weak or spiritually dry, but this made her only all the more faithful to the practice of virtue. Here is how she described her dispositions in a letter she wrote me in September, 1893: "Even if I felt that this fire of love had gone out, I would still throw little straws on the embers, and I am sure it would light up again."[21] Even when, after fervent prayer to God and his saints, she was not heard, she thanked them nevertheless: "I think they want to see just how far I am prepared to go with my hope," she said.

We have a curious paradox here: in the midst of a great temptation against the faith, which concerned chiefly the existence of heaven, the Servant of God constantly showed that she hoped in this heaven, and continually expressed her desire of it. When she heard the doctor say that only two out of every hundred ever recovered from the illness she was suffering from, she said to me quite cheerfully: "What a pity if I should turn out to be one of that two per cent!"

When one of the nuns asked her: "Are you not afraid of death, then?" she said: "Yes, it frightens me when I see it represented in pictures as a spectre; death is not like that, that's a false idea of it. To get rid of that idea, I need only to recall the answer given in my catechism: death is the separation of the soul from the body. Now, I am not afraid of a separation that would reunite me forever with God."

Before she became ill, she used to say that whenever she wished to test whether her love and hope of heaven were remaining constant, she would ask herself whether death was still as attractive to her. A day without trials or a great joy were a burden to her, because they tended to weaken her desire for death. In a word, I can say that I have never seen her falter in her hope. I have never caught her off guard with a sign of human fear; blind hope was her constant attitude.

Love of God

She loved God the Father with all the tender affection of a daughter. She constantly invoked the Spirit of love too. But "her Jesus", as she called him, was everything to her. When writing about our Lord, she wrote "He" and "Him" with capital letters out of respect for his adorable person. It was through Jesus that she approached God. She had special devotion to the mystery of the Incarnation, and celebrated it devoutly every 25 March. She liked to think of Jesus as a child. She used to say: "It would be nice if I could die on the 25th of March; that's when Jesus was littlest." She also had a deep devotion to the Sacred Heart. In her opinion, it was impossible for a person with a love for this heart to be lost; she had great faith in it. There was a certain person whose waywardness caused everyone a certain amount of concern, but Thérèse said: "I tell you God will have pity on her because of her devotion to the Sacred Heart." And of another, whose salvation was in jeopardy, she said: "She will be saved because of her devotion to the Sacred Heart, but in a way that will be like going through fire." When I paid a visit to Paray-le-Monial in 1890, she wrote: "Do pray to the Sacred Heart. You know, I do not see the Sacred Heart like everyone else. I think that the Heart of my Spouse is mine alone, as mine is His alone, and then I talk with Him in the aloneness of that enchanting heart-to-heart, waiting for the day when I shall gaze upon Him face to face."[22]

Her devotion to the Sacred Heart found its complement and fullest expression in the devotion to the Holy Face. In her eyes, the Holy Face was the mirror in which she saw her Beloved's soul and heart. His Holy Face was the meditation book from which she learned the science of love, as she explains in the *Story of a Soul*.[23]

From earliest childhood the Servant of God took great care not to offend God. Her vigilance extended not only to the slightest venial sins, but to the smallest imperfections. Her love gave rise to an increasingly intense desire to sacrifice herself, to prove her love by deeds. So, you might say that her whole life was spent, to use her own words, "strewing the petals of her flowers, her sacrifices, before Jesus", and at the hour of her death she was able to pay this fine tribute to herself: "Why should death make me afraid? Anything I have ever done was for God."

Her life-long dream was to see her generous love crowned by martyrdom. She shared all these feelings of ardent love that burned in her heart with me from childhood, when we had our intimate chats by the window of the summer-house at Les Buissonets, and later in those unforgettable visits to the parlour, when we spoke of nothing but God. "It is about him, about Jesus, that we will talk together," she wrote (15 August, 1892); "without him no conversation has any attraction for us."[24]

She had a very definite attraction to prayer; she found things everywhere that made her think of God. She practised the advice she gave me: namely, to sing a continual song to the Beloved in my heart. One day, in Carmel, I asked her if she ever lost the feeling of God's presence. "Oh, no," she said; "I don't think I've ever been three minutes without it." And that was in spite of her almost continual aridity and her temptation against the faith.

It was the love of God that really animated all her actions; she breathed only for him, thought only of him. On the wall of her cell she had written with a pin the words: "Jesus is my only love." Contrary to the practice of other mystics, who strive for perfection in order to attain to love, Sister Thérèse took love itself as her way to perfection, and at nineteen she wrote to her cousin Marie Guérin: "I know of no other way to perfection but love."

In a poem entitled "Living by Love" the Servant of God sang of the life of love as she understood it. It expresses her thought on the subject fully. She composed it all while she was making her hour's adoration before the Blessed Sacrament on 25 February, 1895.

On 9 June of the same year, the feast of the Blessed Trinity, she received a very special grace during Mass, and felt within herself an urge to offer herself as a holocaust victim to Merciful Love. After Mass she took me with her to mother prioress; she seemed beside herself and did not say a word. When we found Mother Agnes, for it was she who was then prioress, she asked her if both of us could offer ourselves as victims to Merciful Love, and gave her a short explanation of what that meant. Mother Agnes was at a loss; she did not seem to understand too well what was going on, but she had such confidence in Sister Thérèse's discretion that she gave her full permission. It was then that she composed the act called "An Offering to Love", which she carried next to her heart ever afterwards.

Love of neighbour

Sister Thérèse's love for the poor was quite touching. As a child, she had the honour of handing them the alms, and she insisted on it. She approached them with such affection and respect that one would be tempted to think it was the poor person that was doing her a favour. In Carmel, she would have liked to be infirmarian, because that was the job that required most dedication. On this subject she said to me: "Infirmarian is the job I would like best; I wouldn't like to ask for it in case it was presumptuous of me, but if I were given it, I would count myself privileged." As I was assistant infirmarian myself, she urged me warmly to take good care of the sick, not to do it as I would any other job, but carefully and thoughtfully as if I was serving God himself.

Whenever she noticed a tendency in any of her novices to become closed in upon themselves, she fought it vigorously. One day she said to me: "To become introverted is to sterilise the soul; one must turn hastily to works of charity." It was what she did herself.

Shortly after I entered Carmel an elderly lay-sister, Sister Saint Peter, gave me a detailed account of the charitable care which Sister Thérèse took of her. Then she added solemnly: "Such acts of virtue must not remain hidden under a bushel." The Servant of God's virtue must have been of a very special gentleness to impress a rough temperament such as hers like that. What she had found particularly striking was the angelic smile with which her kindly helper left her on each occasion.

Thérèse liked to be constantly at people's service and to please them, at a cost to herself. Her "silences" and her Sundays (times of freedom in Carmel, which every sister is very jealous of) were spent, more often than not, writing poems at the request of other sisters. She never refused anybody. Her time was so taken up with these acts of charity that she had none left for herself.

Her charity found a variety of expressions. While she was ill, she allowed the most repugnant remedies to be administered to her with unfailing patience time and again, though she knew

E

they were utterly useless. She told me she had offered all these painful and useless attentions to God for the benefit of some missionary who was ill and uncared for.

Her charity reached out, too, to the souls in purgatory. She had made her "heroic offering" and entrusted all her daily merits to our Lady so that she might use them for the benefit of those suffering souls; she had made the same arrangement regarding any prayers that would be offered for herself after her death.

Her charity inspired her with zeal for the salvation of souls. This flame was kindled in her heart at the time of what she calls her "conversion", namely Christmas, 1886. One Sunday as she was closing her prayer-book after Mass a picture of Jesus crucified stuck out in such a way that all she could see of it was one of Jesus's hands, pierced and bleeding. At that moment she had a strange inner feeling of seeing this blood drip to the ground and nobody bothering to collect it. She immediately resolved to remain at the foot of the Cross, in order to collect the blood and turn it to good account for sinners.

One special object of her zeal at that time was the notorious Pranzini, a criminal condemned to death for the most heinous crimes. She came to know of him through the newspapers, and decided to convert him. She was about fourteen at the time. For this purpose, she redoubled her sacrifices and had a Mass offered for him, as she told me when asking me to help her. I was surprised to see her, contrary to her normal practice, showing great interest in the newspapers; she was looking out for the announcement of Pranzini's conversion. She was entirely confident that her prayer would be heard, but for her own consolation she had asked God to give her a visible sign of it. Pranzini was, indeed, very unexpectedly and significantly converted.

Recently, I had a visit from Fr Valadier, who used to be chaplain to Roquette prison (a prison for those condemned to death), and was the successor of Fr Faure, who assisted Pranzini at his death. He confirmed the fact of Pranzini's unexpected conversion; Fr Faure himself had told him all about it. Pranzini had ascended the scaffold still refusing any help from religion; it was only after they had bound his hands that he cried out in an anguished voice that was full of repentance and faith: "Chaplain, give me the crucifix!" He kissed it effusively, and exchanged a few words with the chaplain just before the executioner took him away.

The Servant of God used to call Pranzini "her child". Later, in Carmel, whenever she received some money on her feastday, she used to get Mother Prioress's permission to use it to get a Mass said. She would then whisper to me: "It's for my child; he must need it after all he's done. I mustn't abandon him now." After this memorable victory, Thérèse's zeal spread like a forest fire. She undertook to convert a woman who sometimes came to work for us, a complete heathen. She also instructed two poor girls in the faith. It was delightful to listen to her talking about God, and the children listened to her with rapt attention. Later, in Carmel, I saw her furtively slip medals into the overcoats of the workers as they left the convent.

When I had photographed the novices, I painted a portrait of Sister Thérèse; she wanted to hold a scroll in her hand bearing St Teresa's words: "I would give a thousand lives to save just one soul." During her last illness, at a time when she was in great pain, she said: "I am asking God that all the prayers that are said for me may be of benefit to sinners, and not for my relief." She wanted to go on working for souls even after her death; as she told Mother Agnes in my presence, she wanted to spend her heaven doing good on earth. Two months before she died, 22 July, 1897, I was reading her a passage on the happiness of heaven when she interrupted me: "That's not what attracts me." "What, then?" I asked. "Just love: to love, to be loved, and to come back on earth to make Love loved."

During the time she spent in the convent, she bore the sanctification of priests in a special way in her intentions. On 14 July, 1889 she wrote to me: "Dear Céline, let's live for souls, let's be apostles . . . and save especially the souls of priests: these souls ought to be more transparent than glass. Alas, how many bad priests and priests who are not as holy as they should be there are! Let us pray and suffer for them. . . . Céline, do you understand this cry from my heart?"[25] This idea recurs frequently in her letters, as well as in the autobiography and in her poems.

Her charity was not found wanting, either, towards those who gave her cause for complaint. But then, of course, she never complained about anybody. At school, when those older pupils were jealous of her success, she cried silently and would say nothing to me. In Carmel her charity found the same kind of expression. If she had any preference, it was for the most neglected sisters, and at recreation I always saw her with those sisters for whom she had the least liking. She asked Mother Prioress to make her assistant to a person that no one could work with because of her difficult temperament, and that in order to do that person some good.

One day, just to encourage me in my efforts to overcome natural antipathy, she told me how much effort this cost herself. This was a real revelation to me, because she controlled herself so well that it looked effortless. I was still more surprised when she told me the name of the sister who caused her these daily struggles with herself. Indeed, I found the Servant of God so kind and considerate towards this sister that I would have taken her to be her best friend. It looked as if when someone was unpleasant to her, she became kinder, gentler and more considerate towards that person in order to heal the embittered heart which she felt was suffering. She wanted me to follow her example in this, but I said: "It's too hard; I'll never be able to do it. I make good resolutions, and I see clearly what I have to do, but at the first encounter I give in." "If you are that easily overcome," she said, "it is because you do not soften your heart in advance. When you are exasperated with someone, the way to recover your peace of mind is to pray for that person and ask God to reward her for giving you an opportunity to suffer."

While she was ill, she drew a lesson for me from the fact that the infirmarian always chose the softest linen for her, in an effort to give her some relief. "You see," she said, "people must be treated with the same care. . . . How often one hurts them without realising it! . . . So many are sick, others are weak, and all of them are suffering. We ought to be very gentle with them." She told me too that "One should always treat others charitably, for very often what we think is negligence is heroic in God's eyes. A sister who is suffering from migraine, or is troubled internally, does more when she does half of what is required of her than another who does it all, but is sound in mind and body." She had no favourites; I always saw her just as happy in the company of a certain sister who was rather stupid and difficult as she was in anybody else's.

Asked if she was not aware of any deficiency, however small, in the Servant of God's charity, she continued:

In spite of my desire to be absolutely honest with you, I have failed to find any defects. She was sometimes pretty severe on the novices, but I cannot honestly say that that was a defect. It was a holy anger which did not cause her to lose her temper or her peace of mind.

Prudence

The Servant of God always practised the virtue of prudence. She never acted on impulse; she reflected and then acted. All her thoughts, actions and conversations were directed towards God. She behaved with consummate prudence in her own life, never wasting her energy on anything outside her objective, and she tried to guide the novices along the same way by teaching us to avoid any stumbling blocks that would slow us down. She took the Blessed Virgin as her model in prudence, and never ceased to admire her and propose her to us as a model in her reserve with the angel, her silence with St Joseph, and in the way she "kept all things faithfully in her heart" amid the joys and sufferings of life, as the Gospel tells us *(Lk 2:19).*

She was already prudent even as a child: she said little, but she observed a lot and reflected very maturely about everything. About 1883, when I was about fourteen and she was barely ten, we were at our most intimate; we were always together, and shared the same room. For many years she was most discreet and tactfully silent about a delicate matter connected with the difference in our ages. Four or five years later she had this to say on the subject: "I could see that there was something that was being kept hidden from me, but, to please God and mortify myself, as well as in order not to annoy you, I did not try to find out."

Her prudence was evident, too, in the negotiations that were destined to open the doors of Carmel to her at fifteen. The circumstances, as I have already explained, were very difficult, and there was opposition to her project from so many sides that her plan would have failed but for the supernatural prudence she gave proof of. Her great means of overcoming obstacles was prayer; she did not become impatient or annoyed at them, nor had she hard words to say of those who opposed her; she just turned away and explored other avenues by which she might reach her objective, which she considered to be God's will.

The Servant of God never had a spiritual director in the strict sense. Both in the matter of her vocation and for her personal guidance later, she let herself be guided by our Lord. She did so, however, without hurting anybody, and while giving entire respect where it was due.

Asked if she kept away from spiritual directors on purpose, she said:

No, whenever retreat preachers or extraordinary confessors came to the convent, she sought their advice at length. But it was our Lord's will that she rarely found in these sessions the light she was seeking. In this connection she made the following application of a passage from the *Song of Songs*. As the novices used to ask her how they should approach spiritual direction sessions, her answer was: "With great simplicity, but without relying too much on help which might prove inadequate when you come to make use of it. You would soon find yourselves forced to say, like the spouse in the *Song of Songs*: 'The guards have taken away my cloak, they have wounded me; it was only by getting a little beyond them that I found my Beloved' (5:7; 3:4). If you ask the guards humbly and without being over-dependent where your Beloved is, they will tell you. But, more often than not, you will find Jesus only after you have left all creatures behind."

The Servant of God's precocious maturity and her prudence were appreciated in Carmel, so that at twenty-one she was put in charge of the novices, though without the title of novice-mistress. These difficult and abnormal circumstances made her rare prudence stand out all the more. Here is how she defined her task to me in a letter of July, 1894: "I am 'a little hunting dog', I am the one who runs after the game all day. You know, the hunters (novice-mistresses and prioresses) are too big to hide in the bushes; but a little dog . . . well, it has a sharp nose, and naturally it can slip in anywhere! So I keep a close watch, and the hunters are not dissatisfied with their little dog."[26]

But her prudence was not confined to avoiding the pitfalls of the situation; it can be seen at its best in the advice she used to give the novices (I was one of them myself at the time). The real impact of her guidance came less from a purely human prudence than from her self-denial, her love for those in her care, and from her constant recourse to God. I often noticed her raise her mind to God in prayer while conversing with us, and I also noticed that she was never self-seeking. She was very kind, but also very firm; she let us off with nothing. As soon as she noticed some imperfection or other, she sought out the person concerned fearlessly and, whatever it cost, nothing could stop her doing her duty.

What she taught us was full of wisdom; here are some examples of it. She told us that in a community each one must strive to be self-sufficient; that everything should be done as perfectly as possible, but in accordance with custom, because an indiscreet zeal could sometimes damage oneself and others. She also said: "It is a fact of life that one gets tired of doing something over a period of time; so, in the matter of practices, it is better to take on only what you think you can persevere in." In 1889, the time of our family trials, she wrote to me: "Let us look at life as it really is: it is but a moment between two eternities. . . . Let us suffer peacefully. I admit that word 'peace' sounded a bit strong to me, but the other day I was thinking about it, and I found the secret of suffering peacefully. 'Peace' is not the same as 'joy', or at least not the same as 'feeling joyful'. To suffer peacefully it is enough to really want everything that Jesus wants. Holiness is not a matter of fine words, not even a matter of just thinking them or feeling them; it consists in being really willing to suffer."[27] She summed up all her teaching in what she calls "her little way of spiritual childhood and complete surrender".

This "spiritual childhood and complete surrender" was the essential characteristic of her holiness. In the personal guidance she gave each novice individually the same points always cropped up: humility, poverty of spirit, simplicity, trust in God.

The essence of her instructions was to teach us not to be upset when we saw ourselves as the personification of weakness, and to tell us to be diligent in loving, because "love covers a multitude of sins". As she once said: "It is easy to please Jesus, to enrapture his Heart; you have only to love him, without looking at yourselves, without spending too much time examining your own faults."[28] Her thought is also well expressed in her following words to me: "You are very little, remember that, and when one is very little one does not have beautiful thoughts. God is prouder of what he is doing in your soul—your littleness and humbly accepted poverty—than he is of having created millions of suns and the whole expanse of the heavens."

One day she gave expression to a very nice thought, and when I expressed regret at not being able to have such thoughts, she said: "A baby takes its mother's breast automatically, so to speak, and without realising the usefulness of its action; yet it lives and grows. Naturally, it is a good thing to recollect oneself and actualise one's intention often, but it must be done without constraint. God is well able to see the lovely thoughts and marvellous intentions we would like to have."

"Yes," I answered, "but you are always very nice to God, and I am not. I would dearly love to be; would this desire make up the leeway?"

"Yes," she said, "especially if you accept the humiliation of it, and if you go a bit further and rejoice in it; that will please Jesus more than if you had never been lacking in attentiveness to him. Say: My God, I thank you for my not having even one nice thought about you, and I am glad to see that others do."

She used also say: "There is no need for you to understand what God is doing in you; you are too little." Or: "We must work not in order to become saints, but in order to please God." Her "little way" consisted in boasting of her infirmities, of her utter inability to do anything good. The gospel passage about the workers who only worked one hour and yet were paid like all the rest (Mt 20:1-16) delighted her: "Look, if we give ourselves up and put all our trust in God, making our little efforts and hoping for everything from his mercy, we will be just as rewarded and well-paid as the greatest of the saints."

Another element of her "little way of surrender" was to look on the bright side of things, and to moderate our anxiety over our affairs. And she practised this total surrender which she always taught us. One day during her illness, Mother Agnes saw that she was in great pain and said to her: "You look distressed, my poor little one; it's because heaven is not yet just round the corner, isn't it?" She immediately replied: "Oh! Mother dear, do you not know me yet? Take this; you will find all my sentiments expressed in this poem of mine":

> I want to live a long time yet,
> O Lord, if that be your desire;
> or I would like to follow you to heaven,
> if that would give you pleasure.
> Love, that fire from the Fatherland,
> never ceases to consume me.
> What does life or death matter to me?
> Jesus, loving you is all my joy.

One day I read in *Ecclesiasticus* that "Mercy will give to each his place according as his works deserve" *(Eccl 16:15)*. Afterwards, I asked her how it was "as his works deserve" when St Paul had spoken of being "justified freely by grace". She explained to me then with great vehemence that if the authentic spirit of childhood was based on surrender to and trust in God, it was based no less on humility and sacrifice. "We must," she said, "do everything in our power, give without counting the cost, practise virtue at every opportunity, deny ourselves constantly, prove our love by all kinds of attentions and marks of affection, in a word, do all the good deeds in our power for the love of God. But since all that is really very little, it is important to place all our trust in him who alone sanctifies all deeds, and can sanctify without them; he can raise up children to Abraham from the very stones (cf. *Mt 3:9*). Yes, when we have done all that we think we should do, we must admit that we are worthless servants (cf. *Lk 17:10*), but hope nevertheless that God will give us, free, all that we desire. That is what 'the little way of childhood' is all about."

So far was the Servant of God from a vague and lazy piety that she had made the love of the cross the basis of her own. She esteemed the hard work of suffering so highly that she did not think it possibe to live a life of love without it. As she wrote in her poem "Living by Love":

> Here on earth, living by love
> is not just pitching a tent on Thabor;
> it means climbing Calvary with Jesus,
> and looking on the cross as a treasure.
> In Heaven I shall live a life of enjoyment;
> trials will then be no more;
> but in Carmel I want to live by love amid suffering.

Justice

The Servant of God always rendered faithful homage to God and the saints. She valued religious exercises highly; as a little girl, she loved devotional ceremonies and going to the sacraments of Penance and the Eucharist. She prepared for communion four years in advance, and when I, being some years older than her, received God for the first time she looked at me with a kind of holy respect and hardly dared to touch me. She always loved to visit the Blessed Sacrament. Before she went to the Abbey, before she was eight, that is, she went out walking every day with father, and never failed to visit a church; she would not come home without paying God a visit. Nor did she omit this pious practice when she went to school. Every day at half past one, she used her quarter of an hour of free time to visit God instead of taking recreation like most of her companions. After she had left school, she went to Mass daily and received holy communion as often as her confessor would allow her to, which was four or five times a week. She would have liked to receive every day, but would not dare to ask. Whenever the confessor spontaneously permitted her a communion over and above her usual quota, she was beside herself with delight.

She looked on the liturgical feasts of the Church as things of radiant beauty. In Carmel, the recitation of the divine office was a source of great joy to her, and she always looked forward to officiating at it in some capacity or other. Here she greatly edified us novices by the modesty of her bearing, and she urged us to be particularly respectful in our demeanour at it, on account of the dignity of the place of worship; she urged us, in fact, to preserve this decorum at all times out of respect for our guardian angels.

Among her duties to God, the Servant of God attached particular importance to gratitude for favours received. She said to me: "Gratitude is the thing that brings us the most grace. . . . I have learnt this from experience; try it, and you will see. I am content with whatever God gives me, and I show him this in a thousand little ways."

When I entered Carmel I thought God ought to be grateful to me for the big sacrifice I had made for him, and I asked Thérèse to compose a poem for my encouragement, a poem which would list all I had left for God and which would end with the word "Remember". She composed it all right, but gave it a completely different meaning from what I had requested: in it, the soul reminds Jesus of all he has done for her; Jesus is the benefactor now, and it is the soul that is indebted.

The Servant of God loved to get the altar ready, especially on the days when we had exposition of the Blessed Sacrament. For a long time she was sacristan, and it was edifying to see the respect and delight with which she touched the sacred vessels, and the joy she felt when she found a little particle of the host forgotten by the priest. On these latter occasions, I have witnessed some scenes of extraordinary piety, especially once when she found a ciborium that had not been properly purified; she carried it to the oratory tabernacle with indescribable devotion. She touched corporals and purificators lovingly; she said she felt she was touching the child Jesus's linen. When she was getting things ready for the following day's Mass, she liked to look at herself in the chalice and paten, and imagine that the divine species would rest on her since her image was reflected in the gold.

She always had great devotion to and utter confidence in our Lady. When she was very young, she looked on her as her mother. But her devotion grew still greater when, at the age of ten, she was suddenly cured by our Lady of an illness that doctors had deemed incurable. The statue before which she was cured remained always very dear to her. During her last illness, this statue was taken to the infirmary and placed at the foot of her bed.

The Servant of God always recommended all her intentions and all the undertakings inspired by her zeal to Mary. When she wished to encourage the novices in the practice of virtue, she wrote them little letters in Mary's name. At a very advanced stage of her illness she said to me one day: "There is still one thing I have to do before I die; I have always wanted to express everything I feel about our Lady in a hymn to her." Then she composed her poem "Why I love you, Mary".

Her devotion to St Joseph was on a par with that to our Lady. At the time of her trip to Rome she told me that she had no fears for her purity from anything that she might see on the journey because she had placed herself under St Joseph's protection. It was then she taught me to say the prayer *St Joseph, father and protector of virgins* every day, as she did herself. In Carmel she prayed to him a lot to obtain for her the freedom to receive communion more frequently. Pope Leo XIII's decree transferring the regulation of this frequency from superiors to confessors filled her with joy. She was always grateful to St Joseph for this, for it was to him that she gave the credit for the decision.

Sister Thérèse also venerated the angels, especially her guardian angel, of which she had a little statue in her room as a child. To this angel she attributed her preservation from sin, as she told me in a letter of 26 April, 1894.

She venerated all the saints, but she did have some favourite protectors and friends among them. These included her patrons: Sts Martin, Francis de Sales and Teresa. She was also very fond of St John of the Cross because she had liked his writings very much. Her special friends among the saints were: St Cecilia, whom she called "the saint of surrender", Bl. Joan of Arc, and Bl. Theophane Venard. The reason she loved the latter was, to use her own words, "because he is an ordinary, simple saint who had a great love for the Blessed Virgin and for his family, and above all because he lived his life in loving surrender to God". Finally, she also had devotion to the Holy Innocents, whom she saw as a model of the virtues typical of Christian childhood.

Fortitude

Trials were not lacking in the Servant of God's life; she had plenty of opportunities to prove the generosity of her courage. The most poignant of these trials was our father's cerebral paralysis. Other lesser sufferings came from the difficult characters of some of the people living with her. Her constant pleasantness to these people testifies in yet another way to the heroism of her fortitude. Finally, she showed exceptional courage in the way she bore a lifetime of aridity and interior trials without any diminution of fervour, and in this connection one remembers, particularly, the extremely distressing temptation against the faith which troubled her towards the end of her life.

I can now describe in greater detail those circumstances of which I was a witness myself. Already as a little girl she had great self-control; at an age when children tend to exaggerate their sufferings she was able to overcome them, in spite of her excessive sensitiveness, in order to comfort others. She bore everything in silence and never complained.

In the various steps she took towards entering Carmel at fifteen she showed surprising energy; there was something heroic about the way she overcame her shyness at that time. Speaking of her journey to Bayeux to put her case to the bishop, she says: "That journey cost me a great deal. It took a special grace from God to enable me to overcome my great timidity . . . Indeed, it is very true that love finds nothing impossible, because it believes that it can do anything and that everything is permissible."[29]

Where her courage was still more remarkable was in the presence of the Holy Father. "I wanted that day to come," she writes, "and at the same time I was afraid of it; my vocation depended on it. God alone knows what I suffered while waiting with my dear Céline for the audience."[30] And in a letter to her aunt she wrote: "I don't know how I am going to get myself to talk to the Pope. Only that God has taken charge of everything, I really don't know how I would manage."[31] But she was, in fact, quite brave, and presented her request in spite of the opposition of Fr Révérony, the vicar general of Bayeux. More heroic still, however, was the way she peacefully surrendered herself into the arms of Jesus when the Pope's vague answer—"You will enter if it is God's will"—left her broken-hearted. That same day she wrote to her sister: "I am the Child Jesus's little ball; if he wants to break his toy, he is free to do so; yes, I want whatever he wants."[32]

Then there was the painful trial of our father's illness. It was she, with her invincible acceptance of God's will, who supported us all the time. In February 1889 she wrote to me: "What a favour Jesus is doing us by sending us this great sorrow. Eternity will not be long enough to spend thanking him. He is showering us with favours as he did his greatest saints. Why this special love for us, I wonder? It is a secret that Jesus will reveal when we get home to heaven, the day he dries all tears from our eyes (Ap 21:4). . . . Dearest sister, far from complaining to Jesus about the cross he is sending us, I am at a loss to understand the infinite love that causes him to treat us like this. . . . Jesus must love our father dearly if he has to suffer like this. Does it strike you at all that his present misfortune is an exact complement of his beautiful life? I feel I am saying some really silly things to you, but it doesn't matter; there are a lot of other things I think about the love of Jesus, which are perhaps much stronger than what I have said to you here."[33]

In her religious life, too, where she met with many a trial from the very beginning, she showed great strength of character. For, besides the interior trials of aridity and desolation, there was the severity or incompetence of the nuns who had charge of her training in the beginning. She was given neither sufficient nourishment nor sufficient rest, and was treated severely by the Mother Prioress. Her novice-mistress was a very holy person, but somewhat lacking in good sense. For example, she would forget to give her any rest for several weeks and then, suddenly and for no apparent reason, she would make her rest for two weeks together. Then Mother Prioress would miss her at prayer in the morning and start scolding the poor child angrily, so that she did not know whom to obey. Throughout such troubles as these the Servant of God was consistently even-tempered.

Her fortitude was seen at its best in her temptation against the faith. She spoke to no one about this, lest she spread the temptation to them, and she endured it without the slightest sign of discouragement.

Her efforts to correct her own natural inclinations were also unwavering; she would have been very quick-tempered if she had not overcome herself here. When the Servant of God speaks in her autobiography about the sacrifices she made when she was fifteen, she says she "tried to break her will because she tended to be self-willed."[34] She succeeded so well in this that I, who lived always in the greatest intimacy with her, never even noticed this tendency to be self-willed that she is talking about. Both before and after entering Carmel, she always trained herself to repress a rejoinder, to do people little services on the quiet, to do work for which she had no taste, and to overcome her dislikes. We novices used to interrupt her at all sorts of times, we pestered her and asked her indiscreet questions, but I for one never saw her answer anybody even a little abruptly; she was always calm and gentle.

The only help or relief she ever accepted was what was offered to her without any prompting on her part. When, on Good Friday 1896, she had her first haemorrhage, it was after she had observed the whole of Lent without any dispensation;

and even that very day, she was allowed to fast on bread and water, and take part in the tiring work of spring cleaning. She was happy that no one took any notice of her. It was only in the last stage of her illness that she was dispensed from community work (laundry, etc.). She used to come down to the laundry burning with a high temperature, and help to hang the wash out with her back and chest raw with unhealed blisters. I can still see her going up to her cell to rest on her hard straw mattress, after having five hundred hot needles (I counted them myself) applied to her side in one session with the doctor. At that time, the sick who were not confined to the infirmary were not given proper mattresses, even temporarily. This fortitude of hers was still more manifest during the last days of her life.

To conclude, then, there is one fact I have noticed throughout the Servant of God's life, namely: that the divine Master sent her trial after trial and tribulation upon tribulation; everything either went awry for her or proceeded so slowly that she needed to practise patience and acceptance of the divine will at all times. This only makes the firmness of will which she displayed throughout her life all the more remarkable.

She was faithful in keeping her emotions under control; she was always calm and serene. She had a very lively imagination, yet she never got excited, and one was always sure of receiving wise and measured advice from her. Her advice to me was never to hold forth about something that had upset me, while I was still upset. "When you tell someone, even Mother Prioress, about some unpleasantness, never do it to have the sister who caused it corrected, or for the purpose of having the situation remedied; you must speak objectively, with detachment. If you don't feel detached, if there is still even a spark of emotion in your heart, it is better to keep quiet and wait until your heart is pacified, because talking about it would very often only make it worse." She always behaved in this way herself; she always waited until she had recovered control of herself, and was never seen to run to Mother Prioress in the heat of annoyance.

As I have already said, she told me nothing of her struggle to be charitable to that sister whom she disliked, until she had obtained a complete victory. This was because she thought, as I've just said, that discussing one's difficulties while still on the battle-field only made one weaker. This kind of behaviour on her part can be traced back to her childhood, when she would not tell me about her troubles at school until she had left it.

Mortification was something the Servant of God had always been familiar with. She always took the last place or the least comfortable, whether on a journey or at home. As a child she acquired the habit of never letting an opportunity of mortifying herself slip. For example, as soon as it was time to stop reading, she would do so, even in the middle of the most absorbing passage. Later, when she became an enthusiastic student of history and science, it was the same: "I allotted a certain number of hours to it, and, in order to mortify my over-eager desire for knowledge, I would not go beyond the allotted time."[35]

One day my father announced that he was going to let me take art lessons, and he asked Thérèse if she would like to do so too; Marie intervened to object, so Thérèse deprived herself by saying nothing, though she longed to do it. She confided to me later that she was still wondering how she had the strength to keep quiet.

In Carmel, her habit of mortification embraced everything. I noticed she never asked for news; if she saw a group gathered anywhere and Mother Prioress apparently telling them something interesting, she went the other way. In the refectory, she accepted the fact that she was served with left-overs, and never complained. She never supported her back when sitting, nor did she cross her legs; she always sat upright. She shunned anything smacking of comfort or worldly ease, and did not like to see people slumped in their seats even for relaxation. Unless it was absolutely necessary, she would not wipe the perspiration from her brow; she said it was an admission that one was too hot, and a way of drawing attention to the fact.

Speaking with her about instruments of penance, I said that the instinct of self-preservation ensured that one moved as little as possible when wearing them, and that one tensed oneself for the discipline so that it would hurt less. She looked at me in amazement, and said: "I don't think it's worth doing anything by halves; I take the discipline to hurt myself and I want it to hurt me as much as possible." She told me that it sometimes hurt her so much that tears came to her eyes, but she forced herself to smile so that her face would reflect what she felt in her heart, which was so happy to suffer with its Beloved for the salvation of souls.

Regarding instruments of penance which were permitted, but not mandatory, she said she would have liked to wear one on those days when we did not take the discipline, and she did so to the extent that she was allowed to.

In winter she rarely covered her hands, in spite of their being swollen with chilblains. One day, when it was absolutely freezing and we had no fire, I noticed she had her hands uncovered on her knees. That annoyed me, and I drew her attention to it; she just gave me a mischievous little grin, and I knew then that she was doing it on purpose.

Temperance and mortification

The Servant of God mortified her heart and spirit no less than she did her senses. She deprived herself of anything that could give her satisfaction. While Mother Agnes (her dear Pauline, the "little mother") was prioress, she deliberately missed her turn to go to her for direction in order to deprive herself of the comfort it gave her. This degree of detachment really surprised me. I was her novice, so she spoke to me because it was her duty to do so, but I often noticed how she refrained from speaking to me about her own personal affairs. In answer to the prayer she had made when she took charge of them, the novices never became attached to her by purely human affection. I noticed that, though we all loved her, none of us was tempted to have that passionate and inconsiderate affection for her which sometimes takes place between people who are still young and dreamy.

If she was that mortified with me, whom she called "the little companion of her childhood"[36] I know she was even more so with Mother Agnes, her "little mother", because she had a more restricted permission in her case.

When our cousin Marie Guérin (Sister Marie of the Euchar-ist) was being clothed in the habit, the community accompanied her to the enclosure door so that she could see the members of her family again; Sister Thérèse did not go. One of the sisters met her, and said: "Go on down, you too, and see your family!" But she took no notice. It must be noted that the parlours were being built at the time, and we hadn't seen our relatives for a year. Later, I reproached her with being the only one to miss the family reunion; she told me she had done it to mortify herself, and that it had been a very costly sacrifice.

About this subject of mortifying one's affections, she told us (her three Carmelite sisters) before she died: "When I am gone, be careful not to lead a 'family life'; don't tell one another what you hear in the parlour, unless you've got permission, and ask for permission only when it serves some useful purpose, never for your own amusement."

Obedience

Obedience was something the Servant of God practised from childhood. I can never remember seeing her grumble or delay about obeying an order, either at home or at school. We had to be very careful of what we said in her presence, because for her a suggestion became an order, and that not only for a day or a week, but for the rest of her life. It was the same in Carmel, where the circumstances were very favourable for heroic obedience at the time she entered. Poor Mother Marie de Gonzague recommended a great number of things, depending on the whim of the moment. Most of the sisters ignored these after a few days, and mother herself would forget she had ever made them. So they automatically became obsolete for everyone except Sister Thérèse. I have caught her going a roundabout way to get somewhere, or going back to shut a door that was generally left open: six months or maybe two years previously Mother Gonzague would have passed some remark about these things, and it had remained an oracle for Sister Thérèse. She never considered whether something had been recommended with or without reason, or whether it was still in force: Mother Prioress had said it once, and that was enough to make it a lifetime obligation.

She obeyed all the sisters, and was pulled right and left according to their desires without being in the slightest bit upset. One evening while she was ill, the community went to the oratory of the Sacred Heart to sing a hymn. She followed them painfully and had to sit down while they sang. One of the sisters called her to come and sing, and she immediately got up and joined the choir. I was very annoyed at this, because I was infirmarian, so I asked her afterwards who had inspired her with an obedience which, to my mind, was too blind. She answered simply: "I've got into the habit of obeying everybody out of a spirit of faith." If she obeyed everybody that perfectly, her fidelity to our Rule and constitution was absolute.

Three years after their noviceship, the novices leave the novitiate and join the other sisters in a less strict atmosphere. For instance, novices have to ask for their general permissions every week whereas the others do it only every month. Sister Thérèse could have done so too, but she made sure she would be bound by the stricter rules of the novitiate to the end of her life.

Her principle of blind obedience must have cost her many a sacrifice during her long illness, for even in our efforts to give her some relief we often caused her to suffer. But she bore it all, and never even asked for what we should have given her. One day she was told to say what could give her some relief, because she had a very high temperature, so she asked the infirmarian to take off a blanket. This sister was elderly and hard of hearing, and she thought Sister Thérèse had said she was cold; so, she collected all the blankets she could find and covered her up twice as much. When I came back I found her bathed in perspiration. She said she had accepted it all in a spirit of obedience, and that when the sister saw her take everything with a smile, she had gone off to get more.

She judged people by their obedience to superiors, and writings by whether or not they had been subjected to authority. On one occasion, she was given a booklet to read which vas causing quite a stir at the time; she liked it well enough and even had a certain amount of veneration for the author. But when she heard that this author had said something rather critical of a bishop, she would have no more to do with him or his writings.

Poverty

The Servant of God pushed the practice of poverty to extremes, but this was not something she acquired without effort. In her autobiography she says that "she liked to have pretty things for her use, and to have what she needed ready to hand".[37] Being artistic, she naturally liked things to be in good taste and in good condition. I noticed this one day when I stained her hour-glass irreparably, because I could see the effort it cost her to keep it as it was and not to show any sign of the sacrifice I had involuntarily caused her to make.

Another time someone varnished her table and the still wet legs stained the floor of her cell; she could not get the stain out, and I noticed how hard it was for her to suffer it to remain.

It was in spite of this real love of what was beautiful that she nevertheless always chose for her own use the ugliest and most used objects. Even when they were not, she knew how to make them look that way. When her work-basket began to come apart, one of the sisters covered it for her with a piece of old velvet that she found in the attic. Though she was very busy, Sister Thérèse undid the work and turned the velvet inside out so that it would look poorer and uglier. When she worked in the linen room, her workmate gave her a pin to hold down something she was working on; the pin had an imitation pearl head on it, which Thérèse immediately broke off. . . . One of her novices once treated the furniture in her cell with linseed oil; Thérèse made her scrub it all off.

She avoided comfort with great care. Throughout her religious life she had a little lamp that did not work too well; she had to use a pin to raise or lower the wick. But she did this kind of thing so naturally that one was easily inclined to believe that she liked such things. God must have permitted it to happen that way, because we really should have realised that she would prefer to have a good lamp like everybody else. She paid no attention to the state her clothes were in; the plainer and more worn they were, the happier she was.

She once told me that to save time she never made a copy for herself of poems she composed for others, much as she would have liked to have one.

To sum up these ideas on poverty, here is one piece of advice she gave me towards the end of her life: I had expressed the desire that a certain picture she had would come to me after her death. "So, you still have desires!" she said. "When I am with God, don't ask for anything that I had; just take what you are given. To behave any other way would mean that you were not stripped of everything, and that would make you unhappy rather than bring you joy. Only in Heaven will we have the right to possess."

Chastity

Sister Thérèse always exercised the greatest care to keep the beautiful virtue of chastity intact. She told me that she always behaved as modestly when she was alone as she would have in someone else's presence. But she was not scrupulous. Being an honest and intelligent person, she knew everything, and her pure mind saw that everything was beautiful. Her heart was so pure that she did not even know what a bad thought was. She praised God for all his works; they were all stamped with the seal of divine purity. (I am speaking here of her state of soul from the age of fourteen, for I do not know what her earlier scruples were about.)

At the start of her journey to Rome, she commended her purity to St Joseph, and nothing she saw, in museums or elsewhere, gave her the slightest trouble. She told me that when she was little "she was ashamed of her body", and that the only thing that comforted her about having one was that Jesus had not thought it beneath him to take a body like ours. From Carmel she wrote me several letters in which she praised the beautiful virtue of purity: she often spoke of the "white lily", which meant virginity, and emphasised its stainless beauty by comparison with the "yellow lily" of marriage.

When all my sisters had entered religion and I was alone at home with father, she felt a motherly concern for my soul, and it pained her to see me exposed to dangers which she had not known herself. Of course, when I was alone at home I had to go along a bit with the social demands of my environment. She was always a little anxious about me, especially one day when she heard I was going to a party where there would be dancing. She cried as she had never cried before, she said, when she heard this, and she sent for me to come to the parlour in order to exhort me. I told her she sounded a bit exaggerated to me; after all one could not make a fool of oneself. She was quite indignant at this, and said to me quite vehemently: "You, who are Jesus' spouse (I had made a vow of chastity), and you want to come to terms with the world, indulging in dangerous pleasures like this?" I was quite taken aback; she won. I made a resolution to do what she had told me to, and I kept it, troublesome as it was.

Such was the Servant of God's love for purity that when, at her clothing, she was given some relics to wear on her person from then on, she kept only those of virgins and put the others aside, even those of saints whom she loved. She showed me her reliquary, and drew my attention to the fact herself. She also told me that she had never experienced a temptation against chastity.

Humility

The Servant of God always practised humility. As a child, at an age when one is so anxious to grow, she expressed the desire to remain always low-sized. Later, on her deathbed, she rejoiced in the fact that in spite of having been nine years in religion she had always remained in the novitiate, and was thus deprived of a vote in the chapter and always regarded as "a little one".

Going on the fact that she was bad at certain kinds of manual work, the Servant of God always thought of the rest of us as being better than herself. She had a holy envy of the miniatures Mother Agnes made and the poems she composed, and she admired my paintings. One day at prayer she was looking at a picture of the Adoration of the Shepherds, which I had just finished, and she offered to God the sacrifice of not being able to do it herself. After that she had a very vivid light on how the Communion of Saints makes us all share in one another's achievements in the measure that we desire it.

Sister Thérèse was so conscious of her weakness that she was convinced that she would not even attain salvation without a very special grace from God: "With a nature like mine," she writes, "I would have become very wicked, perhaps even damned, if I had been reared by parents who were careless about religion. But Jesus was watching over his little fiancée, and turned everything, even her faults, to good account, because since these were suppressed in time they only helped her grow in perfection."[38]

She attributed her virtue to this preservation, and looked on it as a real pardon. As she wrote to me in July, 1891: "Jesus says of the Magdalen that the person who is forgiven more loves more, but one can say that with even more justification when Jesus forgives the sins *in advance*."[39] She felt she had been preserved from every possible sin committed on earth, because she felt capable of falling into any of them.

On the way to Rome she noticed that one young man was obviously attracted to her. When we were alone, she said: "How timely Jesus is withdrawing me from the poisoned breast of the world; I feel my heart could easily be captured by affection, and I, too, would perish where others do, for none of us is any stronger than the other." On this subject she later wrote in her autobiography: "My not surrendering to human love does not gain me any merit, for it was God's great mercy that preserved me from it."[40] The Servant of God's humility was an attempt at being forgotten rather than an expression of the contempt she felt for herself. On 2 August, 1893, she wrote to me: "To find something that is hidden, we must be hidden ourselves. Our life must be a mystery, therefore; we must resemble Jesus, that Jesus 'whose face was hidden' *(Is 53:3).* 'Do you want to know something useful?' the *Imitation* says: 'then love to be ignored and regarded as of no account'."[41]

It is on humility that her "little way of childhood" is based: feeling weak and incapable of doing what was right (or, as she says herself, "too small to climb the steep stairs to perfection"[42]) she threw herself into God's arms and settled down there.

The Servant of God not only accepted humiliation cheerfully, she humiliated herself as well by always taking the last place, by obeying everybody, and by not speaking until she was asked to; she was humble even in the smallest things.

Here are some of the things she said to me, to teach me humility: "We sometimes catch ourselves desiring what catches the eye. When that happens, let us humbly throw in our lot with the imperfect, and look on ourselves as 'little souls' that God has to support every moment of the day. When he sees that we are really convinced of our nothingness, he gives us his hand; if we still try to do something big for him, even under pretext of zeal, he leaves us on our own. But as soon as I say I have stumbled, you steady me, Lord *(Ps 93:18)."*

Another time she wrote to me: "You probably think that I do as I say. No, I am not always faithful, but I am never discouraged. I drop into the arms of Jesus; the little dewdrop penetrates farther into the calyx of the lily of the valley, and there she finds all that she had lost, and more besides."[43] And elsewhere she says: "Yes, it is enough to humiliate oneself, and bear one's own faults meekly; that is true holiness." "If you could fail in something that would not offend God, you should do it deliberately so as to humiliate yourself."

Asked if the Servant of God had sometimes, perhaps, made much of the favours she had received from God, she answered:

I have heard it rumoured vaguely that some people have accused the Servant of God of a lack of humility in this respect. But I cannot see how such a judgment is possible, unless one reads her life and writings very superficially. It is impossible to look at her any way closely without becoming aware that she was full of humility, and that she never speaks of the graces she received, unless it is to make known with great simplicity what God's mercy did for her, or to express her gratitude, or to edify others. I think the very frankness with which she sometimes speaks of God's favours to her is itself an expression of great humility.

22. Sister Thérèse of the Child Jesus was a very simple person, and she was sanctified by ordinary means. There were, nevertheless, some instances of what appeared to be supernatural intervention in her life.

When she was only a few weeks old, she was cured through the intercession of St Joseph of the same intestinal disease that had carried off our two brothers. She was at death's door herself, and the two doctors who attended her had given up hope.

At the age of ten she was suddenly cured of a strange and serious illness by the Blessed Virgin. At the moment her cure took place, she was favoured with a vision of the Queen of Heaven. She describes all this very accurately in the *Story of a Soul.*[44] I witnessed all the stages of this illness and the sudden cure myself. Here is what I can remember of it in detail.

I felt I could recognise the devil's hand in this extraordinary illness: it was my own opinion, and the opinion I heard expressed around me. In the course of it, I witnessed some terrifying scenes: she banged her head repeatedly off the wooden part of the bed (it was a big, high bed) as if she was trying to kill herself; she used to stand up in bed, bend right down and

better. I would be just as happy to get well as to die." And she wrote: "I am willing to be ill all my life, if that is what pleases God; I have no objection even to my life being a very long one. The only desire I have is to die of love."[46]

She was indifferent to everything. One day, after she had heard us discuss the buying of a new plot in the cemetery, she said to me: "I don't care where they bury me; what does it matter where we are? There are missionaries who have ended up in the stomachs of cannibals, and the martyrs had the bodies of wild beasts for a cemetery." And when one suggested that she might die on such or such a feastday, she answered: "I don't need to choose a feastday to die on; whatever day I die will be the greatest feast of all for me."

She wanted nothing out of the ordinary for herself, whether in the spiritual sphere or the temporal. One day I said to her: "You have loved God very much, he will do wonders for you; we will find your body incorrupt." This idea seemed to pain her, and she answered somewhat sadly: "Oh, no; not that kind of wonder! That would be a departure from my little way of humility; 'little souls' must find nothing to envy in me, so you can expect to find nothing but a skeleton."

Even during her last illness she preserved those childlike and playful ways of hers which made her so likable. Everyone wanted to see and hear her. She was delighted to be dying, and enjoyed the preparations, which we tried to hide from her. For instance, she asked to see the box of lilies which had just arrived to adorn the bed on which she was to be laid out. She looked at them with pleasure and said: "That's for me!" She was so happy, she could hardly believe it. It was at her request that we settled the matter of buying a new plot in the cemetery in her presence; it was something that was brought up in view of her approaching death.

One evening we were afraid that she would not last the night, so a blessed candle and holy water were brought to the next room in readiness. She suspected this, and asked that they be placed where she could see them. She looked at them quite happily, and proceeded to describe to us in detail all that would happen when she died. She cheerfully described all the details of her burial in a way that made us laugh when we would have preferred to cry. Yes, she was encouraging us instead of we her.

One day she suddenly exclaimed: "To think that I am going to die in a bed! I would have liked to die in an arena!" When she haemorrhaged, she rejoiced in the thought that she was shedding her blood for God. "It could not have been otherwise," she said; "I knew that I would have the consolation of seeing my blood spilt, for I am a martyr of love."

Consolations were far from being the Servant of God's ordinary fare. Once, after receiving holy communion, she said to us: "It's like putting two babies together: babies don't talk to one another. I did say some little thing to him, but he did not answer: I suppose he was asleep!"

Her temptation against the faith did not ease off on the threshold of eternity; quite the contrary, the veil became thicker and thicker.

Terrible physical pain was now added to her interior sufferings. Her tuberculosis passed through a particularly painful stage, and the lack of proper treatment made it worse. Just at the time when it affected her intestines and caused gangrene she was without a doctor for a whole month. Besides, the fact that she was so emaciated caused wounds to open. She suffered real torture and we could do nothing for her.

In this abyss of misfortunes she turned to heaven, but she found no comfort there either. I told her I was surprised at this, and she said: "It's true. Very often it is when I pray to Heaven for help that I feel most abandoned." Then, after a moment's silence, she added: "But I don't get discouraged; I turn to God and the saints and thank them all the same. I think they want to see how far my hope will go. . . . It wasn't for nothing that I made my own those words of Job: 'Even if God were to kill me, I would still hope in him' (*Job 13:15*). I admit it took me a long time to reach this degree of surrender, but now I'm there; the Lord took me and placed me there."

Nevertheless, one day after a very painful attack we saw her face suddenly soften and look angelic. We wanted to know what had caused this, and we asked her about it, but she was too overcome to answer. That evening (3 August, 1897) she passed me the following note: "O my God, how kind you are to the little victim of your merciful Love! Now even when you add bodily suffering to my soul's anguish, can I say 'The sorrows of death surrounded me' *(Ps 17:5)*; but I cry out in my gratitude 'I have gone down into the valley of the shadow of death, yet will I fear no evil, for you, Lord, are with me'" *(Ps 22:4)*.[47]

She asked us to pray that God would give her the strength to persevere to the end. One morning in September, she implored me in these words: "Dear Sister Genevieve, pray to the Blessed Virgin; I would pray so much if you were ill, but I dare not ask for myself."

On 21 August she was in such pain that she was groaning and breathing painfully, and with each breath she repeated almost mechanically "I'm suffering, I'm suffering"; it seemed to help her breathe. Then she said: "Each time I say 'I'm suffering' you answer 'So much the better!' That is what I want to say to complete my thought, but I haven't got the strength to say it."

In the midst of all her sufferings the Servant of God preserved her serenity. One day I saw her smile and when I asked her what she was smiling about, she said: "It is because I feel a very sharp pain in my side, and I have made it a habit to give pain a good welcome." No matter how inopportune some visits were, she never showed the slightest annoyance. She never asked for relief, and took whatever she was given. Only in extreme necessity would she call me at night; she would wait until I came of my own accord. The last night she spent on earth Sister Marie of the Sacred Heart and I stayed up with her, in spite of her insistence that we rest as usual in the room next door. But at one stage we dozed off after giving her something to drink; she remained there, glass in hand until one of us woke up.

Her peace was unshakable. She was involved in some rather painful scenes caused by poor Mother Marie de Gonzague, but she did not grumble; it was her gentleness and humility that helped the storms to blow over.

The Blessed Virgin was her kindly beacon. One day, while looking at her statue, she said: "I can no longer look at the Blessed Virgin without crying." Later, on 8 September, she asked to see her little picture of Our Lady of Victories, to which she had stuck the little flower her father gave her when he allowed her to enter Carmel. In a shaky hand she wrote on the back of it: "Mary, if I were queen of heaven, and you were Thérèse, I would want to be Thérèse so that you could be queen of heaven." Those were the last lines she ever wrote.

She often caressed her crucifix with flowers, and when she was not holding it she used to attach a flower to it, which she would replace at the first signs of withering; she could not bear to see flowers that were any way faded on it. Even when she was ill, she used to pluck the withered petals off the roses that were strewn round the crucifix in the cloister garth, so that only the freshest would lie under Jesus's feet.

One day I saw her touching the crown of thorns and the nails of her crucifix very attentively, and I asked her what she was doing. In the tone of one taken by surprise, she answered: "I'm taking out his nails, and removing his crown of thorns."

On one of her last nights I found her gazing heavenwards with her hands joined. "What are you doing like that when you should be trying to get some sleep?" I said to her.

"I can't sleep, so I'm praying," she answered.

"And what are you saying to Jesus?"

"Nothing; I'm just loving him."

Sister Thérèse was never attacked outwardly by the devil, but a few weeks before she died I witnessed a rather strange thing. One morning I woke up to find her in great distress; there seemed to be some sort of painful struggle going on. She said: "Something very strange happened last night. God asked me to suffer for you, and I agreed. My pain was immediately doubled. You know that I suffer chiefly all down the right-hand side; well, I suddenly got a pain of almost unbearable intensity in my left side. Then I actually felt the devil acting on me; he did not want me to suffer for you. He is holding me in an iron grip, and preventing me from getting the slightest relief in order to make me despair: I am suffering for you and the devil does not want it!" We were quite frightened. I lit a blessed candle, and shortly afterwards the devil left, never to return. I shall never be able to describe what I felt when I heard those words. The little patient was pale and her face was contorted with pain and anguish; I felt we were surrounded by the supernatural.

About mid-afternoon on the day she died she was seized with strange pains all over her body. So, she placed one arm on

Mother Agnes' shoulder and the other on mine, and we supported her like that for a few minutes. Just then the clock struck three, and we could not help being deeply moved. What was she thinking then? For us she was a striking image of Jesus on the Cross; I regarded this coincidence as full of mysterious significance.

Her agony began immediately after this, a long and terrible agony. She could be heard repeating: "Oh! This is sheer suffering, because there is no consolation, not even one. O my God! I love him though! O kind Blessed Virgin, come to my aid! . . . If this is the agony, what will death be like? . . . Mother, I assure you the chalice is full to the brim. . . . Yes, God, as much as you wish. . . . But have pity on me! No, I would never have thought it possible to suffer so much . . . never, never! Tomorrow it will be still worse. Ah, well, so much the better!" The poor little martyr's words were broken and heart-rending, but they always bore the stamp of perfect resignation.

Mother Prioress now summoned the community, and Sister Thérèse welcomed them with a pretty smile. Then she clasped her crucifix to her and seemed to hand herself over entirely to suffering, so to speak. Her breathing was laboured; a cold sweat bathed her face, and soaked her clothes, her pillow and the sheets; she was shaking all over.

Sometimes in the course of her illness, Sister Thérèse had said to us (her own sisters): "My dear sisters, you must not be upset if, when I am dying, my last look is for one of you rather than another; I don't know what I will do; it will be whatever God wants. If he leaves me free, however, my last goodbye will be for Mother Marie de Gonzague, because she is my prioress." She repeated these words to us a few days before she died.

Now, during her agony, just a few moments before she died, I rendered her some little service. She gave me a beautiful smile, and a long penetrating look. A kind of a shiver ran through the community. Then Thérèse's eyes sought Mother Prioress and rested on her, but with their habitual expression. Mother Prioress, thinking the agony was going to be prolonged, dismissed the community a few moments later. The angelic patient then turned to her and said: "Mother, is this not the agony, am I not going to die?" And, when Mother replied that it could take a while longer, she said, in a low, plaintive voice:

F

"All right, then! Let it go on. . . . Oh! I would not want to suffer less!" Then, looking at her crucifix: "Oh! . . . I love him. . . . My God. I . . . love . . . you!"

These were her last words. The words were hardly out of her mouth when, to our great surprise, she collapsed, her head a little to the right. Then, suddenly, she sat up, as if a mysterious voice had called her; she opened her eyes and fixed them radiantly on a spot a little above the statue of our Lady. She stayed that way for a few minutes, about as long as it would take to recite the Creed slowly.

I have often tried to analyse this ecstasy since then, and tried to understand that look of hers, which was not just an expression of beatitude. There was an element of great astonishment in it, and her attitude expressed a very dignified assurance. I thought we had been present at her judgment. On the one hand, she had, as the Gospel says, "been found worthy to stand before the Son of man" (*Lk 21:36*), and on the other, she saw that the gifts which were about to be showered on her were infinitely beyond her immense desires. For there was another expression joined with that of astonishment: she seemed unable to cope with the sight of so much love; she was like someone who is assaulted several times, tries to fight back, but because of his weakness he is happily vanquished. It was too much for her; she closed her eyes and breathed her last. It was 7 p.m. on Thursday, 30 September, 1897.

25. I know from all that I have heard around here that Sister Thérèse's body was buried publicly in Lisicux cemetery; hers was the first grave in the new plot acquired by the Carmel. I have also seen photographs of it. Her funeral was modest and uneventful. I also know that on 6 September of this year, the Servant of God's remains were exhumed in the presence of the bishop and a large gathering of people, and that they have been placed in a new coffin and buried not far from where she had been.

26. I have not been to the cemetery myself, because of the enclosure, but I know from the many reports which reach us here in Carmel that the Servant of God's grave has become increasingly a place of pilgrimage. Many priests come there. After the exhumation of 6 September, the wooden cross that had marked her first grave was brought here to the convent. It

was literally covered with inscriptions by pilgrims asking or thanking her for something. The number of pilgrims would seem to be growing daily.

27. Sister Thérèse's edifying death and the ecstasy she had at the moment she appeared before God made a deep impression on all the community, even on those who had least appreciated her during her lifetime. One of these, a lay-sister called Sister St Vincent de Paul (she died in 1905), had pained her with her biting remarks; it was she who said (and loud enough for the Servant of God to hear): "What can we say about Sister Thérèse when she is dead?" But immediately after Sister Thérèse's death she asked her to cure the cerebral anaemia she had been suffering from for a long time. She laid her head on the angelic child's feet, asked her forgiveness, and claimed that she had been immediately and fully cured. From that on she became a tireless collector of rejected photos of Sister Thérèse, and that immediately after her death, before she could be influenced by her subsequent reputation. I know all this from Sister St Vincent herself, who made no secret of her feelings in the matter.

Sister John of the Cross (died 3 September, 1906), one of the elderly sisters who sometimes sought the Servant of God's advice, wrote the following prayer, and always kept it in her breviary: "My dear Sister Thérèse of the Child Jesus, I thank the Sacred Heart for all the graces he showered on you. I ask you to let me share on earth the love that you have for him in heaven. Ask the angel who pierced your heart with the dart of divine love to please do for me what he did for you."

Mother Marie de Gonzague told me of a favour she had received before a portrait of Thérèse as a child. It must have been a very vivid experience, because our poor Mother could not look at this picture without crying. I often saw her moved in this way, and she said to me: "Oh! The things she said to me! . . . How much she reproached me with! . . . But how gently!" The good Mother often took up this picture, and in her latter years there was a marked improvement in her, under the gentle influence of Sister Thérèse.

The Servant of God's reputation for holiness had really spread throughout the community, therefore: all the sisters prayed to her, recommended their relatives to her, and rejoiced as Mother Prioress told us each day at recreation of the accounts that were coming in of the wonders she was working.

As soon as some people began to read her life, it was like a spark that caught fire in all directions; we could not have stopped its progress even had we wished to. Editions poured out without interruption, and we still could not meet the demand; the 65th thousand copies are in the press at the moment. This book is not one of those you just read once; when people read it, they do not want to be without it any more. As a friend of mine wrote: "I will read this book again, not once but ten or twenty times; I have spiritual nourishment here for a long time to come." We have heard this kind of appreciation a hundred times or more. In the past few days we had a letter from Constantinople telling us that the *Story of a Soul* had been lent to Bishop Sardi, and that he had read it three times since July.

With this kind of reception, the book became known all over the world, and we had requests for translations from several countries. Then there were letters from bishops and other personages recommending it in very glowing terms in the prefaces to these translations. Those in the Dutch and Portuguese editions were particularly remarkable.

From the start, there were people looking for souvenirs of the Servant of God. We have had to send them out in thousands. I am responsible for any objects that once belonged to Sister Thérèse, and I am amazed to see sheets, bed curtains, and articles of clothing already gone, though we cut them up into tiny fragments.

Nearly all the letters we have received since the appearance of the *Story of a Soul* (1898) express the desire to see her Cause introduced and brought to a happy issue. One often gets a glimpse from them too of the reason why the veneration given to Sister Thérèse has something special about it. "What I like about the life of this Carmelite nun," writes one person, "is that she is a likable saint, one whom we can imitate and who does not discourage us by being too ascetic or too forbidding." That is the general impression which comes over to us in a thousand different ways: thanks to Sister Thérèse, one person learns to cover her crucifix with flowers and smile in the face of suffering; her example reminds another of the childhood that our Lord praised so much. Many ordinary, simple people feel attracted to this way of love and trust in God, and find in Sister Thérèse's example the encouragement they need to travel this way without fear. Such attraction or encouragement is often expressed in the letters we receive. Many communities claim to have been transformed by this "spirit of childhood", and from all sides comes the wish that her glorification would set the seal of approval on "this way of surrender and littleness".

The simple people referred to include doctors and scholars as well as the uneducated. Fr Pichon, s.j., wrote to me on 11 May, 1900: "Yes, God wants to glorify his humble little spouse. Then we shall have no choice but to become little children; it is what I am trying to do myself at sixty-six."

The idea that Sister Thérèse's glorification would encourage people to be holy has raised up apostles for her cause everywhere; priests especially have a particular devotion to her. Fr Flamérion, s.j., who runs a retreat-house for priests in Paris, has given us some touching examples of this. In seminaries Thérèse is very well known and loved. Many priests and religious take her as a "sister," or partner, in their priesthood. We have had a lot of visits from bishops and priests asking to be allowed to visit Sister Thérèse's cell. There is real veneration in the way they kneel before the statue of our Lady that smiled at her, and visit the places that were sanctified by her presence. We have had to refuse requests for objects that had belonged to Sister Thérèse to be brought to the grille. We have so many requests for prayers that going to the parlour and coping with the correspondence has become extremely difficult. Mother Agnes, Sister Marie and myself have had to be withdrawn almost entirely from this kind of thing, for, being the Servant of God's sisters, it would have become impossible for us to lead any religious life at all.

28. I have heard no serious objections to her reputation for holiness. At first, some of the Carmels were suspicious, thinking that her sisters had exaggerated her merits out of love. But these impressions disappeared as the facts began to speak for themselves, and people reflected a little.

29. In answer to this question I can speak of three categories of favours: 1, many extraordinary favours to myself; 2, some favours received by the sisters; 3, her widespread reputation for special favours and miracles

During the months immediately following the Servant of God's death I received considerable interior enlightenment, often accompanied by perceptible favours. The most important, for the intensity of the interior graces if not for the accompanying sign, took place in October 1897, only two weeks after her death. It was the vigil of the feast of the Motherhood of Our Lady, and I was making the Way of the Cross in the cloister. Suddenly, I saw a kind of flame coming from the depths of the sky. At the same moment, I felt something supernatural and exclaimed: "It's Thérèse!" The interior grace I received then is beyond my powers of expression; it was one of the greatest graces I have ever received. In a flash, I had the answers to difficulties that had depressed me for a long time. All my groundless worries disappeared; Thérèse's "little way" of trust, surrender, humility, and childlikeness was explained to me and I understood it fully.

One day a sister took something from me that I needed, and I was just getting ready to recover it from her in a rather brusque manner when I distinctly heard the words: "Very humbly!" I recognised Thérèse's voice, and my heart was immediately transformed and inclined towards humility.

In June 1898, during the retreat I made in preparation for the anniversary of my profession, I renewed my commitment to Love, but I was asking myself at the same time how I would know that I was fully committed. About 4 a.m. I was woken by the sound of words; someone was saying into my ear: "One is committed to Love only to the extent that one is committed to suffering." I had no doubt that this was the Servant of God's voice, and these words brought great light to my soul. I understood that more and less in the giving of oneself was not a once-only act, but a work that was carried on every day and every minute of the day.

At the end of 1908 the time appeared to have come for the Servant of God to manifest herself more widely. One heard of perfumes by means of which she made her presence felt. I don't know why I rebelled against this kind of manifestation; I suppose I thought it was rather vulgar because of its appeal to the senses. Anyway, I decided that I did not believe in it. One evening in November I was returning to my cell, which is the one that Sister Thérèse used to occupy, when I smelled a strong scent of roses from the oratory next door. I was startled, but that passed and I remained still incredulous, saying to myself: "Now people put perfume on everything; it could be a scented letter." I knew deep down there was no letter in the place, but I left the room without further investigation. Then near the stairs, and fairly far from the cell, I felt a little puff of rose-scented wind. That convinced me and I wanted to thank Thérèse, but it vanished immediately. This kind of thing has happened to me about fifteen times during the last two years.

It is noteworthy that these phenomena involving perfumes never happened during the eleven years immediately following the Servant of God's death; only since 1908. With two or three exceptions, when the fragrance lingered for some time, I noticed that the scent vanished as soon as I realised that it was Sister Thérèse. They always underscored some particular fact or were sent as a consolation in time of trouble. I also noticed that such phenomena never took place when I wanted them to; it always happened when such things were farthest from my mind, so that it always took a few moments for me to realise it was from Sister Thérèse.

We omit her accounts of wonders that took place in the convent and elsewhere, as they are sufficiently covered by other witnesses.

5 Françoise Thérèse Martin, VISITANDINE

Léonie, the third eldest of the Martin sisters, was born in Alençon on 3 June, 1863. She was always a worry and a problem to the family because of her delicate health and over-sensitive nature, but she was also a very good-hearted person. Until 1877 she went to school mostly in Alençon; twice she was sent to boarding-school at Le Mans, where her sisters Marie and Pauline were, but each time she returned home after a few months.

In June 1877 Mme Martin took her with her on pilgrimage to Lourdes to ask our Lady's blessing on the two of them. Two months later, Mme Martin died. Léonie continued to be extremely temperamental for some time, but gradually she showed signs of improvement.

After the family moved to Lisieux, she became a boarder at the Benedictine school there (1878-81). She tried her vocation with the Poor Clares in Alençon in 1886, but left them after two months. The following year she entered the Visitation Order at Caen; she was home again after six months. Thérèse followed her sister's vocational problems closely from Carmel, and on 8 September, 1890, while prostrate at the foot of the altar during her profession ceremony, she implored God that her sister would be able to enter the Visitation convent again. Léonie did, in fact, return to the Caen convent again in July 1893, but two years later she left it for the second time; her uncle, M. Isidore Guérin, took her into his home.

Thérèse still did not despair; she told Sister Marie of the Sacred Heart: "After my death I will make her return to the Visitation nuns, and she will persevere." And she did: Léonie was received back into the convent at Caen on 29 January, 1899, and made her profession as Sister Françoise Thérèse on 2 July, 1900. She was to live there for almost forty-one years.

She lived as a true disciple of Sister Thérèse's; the more the

*latter was glorified and widely known, the more the Visitandine
hid herself away. She used to say:* "Noblesse oblige: *I belong to
a family of saints, and I must not stain the record."* She became
a really spiritual person. Her health began to give way in 1927;
frequent illnesses followed, as well as rheumatic and arthritic
pains. She died on 16 June, 1941.

*Léonie comes seventh in the series of witnesses; she gave her
testimony on 29-30 November and 1-2 December, 1910.*

The testimony

8. From the time of the Servant of God's birth until she
entered Carmel, I lived at home with her about two thirds of
the time. The other third I spent away at school at various inter-
vals in Le Mans and Lisieux, or preparing to be a nun. Some
details of her life I have learned from family conversations and
correspondence, particularly from my three Carmelite sisters
(Marie, Pauline and Céline). I also received letters from the
Servant of God herself. I do not remember having drawn on any
sources outside the family circle for my information.

Finally, I also used the *Story of a Soul* in preparing my
testimony. That reminded me of many incidents I had forgotten, but which, when I read about them, I could see were
described with perfect accuracy. The book also told me a lot
about her interior life, during the periods when we were together
as well as during the periods when we were separated. Even as a
girl, Thérèse was very spiritual, but because I was relatively
young she confided less in me than she did in her two elder
sisters, who were like a mother to her.

Asked if the Story of a Soul *was objective or whether,
perhaps, some of it was a bit imaginative, she replied:*

I am convinced that it is all true. Thérèse was a very sincere
person, and as simple as a child. There is nothing in her book,
any more than in her letters to me, that is not the true expression of what she thought.

9. I desire this beatification, because I think it will contribute to the glory of God and inspire people to love God. Were
the Church not to beatify her, for me the only thing to do would
be to accept the Church's judgment serenely; that is the better
thing of the two, and I would certainly prefer it to my little
sister's glorification.

10. The Servant of God was born on 2 January, 1873 in Our Lady's parish in Alençon. It was during the New Year vacation, so we were all at home. She was the ninth and last child born to our parents, and the only one to be born in Our Lady's parish; all the others were born in St Peter's parish. It was in the latter that my father had his jewellery business. As far as I can remember, he left this business to his nephew about 1871, and we went to live in a house that belonged to our maternal grandparents in Our Lady's parish.

Of the nine children, four died when they were very young; so when Thérèse was born we were five, all destined to become nuns: Marie, the eldest, then aged thirteen, then Pauline. then myself, Léonie, and finally Céline and Thérèse.

Father had been a successful businessman, and after retiring he helped my mother with her Alençon lace business. We were reasonably well-off members of the business class.

Thérèse received her earliest education from mother, who was unfortunately taken from us too soon; she died when Thérèse was four-and-a-half years old. After mother's death, the younger sisters were brought up by the elder ones, under father's supervision. This was in Lisieux, where father had moved after our mother's death to be near our uncle and aunt, M. and Mme Guérin.

11. Our family was what is called patriarchal. Our parents had both thought of entering religious life when they were young, and they kept up a very high standard of Christian living during their married life. Father made the closing of his shop on Sunday an absolute law for himself, in spite of the fact that all the other jewellers remained open, and in spite of pressure from friends, who pointed out to him that he was thus losing the custom of those people who liked to take a walk on Sunday and do their shopping then. Besides, he was very much given to religious practices. and willingly sought the company of the clergy. He always saluted a priest, even a stranger, out of respect for the priesthood. Mother was very devout, and a member of the Third Order of St Francis. In rearing her children she paid a lot of attention to training them in devotional practices and to making them think in accordance with their faith.

12. The Servant of God was baptised on, I think, 4 January in the church of our Lady in Alençon. Fr Dumaine, then vicar

of the parish, but now vicar general of the diocese of Séez, performed the ceremony. Her godfather was a young man of about fourteen called M. Boule, the son of a friend of my father's. He is no longer alive. Marie, our eldest sister, was godmother.

13. We received our post-primary education mostly in convent schools: the Sisters of Providence at Alençon and the Visitandines at Le Mans in the cases of Marie and Pauline; the Benedictines at Lisieux in my own case and in that of Thérèse. The upbringing we received from our parents at home was kindly and affectionate, but also watchful and conscientious; we were not spoiled. Thérèse was indisputably father's pet, and indeed mother's too, while she lived. But the rest of us were not jealous of this. On the contrary, she was our pet too. She was the "Benjamin" of the whole family, and such a charming little child. Thérèse, for her part, did not abuse this affection; she was just as obedient as the rest of us, if not more so, and I never noticed the slightest trace of superiority to the rest of us in her attitude.

14. In Lisieux, our little sister was educated at first by Marie and Pauline. During this time I was a boarder at the Benedictine school there. I left this establishment in August 1881, at the end of the school year, and Thérèse took my place there in October, but not as a full boarder; she came home to Les Buissonets every evening.

Thérèse was four years at this school; she made her first communion there in 1884, and was confirmed there the same year. She suffered a lot of moral conflict within herself at this time. Even as a young girl she thought very seriously about things, and the contrast between her state of soul and the school environment, which was very different to that of Les Buissonets, disturbed her. Besides, Pauline, who had been like a mother to her, entered Carmel in 1882, when Thérèse was only nine and a half, and she felt this separation very much. Indeed, I am inclined to think that this upset had something to do with the serious illness she had the following year.

Anyway, after her first communion a severe bout of scruples was added to the troubles she already had. I must point out that she was never rebellious or restless in the midst of her sufferings, either physical or moral. She cried easily, especially since her mother's death, but she neither objected nor grumbled when asked to do anything. I think it is relevant to note that this extreme sensitiveness resulted from the disturbing effect her mother's death had on her. I myself noticed the sudden contrast between the vivaciousness that was so typical of her before this bereavement and the habitual hyper-sensitiveness that followed it, something she overcame only later by dint of virtuous effort.

The illness I mentioned above deserves to be described in some further detail. It started with violent headaches, and she began to have these almost immediately after Pauline entered Carmel (October 1882). At the end of March 1883, she became delirious and had convulsions. As if by an act of providence, the illness ceased entirely for the whole of the day on which Pauline received the Carmelite habit. Thérèse was the only one who thought she was fit to go to the ceremony; the rest of us thought this was impossible, and we opposed the idea strenuously. But she was able to go, nevertheless, and remained perfectly calm for the few hours that we spent at the convent. She lovingly kissed and caressed her "little mother", now become Sister Agnes of Jesus.

Once this happy day was over the illness returned, and she remained continually in the throes of it until 10 May, when she was miraculously cured. She suffered one attack after another without intermission. They looked to us like continual attacks of delirious terror, often accompanied by convulsions. Her screeches were frightening; her eyes were full of terror and her face was contracted with pain. Nails in the wall took on terrible forms in her eyes, forms that frightened the life out of her. Often, she did not even recognise us. One evening especially she was terrified when my father approached her with his hat in his hand; to her it looked like some horrible beast.

When she had convulsions she would try to throw herself off the end of the bed, and we had to hold her down. One Sunday I stayed behind alone to mind her while the others were at High Mass. I saw that she was quite calm, so I risked leaving her for a few minutes. When I returned she was stretched out on the floor; she had jumped over the head of the bed and fallen down between the bed and the wall. She could have killed herself or done herself a serious injury, but thank God, she did not even have a scratch.

FRANÇOISE THÉRÈSE MARTIN, VISITANDINE   173

She says in her Life that she never lost consciousness of what was going on around her. I did not know that until I read what she says herself. If she hadn't said it we, judging by appearances, would have thought that she was more or less completely and almost continually delirious.

On 10 May she had an attack which was, perhaps, worse than any that had gone before it; she did not recognise her sister, Marie, who was holding her in her arms. We were desolate over this nerve-racking state which no artifice of our affection could overcome. It was then that Marie and I fell on our knees before the statue of the Blessed Virgin, and, with our hearts full of hope, implored our heavenly Mother to cure our little sister. Suddenly, Thérèse was perfectly calm; she was smiling at the statue, her face was composed, and she was in full possession of her faculties: she was perfectly cured. Sister Thérèse says in her autobiography that she was favoured with a vision of our Lady at that time, and she repeated this on her deathbed; but she said nothing to me about it, neither then nor afterwards.

Asked if the Servant of God had any further trouble from this illness, she replied:

The doctor who had treated her unsuccessfully with hydrotherapy told us after she was cured that we should shield the patient from violent emotion of any kind. I upset her twice in the months immediately following her cure. She fell down and remained stretched out for several minutes each time; she went completely stiff all over, but this passed off of its own accord. On these occasions, however, she did not become delirious or convulsive as she did during her illness. These were the only two instances; after that there was no further trace of the illness.

When she was well again, Thérèse returned to the Benedictine school, and made her first communion there on 8 May, 1884, at the age of eleven-and-a-half. There was a rule at that time that one had to be ten before the preceding 1 January before one could be admitted to first communion. Thérèse was born on 2 January, so she was put back a whole year.

She had shown a desire for holy communion at a very early age. I remember when Céline was preparing for her first communion, Thérèse, who was only seven, was very keen to assist at the lessons Céline was getting from our elder sisters in preparation for the event. She was sometimes told she was too

young, and sent out to play. You could see she was very disappointed at not being allowed to stay.

Every year her longings were renewed, as first communion
time came round. I remember a very touching little incident
in this connection. Thérèse was, I think, going on nine at the
time. Walking along the street with her sisters one day, she
saw the bishop on his way to the station, and she said to us:
"Shall I go and ask his Lordship if I can make my first communion next year? It's hard being put back a year just because
I was born on 2 January." I was very well aware of the anguish
this caused her. However, we dissuaded her, telling her that it
would not be proper, and that anyway she would be refused.

I am not afraid to say that the Servant of God was perfectly
capable of making her first communion even well before she
was seven: she was devout and enlightened about heavenly
matters to a degree that was well beyond her years.

Finally the longed for day arrived; she made her first communion on 8 May, 1884. She lived and breathed only for Jesus
in the Blessed Sacrament; he had won her heart completely. She
was hungry for the bread of angels, and some days later (15 May)
I saw her radiantly happy as she made her second communion
between our beloved father and Marie, who is today a Carmelite
nun and known as Sister Marie of the Sacred Heart.

My Carmelite sisters have given me a little note, written in
a little notebook by the Servant of God herself, which contains
the resolutions she made at her first communion:

1. I will never allow myself to be discouraged.
2. I will say the *Memorare* every day.
3. I will try to humiliate my pride.

She carried out these resolutions fully, because her distinctive
characteristic was, in fact, that spiritual strength which prevented her from ever being discouraged, and drove her to total
surrender to God's will and a blind trust in him.

She was confirmed at the Benedictine Abbey on Saturday,
14 June. I was in a better position than anyone else to see the
recollection and almost angelic bearing with which she received
this sacrament, because, as it was my privilege to be her godmother that day, I accompanied her right to the altar with my

hand on her shoulder. It was obvious that she was deeply aware
of the great mystery that was about to take place in her soul.
Usually at that age children do not grasp the full significance
of this sacrament, and they receive it rather light-heartedly.
But Thérèse was wholly immersed in the love that was already
consuming her. I could hardly control my emotion as I led this
dear child to the altar.

15. After the first anniversary of her first communion (May
1885), father decided it was better to keep Thérèse at home,
and as soon as the school year finished (August), he did so. This
departure of hers from the school was not asked for by the
teachers there; they would much rather have kept her. Her
precarious state of health (she was frequently unwell) was the
determining motive in my father's decision: this delicate flower
could blossom only in the family circle.

After leaving school she was sent into town for private
tuition several times a week, to complete her education. Her
tutor had a very high opinion of her, and was very proud of her.
She was passionately fond of reading, and it was by this means
that she now made progress, especially in science. Even when
she was much younger, her serious, thoughtful mind enjoyed
nothing better than books.

At this time of her life, Thérèse was always at home, and
was the family's pride and joy. Even the servant-maids loved her,
because her whole person radiated peace and kindness. She was
always forgetful of her own convenience, in order to please
others; making everybody happy was her element. She was
sweet-tempered in such a simple, natural way that one would
have thought this constant renunciation cost her nothing. She
was so friendly and playful that everyone felt at ease with her;
she won everybody's heart. Pride and vanity had no hold over
this innocent soul. She was very pretty, but she was the only one
that did not seem aware of the fact; we were all living together
at home at this time, and I never once saw her look at herself
in the mirror.

She took great care not to humiliate or annoy anybody.
I noticed this especially in a matter which concerned me personally. I was then twenty-three, but I was backward at writing
and in my studies generally, having always had considerable
difficulty in learning things. Thérèse, who was ten years younger,

went to great trouble to try and fill up the gaps in my education. I admired the tactful way she went about this without humiliating me, and her inexhaustible patience.

She was very cheerful and witty, and was very good at doing impressions of people's voices and mimicking their gestures. But never, to my knowledge, did this little amusement degenerate into mockery or give rise to the slightest uncharitableness on her part; she had the tact to know exactly when to stop.

Thérèse loved little children. I shall never forget the delightful smile and the caresses she had for them, especially for the poor ones; they were her favourites, and she lost no opportunity of telling them about God. She had a charming way of getting things across to them. It is noteworthy that the unkempt appearance of these poor children did nothing to lessen her signs of affection for them. Since she liked beautiful things and was very proper and neat about her own dress, this seeking of the poor on her part must have been the effect of solid virtue.

Because she was young, my sisters did not always take her with them to church, which was rather a distance from Les Buissonets, even though she longed to be present at all the religious ceremonies, especially the May devotions, which were always in the evening.

She went to communion as often as she was let, which was at least once a week, but she would have liked to be allowed to go more often; in fact, I think she would have liked to go every day. Her great desire to join the Children of Mary, a sodality established in the Benedictine Abbey, made her decide to spend two afternoons a week at the school. When she had fulfilled this condition, she was admitted to the sodality.

16. I don't remember the Servant of God ever speaking to me about her intention to become a nun, but as I have said, she was not as open with me as she was with her elder sisters, who were like mothers to her, or Céline, who was almost her own age. However, I was not at all surprised when she announced that she was going to enter Carmel. It was not hard to foresee from her attitude and her virtues that she was made for the religious life.

Asked if she thought the presence of Pauline and Marie in the convent had had any influence on her vocation, she replied:

I don't think so; she thought only of loving God. She would have entered Carmel anyway, even if Pauline and Marie had not been in Lisieux. Besides, there are a lot of details in the autobiography that guarantee her purity of intention, like when she says that if she had failed to enter Carmel she would have gone to a "refuge" and hidden herself among the "repentant girls". I was at home that Pentecost Sunday in 1887 when she told her father of her desire to be a Carmelite nun, but she did not tell me, and I noticed nothing. At the time of her journeys to Bayeux and Rome, I was in the Visitation convent at Caen, and I learned of these events only from letters and, since then, from her autobiography.

17. I was present when my little sister left home for Carmel. I did not enter the Visitation Order definitively until 1899, but I had made two attempts: one, which lasted six months, in 1887, and another of about two years, in 1893. So when Thérèse was bidding us farewell, I had returned from my first stay with them. I found her strength of character particularly striking on this occasion; she was the only one of us who was calm. Only her silent tears bore witness to the pain she felt at leaving father, whom she loved so much, and for whom she was the only consolation of his old age.

I told her to think well on it before entering a convent, that my own experience had taught me that such a life demanded many sacrifices of one, and was not to be entered into lightly. Her answer and the expression on her face told me that she expected sacrifices and accepted them joyfully.

At the entrance to the Carmelite enclosure, she knelt before our incomparable father for his blessing, but as far as I can remember, he was prepared to give it only on bended knees. Only God can measure what a sacrifice he was making, but for that great and generous Christian to know the will of God and to do it were one and the same thing.

Until I entered the Visitation again (1893) I visited my three sisters fairly often in the convent parlour, and again after I left in 1895. On these occasions I could see for myself how virtuous our young sister was, and my elder sisters told me several stories which illustrated that same fervour which is to be found in her own account of her life.

Among other things, I was very edified by her great regularity. The Carmelites have a half-hour sand glass in the parlour to regulate visits. She was so faithful that as soon as the last grain of sand dropped, she bid us a pleasant farewell, closed the grille and curtain, and was gone. When she was with my other sisters she was always the first to leave. Even in the parlour, her humility kept her very much in the background. She willingly remained silent when my other sisters were there, which was very remarkable because she was a very talented and lively person.

Léonie's testimony about Thérèse's virtues is taken almost wholly from the letters she received from her. We omit most of this section because it is readily available elsewhere.

After three pages on Thérèse's faith, hope and love of God, Léonie has this to say of Thérèse's love for her neighbour:

I have already said that, as a child, Thérèse loved the poor and sought them out. Father made her very happy when he entrusted her with the distribution of his alms. Any money she received, she always kept it in a money-box for the poor.

I was a witness of her constant charity towards a cousin of ours who was very sickly as a child. Although she was very young at the time, and three years younger than her cousin, Thérèse willingly distracted and amused her, and was not at all put off by the whims and moods which were an effect of her illness.

On these occasions, and they were frequent, Thérèse showed admirable unselfishness and patience. Once, when they were playing, Thérèse referred to her aunt (Mme Guérin) as "Maman". Her little cousin sharply reminded her that *her* mother was not Thérèse's, and that Thérèse had no mother. This hurt her, and she could not hold back the tears, but she neither answered back nor showed any annoyance, and she continued to take the same loving care of her cousin.

This same cousin was later trained in the religious life by Thérèse herself. She became Sister Marie of the Eucharist in the Lisieux Carmel, where she died a holy death in 1905.

I could give many other instances of her charity, but they are all told accurately in the *Story of a Soul*.

Prudence
    Thérèse's prudence, she says, showed itself in the good advice she gave to people concerning the spiritual life, and in

*her apt use of Scripture. By way of example, she quotes at length
from a letter of Thérèse to herself (Sheed, Letter 143).*

Justice

The devout way she bore herself when praying, and the
respect and love she had for every kind of religious expression
were remarkable even as a child, when I was living with her.
There was nothing affected about her in all this; it was a joy to
watch her pray: completely rapt in the presence of God, her little
hands joined properly, and kneeling upright and still. That was
how she prayed, whether in church, which she liked so much, or
at home with our father, whose own posture in prayer edified
us deeply. I cannot describe her happiness.

The first time Thérèse went to midnight Mass, she cannot
have been more than eight. The mystery of a God lying as a babe
in a crib for love of us captivated her innocent and pure heart. I
can still see the heavenly expression on her beautiful face as she
contemplated Jesus in the crib.

At the Corpus Christi processions she went with the
children's group, and she was the most recollected and best
behaved of them all. It was the same in church, even when the
service was long. The kind young lady who minded the children
in their own little chapel never tired of admiring her. She spoke
very highly about her several times.

No doubt her religious spirit gave the same kind of edification in Carmel, but my sisters are more cognisant of that than
I am.

22. . . . My Carmelite sisters told me that they knew of a
Benedictine nun in Lisieux who received the following prophetic
answer concerning my future from the Servant of God in 1888:
"You must not worry about Léonie's failures to become a nun.
When I am dead, she will enter the Visitation Order; she will
persevere, and will take my name and that of St Francis de
Sales." This prediction came true to the letter. I don't know who
that Benedictine nun was, but I think it would be easy to find
out by enquiring in Lisieux.

23. I have often heard friends of ours admire Thérèse's
"heavenly expression" when she was a child. Later, her simplicity made her pass almost unnoticed. But I can testify that
our superior, Mother de Sales, read the letters which Sister

Thérèse wrote to me from Carmel, and she said that it was extraordinary how so young a nun could have such lofty thoughts. She admired her greatly, and said so to the community and to the novices.

24. I was in Lisieux for the last stages of Thérèse's illness and for her death, but from July onwards I was no longer able to see her in the parlour; she was then moved to the infirmary, and I was not able to go in there. I used to get news of her from my sisters. The last time I met her, towards the end of June 1897, I could not hold back the tears at the thought of her imminent death, but she made me understand that there was nothing to be sad about. Two of her letters admirably express how she felt about dying.

She quotes from Sheed, Letter 171 and gives Letter 228 in full.

25. Sister Thérèse died on 30 September, 1897, and was laid out, according to custom, by the choir grille. Many people came and had their rosaries or other objects touch her. I saw her myself in the coffin, and I thought she looked remarkably beautiful.

I was at the funeral service in Lisieux cemetery; she was the first to be buried in the new Carmelite plot there. The only remarkable thing about the ceremony was the great recollection of the crowd.

26. During the eighteen months that I remained in the world after her death, I visited her grave many times, but I did not notice that there were any pilgrims there then. I have not been able to return to the cemetery since I entered the convent. But from my sisters' letters and from what I hear in the parlour it is obviously well known that pilgrimages have increased steadily and are now quite numerous.

27. I don't receive nearly as many letters as my Carmelite sisters do. Still, I do receive a certain amount of correspondence both from within France and from foreign parts (Portugal, Italy, England, etc.), and all these letters are a witness to the Servant of God's fame for holiness. A lot of these letters come from around the Visitation Order, and they show that there is great devotion to her in all our convents. This is not surprising, however, because her piety is the same in spirit as ours and as that of our holy founder St Francis de Sales. Several of the letters are

from people in the world, and they express the same sentiments.

The devotion to and confidence in Sister Thérèse which our sisters in Caen have is unbounded. Both our present mother superior and her predecessor have the highest esteem for the Servant of God's holiness. Sister Marie-Pauline here tells me that she obtains everything that she asks of Sister Thérèse. Because of requests from people outside, we are nearly always making novenas to her in this convent.

28. I have heard nothing derogatory to her fame outside the convent. Among ourselves, there were several sisters who thought when the *Story of a Soul* was first published that a lot of the impact was but a passing enthusiasm. But they have seen what has happened since and the graces that have been obtained, so that today they are all unanimously in her favour.

Pressure of space forces us to omit her last section, which recounts several favours and miracles.

6 Marie-Joseph of the Cross, o.s.b.

The importance of this witness is that she can illustrate and corroborate several details about the childhood and adolescence of Thérèse Martin.

Marcelline-Anne Husé, daughter of Norbert Husé and Frances Baubier, was born in Saint-Samson (Mayenne) in the diocese of Laval on 19 July, 1866. At the age of thirteen she entered the service of Thérèse's uncle, Isidore Guérin, as maid and governess. Thérèse was then seven years old, and went frequently to her uncle's house to play with his two daughters, Jeanne and Marie. Besides, whenever M. Martin and his older daughters were away, Thérèse and Céline were left in Marcelline's care. So, she had ample opportunity to know Thérèse well.

Marcelline remained in service with the Guérin family until she went away to join the Benedictine nuns of the Blessed Sacrament at Bayeux, where she became Sister Marie-Joseph of the Cross. She was professed on 10 August, 1892, and lived out her life there as a humble disciple of Sister Thérèse until her death on 26 December, 1935, after a long and painful illness.

She was the eighth witness, and testified on 12-15 December, 1910.

The testimony

8. In 1880, when I was thirteen years old, I entered the service of M. Guérin, the Servant of God's uncle, as maid and governess. The Servant of God was then seven, and had been in Lisieux two or three years. She came to her uncle's house every day, and I took care of her, as I did of her little cousins Jeanne and Marie, M. Guérin's daughters. I was always with them and took part in their games. I remained with the Guérin family until 1889—the year after the Servant of God entered Carmel—

and then I left to become a nun in Bayeux. I will draw chiefly on my personal recollections for what I have to say to the tribunal; reading the *Story of a Soul* has only confirmed what I had observed myself.

9. I have a very special affection for the Servant of God; I was already very fond of her when she was alive, and I love her even more now. But that will not hinder me from saying what is right and true in what is relevant to the present enquiry. I desire her beatification very much indeed, because she richly deserves it. I pray to her with all my heart, even though I lived on familiar terms with her, and I will continue to pray to her more and more.

11. M. Martin was looked upon in Lisieux as "an old-time patriarch", and a saint. I witnessed the fervour of his Christian practices myself. He attended six o'clock Mass every morning with his older daughters. He was a member of the Association for Nocturnal Adoration of the Blessed Sacrament, as indeed was his father-in-law, M. Guérin. He was also a member of the St Vincent de Paul Society for visiting the poor.

13. M. Martin was an excellent father: he brought all his children up very carefully and was very fond of all of them. He was especially fond of the Servant of God, she being the youngest; he used to call her his "little queen". But this in no way detracted from the seriousness of her upbringing: he tolerated no faults in her. Without being severe, he brought all his daughters up to be always faithful to their duties. I do not know whether Thérèse in her simplicity was aware that she was loved more than the others, because all the members of this family were very fond of each other. In any case, she was not a spoiled child, and she never took advantage of her privileged position. As for her sisters, they loved her so much themselves that they were in no way jealous of her.

14. The person responsible for the Servant of God's earliest upbringing was her second eldest sister, Pauline, who was about eighteen years old; Thérèse called her "little mother". In 1882, Pauline entered Carmel, and it became Marie's turn to be a mother to her. In 1881, the year after I came to live at M. Guérin's, Thérèse attended the boarding-school in Lisieux, run by the Benedictine nuns, as a day-pupil. At that time I had to take herself and her young Guérin cousins to school. When-

ever she was alone with me on the way to school or at home, she was always very affectionate and trusting, and freely confided in me. These intimate conversations always seemed to veer spontaneously towards pious subjects. She was exceptionally intelligent and thoughtful for her age. I particularly remember how, even before her first communion, whenever she heard workmen using foul language, she would explain to me, in order to excuse them, that these people had received less grace than we had, and were more unfortunate than blameworthy.

In the family circle, or with us (at the Guérin's) she was very cheerful and talkative, as if compensating for the constraint of the school hours. She had great esteem and affection for the nuns who taught her, but she suffered a kind of frustration where her school-mates were concerned, for they did not respond to her habitual outpourings as her family did. But this was something we only guessed for ourselves; she never accused or complained of anybody. She always had the highest marks in her class, but found no pleasure in the noisy games of children her own age. Her idea of enjoyment was to pick flowers, or to go away by herself in the garden or in the country "to play the hermit". She loved nature and the singing of the birds.

During the 1883 Easter holidays, M. Martin took the two older girls, Marie and Léonie, with him to Paris, leaving Céline and Thérèse with us. Pauline had entered Carmel the previous October. The Servant of God found this separation extremely painful. I think she was trying to hide a deep loneliness, and that this was at least partially responsible for the sudden illness that laid her low about this time. After a conversation with M. Guérin she was seized by nervous trembling, followed by attacks of fright and hallucinations several times a day. In between these she was very weak, and could never be left on her own. I think she retained consciousness during these attacks: after they had passed she certainly remembered what had happened. She insisted all the time that she would be able to go to Pauline's clothing ceremony, which was due to take place a few days later. Contrary to all expectations, and in spite of having had one of her attacks the previous day, she felt perfectly well at the time of the ceremony, and followed it with interest and delight. She seemed to be cured then. She went back to Les Buissonets, but the attacks recommenced the following day.

After that I saw her only from time to time, when I visited her. But I had news of her every day, because her aunt, Mme Guérin, went to see her daily. I knew that the doctors found her illness strange, and that their energetic treatment was of no avail. On the contrary, she seemed to grow worse. I prayed fervently for her with her sisters. Then suddenly on 10 May someone came to tell us that Thérèse was well again; the following day she came to see us herself. The only trace of her illness was a certain weakness, and that quickly disappeared. At the time, nobody associated with her doubted that her cure was a miracle worked by the Blessed Virgin, just as no one really believed that her illness was entirely due to natural causes. But at the time, I knew nothing of an apparition of the Blessed Virgin.

The Servant of God made her first holy communion at the Benedictine Abbey on 8 May, 1884. She was then eleven, but she knew what the Eucharist meant a long time before that, and longed to receive it. I noticed that particularly when Céline (1881) and her cousin Jeanne (1882) made their first communions. I also noticed how much she felt being unable to receive with her father and sisters on Sundays and Holydays. As the day of her first communion drew near, I noticed how carefully she prepared herself for it, and how she used to make little acts of self-denial, and even sought opportunities for them. I remember too that on the day itself, I had the impression that she was much more deeply aware of the grandeur of what she was about to do than children of her age usually are.

15. When she was about thirteen years old, the Servant of God was plagued by frequent headaches, and her father decided to take her away from school. I have never heard any reason other than ill-health for this decision. I have read in the *Story of a Soul* that the Servant of God suffered from scruples about this time, but she never confided that to me. All I noticed was that she became less talkative, and more reserved towards me. Back at home, she completed her education under private tuition. We no longer met as frequently as we used to when she came to Guérin's every day, but I was still able to see her great piety, her recollection at Mass and other devotions, and the fervour with which she received Holy Communion every Sun-

day. She probably received during the week as well, but I was not there on weekdays.

20. While I was still with her, I was already convinced that her virtue far surpassed that usually seen in children, even very pious ones. I do not know how to put it any better, but she was a soul apart, something special, and not at all like the rest.

I have been asked about her faults, but I really feel hard put to it to find any. Perhaps you could say she was rather sensitive and impressionable, but she had such control over her natural impulses that she never showed impatience. Sometimes a little blush would reveal her effort to check herself, but that was all.

21. Even before her first communion, the Servant of God showed great faith in and devotion to the real presence. When she was chosen with other girls to strew flowers in the Corpus Christi procession, she took care to throw her petals up high "so that they could caress Jesus", as she used to say herself. Her piety and angelic expression was noticed by those present, and I have often heard them express their admiration of her.

I also noticed her delicate love for her neighbour. The first time she was introduced to me at Guérin's she was only seven. Someone had told her that I was still lonely for my mother, and she took it upon herself to comfort me with a great demonstration of affection. When out walking, she was always delighted to be sent to give an alms to the poor. Later on, when she was about fourteen, she used to visit poor families herself, and teach their children the catechism. I often accompanied her on these trips, and witnessed her joy and the children's appreciation of her. Shortly after her first communion, when she was about twelve, she used to talk to me about God: how good he was to those who loved him, the love he bore each of us individually. As I did not feel all that much love for him, and said as much to her, she explained that love was not a matter of what you felt but of practising virtue, and that we should always try to please God in the least of our actions, without any attempt to draw attention to ourselves.

One characteristic of her charity towards her neighbour which I remember especially was that even before her first communion, she used to do little acts of charity for her cousin Marie Guérin who was always ill. What patience she had with her! Though three years younger, she lavished the most charming care upon her, giving in to all her whims, dissipating the boredom and sadness caused by her illness, teaching her how to live alone, and inviting her to practise virtue. Her pains were rewarded, for Marie afterwards joined her in Carmel, and was her novice. Even when she was only a child, Thérèse used to ask us to put her share of cakes and other dainties aside for the poor.

I have one very vivid memory of her devotion to the Blessed Virgin. She was ten, or maybe twelve, and we were spending May by the seaside, at Trouville. Where we were staying was rather far from the church of Our Lady of Victories, but we usually went there every evening for the May devotions. If any of us pleaded weariness after a long day, or the distance as an excuse for our reluctance, Thérèse would insist that this was just not good enough. Her greatest joy was to go to Mass every morning at this church of our Lady, and neither cold nor bad weather could put her off.

Her love for the Blessed Virgin showed itself, too, when she joined the Children of Mary. In order to do so she had to return to the school she had left, and where she no longer found any of her own companions.

Her prudence displayed itself in the wisdom of her advice, and in her concept of holiness. Even before she entered Carmel, not long after her first communion in fact, she already understood the value of sacrifice. One day I told her how good and perfect I thought her uncle and aunt were, especially the latter, who was a real saint. "That's true," she said, "but one day she will be even more of a saint, because she suffers, and always will. This suffering, united to her deep love of God, will make her grow in perfection." Later, during her first year in Carmel, I confided to her that I intended becoming a nun. On this occasion, too, she gave me some excellent advice. Her last recommendation to me before I left the parlour was: "Dear Marcelline, we must always love God a great deal, and to prove that love we must make all the sacrifices he asks of us. Don't worry; I'll be praying for you. Love God so that you won't be too afraid of him; he is so kind really! Remember too to pray for those who do not love him, so that we can convert many souls."

On the subject of temperance, while we were staying at Trouville, and living in closer intimacy than usual, I noticed that she accepted whatever was put in front of her at meals. If she showed any preference, it was for what was less appetising.

27. There is great devotion to Sister Thérèse in our community; we all love her very much, and she has obtained private graces for several of the nuns. Lay people have asked us many times for novenas in her honour, and many others ask us to pray to her for their intentions. As for her fame for sanctity outside the convent, that is already a well-known fact; I know it myself from the reports that come from all sides.

28. I have never heard anyone dispute her reputation for holiness, or object to the measures being taken to make her life better known. Many people, knowing that I was personally acquainted with her, have asked me if the account she has written of her life is really true, and I have always answered with conviction that it is perfectly true.

29. I earnestly recommended the conversion of my brother-in-law to the Servant of God; he had not practised his religion for many years. I sent him a relic of her. He was converted on his deathbed, and died a very Christian death two years ago. I am still convinced that the Servant of God's prayers had something to do with his return to God.

I know from a letter my brother wrote me, and have heard from Mlle Aimée Roger, who was an eye-witness, that Mme Poirier, a niece of my brother's, had been suffering for two years from a serious internal disorder, the precise nature of which I do not know. I sent her a relic of Sister Thérèse of the Child Jesus (a little piece of cloth) and urged her to pray to her. Recently, she astonished my brother in Lisieux by paying him a visit; a short time previously she was scarcely able to move from one room to another. She had come to pray at the tomb of the Servant of God and to thank her for the cure. I have heard and read accounts of a multitude of other favours, but I have not witnessed any of them myself.

30. I would like to add to my answer to Q. 15 a few details about the Servant of God's conduct during the period immediately after leaving the Benedictine school.

I can truthfully assert that since her first communion I saw Thérèse grow in grace and virtue in a very remarkable manner.

Only her love for God and her desire for sacrifice could make her undertake all she did in connection with her vocation, and overcome all those obstacles in order to realise her ambition. One felt about her that she was a person who always lived in God's presence, because if one spoke to her of little matters of female vanity there was no holding her attention for very long, but when I talked with her on pious subjects, she immediately opened up and her heart overflowed with happiness.

7   Teresa of Saint Augustine, o.c.d.

The thirteenth witness to take the stand was a nun whom St Thérèse disliked intensely. But Thérèse was so well able to hide her dislike that the nun thought she was very fond of her.[1] Her testimony is rich in day-to-day detail and quotations from the Saint which are not to be found elsewhere.

Julie-Marie-Elisa Leroyer was born in Cressonnière, in the diocese of Bayeux, on 5 September, 1856. She received the habit as Sister Teresa of St Augustine on 15 October, 1875, and was professed on 1 May, 1877. A peaceable, unassuming nun, she was sacristan for many years. Shortly after the Servant of God's death she wrote a little work entitled Memoirs of a Holy Friendship, *in which she speaks of Thérèse's joy every time she went to see her in the infirmary.*

Sister Teresa testified on 14-15 February, 1911. She died on 22 July, 1929.

The testimony

8. I knew the Servant of God from the time she entered in 1888 till her death in 1897. During that time I lived close to her, and enjoyed a certain amount of intimacy with her. In my deposition I will make little use of what I have heard Mother Prioress or the other nuns say about her, and I will make hardly any use of her autobiography. My whole testimony is based on my own personal memories.

9. I am very anxious for her beatification, because I think that once the Church has officially recognised her holiness many people will be drawn to imitate her virtues and follow her "little way", which, in my opinion, leads one easily to progress and perfection.

17. When in April 1888 the Servant of God crossed the threshold of our enclosure, I was struck by the recollection and seriousness with which she did it.

18. Sister Thérèse's role in the community was that of advising and directing the novices, but she also worked in the sacristy, the linen-room, etc. I was already a professed sister at the time, so I did not have the opportunity of availing of her counsels. I will relate whatever I know of her life as a Carmelite under the headings of her various virtues.

19. I was not aware that she was writing anything. Like the rest of the sisters, I knew she composed poems and songs for the convent feasts, but it was only after she had died that I learned about her autobiography.

20. I think I know what "heroic virtue" means. It means practising perfection unfailingly. That surpasses what we usually see even in very fervent religious. These always have their moments of weakness, whereas I noticed that the Servant of God maintained an ever-even fervour, especially in her fidelity to the very little things.

21. *Faith*

Her greatest pleasure was holy communion. She was prepared to suffer a lot rather than be deprived of it. All the sisters who lived with her knew that during the last years of her life, when her health was already broken, she used to get up for morning Mass after sleepless nights in pain, even during the worst cold of winter. It pained her deeply to be deprived of daily communion, which was not customary in our convent at the time. Speaking to one of the sisters about how much she felt this privation, she said: "It won't always be like that. The time will come when we may have Fr Hodierne as chaplain, and he will give us holy communion every day." It was Sister Marie of the Sacred Heart she made that remark to, and Sister Marie told it to me before Sister Thérèse's death. When Sister Marie asked her: "What makes you think Fr Hodierne will be our chaplain? There's nothing to indicate that he will," she replied: "I suppose not, but I hope he will come, and we'll be very pleased with him."

Our chaplain at the time was Fr Youf, and his health gave no cause for alarm. There was no reason to think he would die soon, nor did he for many years afterwards. Yet, Sister Thérèse's presentiment about Fr Hodierne turned out to be right. He was appointed chaplain on 15 October, 1897, and for his very first instruction he took as his text the words "Come and eat my bread" *(Prov 9:5)*. It was an invitation to daily communion, and he made it without any of us telling him about this desire of ours.

Sister Thérèse had a remarkable liking for the Bible. The Gospels especially enchanted her, and she carried them day and night next to her heart. She was also very fond of the *Imitation of Christ*, and had already learned it all by heart before she became a nun. She had great respect for God's word, and would not allow herself even the slightest criticism of a mediocre sermon.

She had a tender love for the Blessed Virgin. When the statue that had smiled on her in her illness was brought to the convent, none of the sisters could lift it—they all found it too heavy. "She's not too heavy for me," said the Servant of God, and, with a heave that admirably expressed her sentiments, she lifted the statue and carried it effortlessly to the oratory which had been prepared for it.

Hope

You could say that Sister Thérèse lived mostly in heaven; her spirit dwelt on it continually, and her heart longed unceasingly for the sovereign good. She spoke to me so many times about her desire to die, and her eyes shone with happiness every time the subject was brought up. The thought of her approaching death was something that brought her only joy and hope. I must say here that whenever I quote certain things Sister Thérèse said to me, I quote them literally. In April 1895 she confided to me: "I am going to die soon. I'm not saying that it will be in the next few months, but in two or three years. What I experience in my soul makes me feel my exile is nearly over." She was still perfectly healthy when she said this.

She soared above earthly things: nothing seemed to be able to captivate her soul even for an instant; nothing worried her. "I cannot understand," she used to say, "why people get so upset when they see their sisters die; we are all going to heaven and we will meet one another there again." If she desired heaven it was only because of the love she could thus give to God; her own interest was entirely set aside. She was not anxious about her crown; she used to tell me to "let God take care of that".

Charity

In Sister Thérèse, the love of God dominated everything else; her dream was to die of love. But then she would add: "To die of love we must live by love." So she strove to develop this love day by day, because she wanted it to be of the highest quality. Her ambition was to love like a seraph, to be consumed by the devouring flames of pure love without feeling them, so that her self-sacrifice would be as complete as possible. She admitted quite simply that not even a second passed without her thinking of God, and you could see this habitual thought of God reflected in her features. One of the sisters was so struck by this that she remarked to me one day at recreation: "Look at Sister Thérèse, wouldn't you think she came from heaven, she's so angelic-looking." She loved to talk about our Lord, and was always delighted to meet someone who felt the same way.

She was ever so careful to avoid the slightest imperfection, or anything that savoured of lukewarmness or softness in God's service. So eager was she to find ways of pleasing our Lord that she seized avidly on every opportunity of making a little sacrifice. During her illness, I used to tell her that although she was suffering a great deal, God would richly reward her. "No, no," she would say, "it's not for the reward, it's just to please God."

Her trust in Providence was unwavering. People used to talk about the persecution of religion, and the consequences this could have for our convent, exile even. "What do you think about it?" I asked her. "I am prepared to go to the other end of the world in order to continue my religious life," she said, "but I'm like a baby: I just let things happen; I will go wherever God wants me to." And during her last illness: "How unhappy I would be now if I were not wholly in God's hands! One day the doctor says I'm finished, the next I'm better. This continual change could be wearisome, but it does not affect my peace of soul; I just take things as they come." When I told her I was worried about how much she was suffering: "Oh! Don't worry about that; God will not give me more than I can bear."

She also had a burning zeal for the salvation of souls. "My greatest devotion," she used to say, "is to pray for sinners and pure souls." Priests and missionaries were the chief object of this zeal. She also had an intense desire for martyrdom. I noticed this all the time. When she was ill, she wistfully remarked: "You are

G

more fortunate than I am; I am going to heaven, but you might yet obtain the privilege of martyrdom." It showed how disappointed she was at not being able to win that coveted crown.

Sister Thérèse's love reached all her sisters; she allowed herself no favourites. She gave everyone her affection unselfishly and did all in her power to serve each one with perfect self-denial. She was always kind, even to those who were rather rude to her. She received them with the same smile, tried to please them, and avoided hurting or provoking them.

One might have thought that entering at fifteen and living with her own sisters she might have been seeking the comforts and joys of family life, but there was nothing of the kind; her self-sacrifice was complete in every respect. She never showed any preference for the members of her family over her sisters in religion. Once, when the community was free to speak, I said to her: "I'm not asking you to join us for a while; you have your own sisters, so you must have very little free time." "Oh, don't think that," she said, "I don't spend any more time with them than I do with the rest: you are all my sisters."

She showed great zeal for the relief of the souls in purgatory. "After my death," she said, "if you want to please me, offer up the Stations of the Cross often for my intention. If I don't need them myself I'll be delighted to make a present of them to the souls in purgatory."

Prudence

In guiding her novices, Sister Thérèse showed a rare degree of prudence. She knew how to wait for souls, how to urge them towards virtue without hurrying them any faster than they were able to proceed. She told them their faults firmly, and was not deterred by the fact that some had rather difficult temperaments. Her clear-sighted judgment gave her a remarkable aptitude for seeing what was best and most perfect in each case.

Justice

Everything connected with the worship of God delighted her. You should see the care with which she decorated the statue of the Child Jesus with flowers and the joy she got out of preparing the Christmas Crib. As a postulant, she spent a long time carrying quite heavy stones a considerable distance in order to build the stable; she was tireless when it came to proving her love for our Lord. Then there were all those rose petals which she used to spread at the foot of the Calvary in our cloister garth and on the feet of her crucified Lord when sickness nailed her to a bed of pain. She used up every last ounce of strength proving to our Lord that she loved him.

She was very devoted to St Joseph and St John of the Cross. She would have liked to see us give due honour, too, to the patrons we received in baptism and in religious life, as well as to the saints under whose protection each month and year were placed. She said that if they were given the responsibility of looking after us, we ought to show them our appreciation. She became even more fervent than usual when those who had shed their blood for our Lord were being honoured. On 17 July, 1894, the centenary of the martyrs of Compiègne, the Carmel of Compiègne wanted to celebrate the event, and they asked the Lisieux Carmel to help them. The two of us were given the task of making little banners to decorate the chapel with. I was thus able to see the eagerness with which she set to work; she was almost beside herself with happiness as she explained: "If only we could be fortunate enough to share their lot! What a privilege!"

Fortitude

Mother Prioress was not sparing in her use of reprimands and humiliations where Sister Thérèse was concerned, but she bore them all patiently, meekly and humbly. She never made excuses, even when they were too harsh. One day during dinner she had a violent fit of coughing. The prioress got tired of listening to her, and said sharply: "All right, Sister Thérèse; leave us!" I was struck by the calmness with which she received this unpleasant outburst.

The heroic courage she showed during her father's illness was particularly edifying.

She once told me something in confidence, which rather mystified me. "If you only knew what darkness I am plunged into!" she said. "I don't believe in eternal life; I think that after this life there is nothing. Everything has disappeared on me, and I am left with love alone." She spoke of this state of soul as a temptation; yet she seemed always so calm and serene.

Virtue seemed to come so naturally to her that people thought she was inundated with consolations. I heard one sister say: "Sister Thérèse gets no merit for practising virtue; she has never had to struggle for it." I wanted to know from herself if there was any truth in this, so, availing of my intimacy with her, I asked her if she had had to struggle during her religious life. This was two months before she died. "Oh!" she replied, "but didn't I though! I didn't have an easy temperament. It might not have looked like that, but I felt it. I can assure you that not a day has passed without its, quota of suffering, not one!" It was above all during her last illness that we were able to admire her courage in the face of suffering. Fearing that her pain would get even worse, I told her that I would ask God to give her some relief. "No, no," she exclaimed, "he must be allowed to do as he pleases."

Temperance

Sister Thérèse was very attentive to the practice of interior mortification. If her sisters went to the parlour, she would never inquire who the visitor was, interested though she might be to know. When her sister was prioress, the Servant of God never once went along during night silence to talk to her. She had a very religious bearing; she walked quietly, with an air of deep recollection.

Obedience

For the Servant of God the simplest recommendation was an order and she always carried it out. It was never necessary to tell her anything twice. Her obedience was heroic; I mean she never failed in it. When she was ill someone made a suggestion which was meant to bring her some relief. The effect, however, was just the opposite, but, without a word, she did exactly as suggested, though this renewed her pain. She obeyed even those sisters who had no right to order her.

Poverty

During her postulancy and part of her religious life she had a sister next to her in the refectory who took almost everything for herself and never spared a thought for her neighbour. The Servant of God never commented on this; she just went without.

It was only a long time afterwards that her office, and motives of charity towards that same sister, obliged her to speak about the matter.

Humility

On one of my visits during her last illness I found her radiant. I asked her what she was looking so pleased about. "Something great has happened to me," she said, "and I'm going to tell you about it. One of the sisters came to see me, and she said: 'If you only knew how little you are liked or appreciated!' The other day I heard another saying: 'I don't know why they talk so much about Sister Thérèse; she doesn't do anything remarkable. We never see her practising virtue; in fact she could hardly be called even a good religious!' " (I know the sister said that in a moment of bad humour.) "Oh!" continued the Servant of God, "just imagine hearing that I was not a good religious, just when I am on my deathbed. What joy! Nothing could have given me greater pleasure."

I told her about the glory that would be hers in heaven. "No," she said, "it won't be like you think; God always grants my desires, and I have asked him to let me be a little nothing. When a gardener makes a bouquet there's always a little space between the magnificent flowers. To fill this up and make it all look prettier, he puts moss in there. That's what I'm going to be in heaven, a little pinch of moss among God's beautiful flowers."

22. I have never heard that Sister Thérèse experienced any extraordinary phenomena during her lifetime.

23. I have heard different opinions expressed about the Servant of God in this convent during her lifetime. The nuns who knew her best, especially her novices, admired her for her outstanding virtue. She passed unnoticed as far as others were concerned; chiefly, I think, because of her simplicity. There were some, however, who viewed her unfavourably. Some of these accused her of being cold and proud. As far as I can judge, that was because she did not speak much, and remained recollected and reserved. It may be, too, that the presence of four sisters in the same community aroused some sparks of opposition and jealousy. But I can assure you that since her death, those of her critics who are still alive have completely changed their opinion of her.

Asked what she thought of the Servant of God's character herself, she replied:

I have always thought of her, even when she was alive, as a charming child and an excellent nun. Strictly speaking, therefore, I have never had to change my mind on this subject. I admit, nevertheless, that her great modesty and the extreme care she took to hide her virtue under the appearance of a very simple, ordinary way of life prevented me at the time from noticing a lot of acts of perfection that I have since come to recognise for what they were.

24. I was present when she died, and was struck by a phenomenon which seemed extraordinary to me. After her head had fallen back, and we thought she was dead, she raised it again, opened her eyes and gazed upwards for a considerable space of time. There was such depth in her gaze that I had to turn my eyes away, so near was I to being overcome.

27. The Servant of God's reputation for holiness is universal. The enormous volume of correspondence that Mother Prioress receives from all over the world could prove this, but I have made no detailed study of it. Not many people come to see me in the parlour, but those who do vouch sufficiently for the fact that her fame is very widespread.

28. Nobody has ever expressed objections to this reputation for holiness to me personally. But I have heard in the parlour that there are a few people in Lisieux who at one stage accused the Carmel of making too much fuss about the Servant of God and exaggerating her merits. They were generic criticisms; no specific charges were made. On the other hand, I know from the same source that these people have since changed their attitude and now do full justice to her holiness.

29. From my conversations in the parlour I am aware in a general kind of way that a lot of people pray to the Servant of God, and are confident that they will obtain exceptional favours through her intercession. I would like to dwell particularly, however, on three categories of facts:

a) Sister Thérèse said that as soon as she reached heaven she would visit the missions, and help the missionaries in their conquest of souls. She left this exile towards the end of 1897, and here is what the Rue de Bac missionaries accomplished the following year. I was so struck by the coincidence when we read the *Annales de la Propagation de la Foi* in the refectory that I took a note of it. Here are some extracts from the July 1899 issue:

"Asia. The year 1898 will be remembered in our Society as the year of God's great blessings. The number of adult baptisms rose to the almost unbelievable total of 77,700. In its 235 years of existence our Society has never recorded a similar result. The zeal and activity of our missionaries are not enough to account for it. It must be attributed to the breath of the Holy Spirit passing over some of our missions and instilling into the pagans an irresistible impetus towards our holy religion."

And from the November issue: "In reporting to you on last year's work, we thank God for enabling us to reach numbers which, while still far short of our desires, are very encouraging, and almost double those of the previous year. The number of adult conversions was higher than in any other year, and we have so many catechumens that we expect a plentiful harvest. The crown of angels who have gone to swell the heavenly ranks has also surpassed that of any other year. Catholic marriages, the indispensable foundation of any Christian society, are also increasing. They provide the pagans with the eloquent witness of a holy union."

b) The following account is from my mother, Mme Veuve Leroyer. About a year ago she had sufficient devotion to Sister Thérèse to ask her to be a kind of guardian angel to her and to help her in everything. One day when she was shopping the shop-assistant, who knew nothing of my mother's devotion, said to her, "What a delightful rose scent you are wearing, Madam!" My mother told her the simple truth: she was wearing no scent, nor was she carrying anything that could account for such a scent. Another day someone who was visiting my mother at home expressed surprise at finding a strong smell of violets in the house. This had no natural explanation either.

Asked by the judge what kind of person her mother was, she said:

My mother is a level-headed and discreet person. I am sure she had not told anyone of her request to the Servant of God to help her like a guardian angel. Besides, she is not at all inclined to believe in extraordinary phenomena, and she attached no great importance to these happenings when she told me about them. Mme Leroyer lives in Lisieux and devotes her time to good works, especially that of teaching catechism. It is remarkable that on the two occasions I have mentioned she did not smell anything herself. I, too, have twice found the smell of lilac or violets in circumstances that afforded no natural explanation. Nor was I expecting anything of the kind to happen at the time. Besides, I have no desire to be favoured in this way; what I expect from Sister Thérèse are hidden graces that will benefit me spiritually.

c) It is in this realm of graces which help one towards perfection that I have noticed the special efficacy of praying to the Servant of God. There is no denying that her supernatural influence has produced extraordinary results in this convent in the way of spiritual progress. To tell the truth, a great change has come over us. I have noticed it particularly in the care being taken to be faithful even in small things, in greater kindness to one another, and in obedience which has become prompt and uncritical—a really cheerful obedience to the least wishes of our Mother Prioress.

8 Marie of the Angels and the Sacred Heart, o.c.d.

The fourteenth witness is none other than St Thérèse's own novice-mistress.

Born at Montpinçon in the diocese of Bayeux on 24 February, 1845, Marie-Jeanne-Julia de Chaumontel entered the Lisieux Carmel on 29 October, 1866, after overcoming, with some difficulty, the ties of affection that bound her to her family. She received the habit on 19 March, 1867, and made her profession on 25 March, 1868. Her novice-mistress was the venerable foundress of the Lisieux Carmel, Mother Genevieve of St Teresa.

After a difficult novitiate, she found perfect peace from the day she was professed, and was a model of silence and availability to the rest of the community. She shirked no task, no matter how lowly, and showed a real talent for sewing and embroidery. She first became sub-prioress in 1883, and was novice-mistress from 1886-93. She was then re-elected sub-prioress for a further six years, and became novice-mistress again from shortly after St Thérèse's death until 1909. She died on 24 November, 1924.

St Thérèse describes her as "a real saint, cast in the mould of the first Carmelite nuns"[1], and the community as a whole concurred in this judgment. Thérèse found it difficult at first to take her fully into her confidence, but when she eventually did, she found her very helpful. Mother Marie was rather absent-minded, and her habit of forgetting what she had said was sometimes an unwitting source of pain to Thérèse. After the latter's death, she experienced the power of her intercession. In the various stages of the Process of Beatification and in some jottings entitled Memories of my little Thérèse *she recorded for posterity the favours she received.*

In her testimony, dated 15-17 February, 1911, Mother Marie underlines, among other things, the discretion with which

Thérèse handled the inevitable sufferings of community living,
and her firm detachment from her three sisters. Her testimony
also preserves several of the Saint's sayings, which would other-
wise have been lost.

The testimony

8. I knew the Servant of God from the time her sister
Pauline (Agnes of Jesus) entered in 1882. I used to see her
in the parlour, a little child of nine who would soon consecrate
herself to God. When she entered (1888) I was novice-mistress,
and as such I was able to observe and get to know her very
well. I left that office in 1892, and after that my relations with
her were only those of any two nuns living together. In preparing my testimony I have made use chiefly of my own recollections and observations. I have used her autobiography only to
complete them and make them more precise. I do not think
this writing of hers is in any way tainted by illusions: the
Servant of God sets down her experiences with great sincerity
and precision.

9. I pray every day for the success of her Cause of Beatification. The accounts which reach us daily of marvellous favours
make me believe that the glorification of the Servant of God
will contribute to the exaltation of the Church, the glory of our
Order, and the salvation of France and many people.

10. I have no personal knowledge of her early years. I note
only that when, between the ages of nine and fifteen, she came
to the parlour to visit her sister, Agnes of Jesus, and, later,
Marie of the Sacred Heart, I could easily see that this beautiful
child was blessed by God. Whenever I was near her the effect
it had on me was similar to what one feels before the tabernacle.
She radiated an atmosphere of calm, silence, gentleness and
purity that made me regard her with a very real respect.

16-18. Having been novice-mistress at the time, I am in a
good position to speak about this period of her life. From the
day she entered she grew in grace and wisdom before God and
the community by responding faithfully to every grace. For me,
this is the explanation of the rapid rise of so young a girl to
the highest holiness. It was only recently that an elderly and holy
nun said to me: "Indeed, we had never seen anything like it";
she was referring to Sister Thérèse's novitiate.

From the day she set foot in our convent the Servant of God had an extraordinary insight into religious perfection and the sacrifices it entailed. She set to work with invincible courage, and did not baulk at any obstacle. I can assure you, too, that even if she was made the equivalent of novice-mistress shortly after her own profession, she was already so perfect in every respect that she was just as fit to be placed at the head of our community. All I had to do, so to speak, was to instruct her in the Rule and in the various customs of the community. I must also state here that in the whole course of her novitiate I never had to draw the attention of this dear child to the least imperfection. In the fifteen years of my experience as novice-mistress I have never had a novice who was her equal in virtue or perfection. This will be confirmed by what I have to say about her virtues later on.

19. It was only after she was dead that I learned about her writing an autobiography.

20. Heroism in the Christian life seems to me to consist of a constant generosity to practise all the virtues in their tiniest detail. This perfect consistency must be a very rare thing; it presupposes an exceptional grace from God and an equally exceptional degree of correspondence to it. I think Sister Thérèse displayed this consistent fidelity and surpassed even the most fervent nuns in this regard.

21. *Faith*

During her novitiate her respect for Mother Prioress and the novice-mistress showed remarkable faith. With childlike simplicity she used to come and tell me the trials she underwent because of Mother Prioress. The prioress sometimes treated her with a severity that hurt her deeply, especially as Sister Thérèse was very much aware that the prioress's behaviour was all too human; but she kept her feelings about this to herself. I can still see her as she came to me one day and threw herself into my arms to confide her heartbreak to me, though she did so without the slightest complaint. In this painful trial she saw God acting on her little soul, and she kept on smiling in spite of it all.

When she was feeling spiritually miserable, she told me about it quite cheerfully and accepted the fact generously, so that God could give his consolations to others and thereby attract them. She gave proof of heroic faith in the terrible trial which afflicted her venerable father. This caused her hours of terrible anguish. But, as she relates in the *Story of a Soul*,[2] she surprised me one day by saying, as she looked intently up at the sky: "Oh, sister, I can still suffer some more." Whatever the tempest, she remained as calm as a rock lashed by the waves.

She had an unusually keen understanding of the Sacred Scriptures—a thing readily apparent from the way she uses them in her writings. She always carried the Gospels on her person. She saw only God in authority; the ciborium might be of gold or copper, but it was always to our Lord that she paid her respect, her love and her obedience—in a word, her faith.

The day before her profession she was very upset by the devil: he tried to persuade her that this was not her vocation. She regained her peace of mind quickly by humbly confiding the temptation to me, and accepting my words as if God himself had spoken to her. As for the long temptation against the faith which she suffered during the last year of her life, she says herself that she made more acts of faith in that year than she did in her whole lifetime. In that trial Jesus saw fit to associate her with himself in the darkness of Calvary; but her unspeakable suffering only purified her love and rendered it still more ardent.

Hope and trust in God

The Servant of God experienced numerous trials, both internal and external, in the course of her life, but her trust in God was so unshakable that she never lost her peace of soul, or even her joy, however sorely tried she might be. There are several examples of this in the story of her life. What struck me was her constancy in the face of all the obstacles she had to overcome in order to enter Carmel at the age of fifteen, and the serenity with which she bore the prioress's severity during her first years in religion. Neither in the midst of spiritual desolation nor when the news of her father's condition became steadily worse did she ever lose her serenity. Even before she became a Carmelite the confidence with which she prayed to God for sinners was such that in the case of Pranzini, the murderer, she had the audacity to say: "I am sure you'll forgive him, God; even if he does not go to confession, I will believe that you touched his heart at the last moment."[3]

Later, she was asked how she kept from being discouraged during periods when God made it look as if he had deserted her. "It is not for nothing that I made the words of Job, 'Even if God were to kill me I would still hope in him', my own," she answered. And on another occasion she said: "For a long time now, O Lord, you have allowed me to be daring with you. Like the prodigal son's father, speaking to his elder son, you say: 'Everything I have is yours' " (*Lk 15:31*).[4] She also said: "I know that God loved the prodigal son; I have heard his words to Mary Magdalen, to the woman caught in adultery, and to the Samaritan woman. No; nobody can frighten me, because I know where I stand on his love and mercy."[5] Shortly before she died, she said: "I have no fear of last-minute struggles. . . . I depend on him; I am sure he will never desert me."

Love of God

There are numerous instances in her autobiography to show the high quality of her love of God, her ardent desire for holy communion, her devoutness in prayer, and her attraction to religious things generally, even when she was still only a child. I can add some instances from her religious life, to which I have been a witness myself. From her very first day in Carmel she accepted everything that she had to suffer there in a spirit of love, for the sake of the souls she wanted to win over to the love of God. She had a special zeal for the salvation of great sinners, among others the misfortunate Fr Hyacinth for whose conversion she offered up so many prayers and sacrifices. Like St Cecilia (who had become her close friend ever since Thérèse visited her tomb in Rome) everything in her soul sang. During her postulancy she explained to us one day why St Cecilia had been proclaimed patron saint of music: "It was because of the virginal singing that her heavenly Spouse caused her to hear in the depths of her heart."[6]

Shortly after leaving the novitiate she got permission to come and see me. She told me what God had wrought in her, and about the lights she received concerning the life of grace in us. I was amazed. It was a few days after this, when I was presiding over the laundry work, that she asked me to sing her wonderful canticle "Living by Love", and to invite the other sisters to join in. I thought it was beautiful, sublime even.

The whole of chapter 11 of the *Story of a Soul* is the song of a seraph. "O Jesus," she wrote in these lines penned on her death-bed, "allow me to tell you that your love reaches the point of folly. Faced with this folly, what else can my heart do but fly to you? My hope is that one day you will carry me off to the home of love, and finally plunge me into that burning abyss, and make me its lucky victim forever."[7]

Love of neighbour

No sooner had the Servant of God entered Carmel than she seemed to us to be full of kindness to all the sisters; she obliged them in every way she could. In the novitiate she showed her charity towards one of her companions of whose faults she was well aware. She gave her little pieces of advice, tried to lead her to virtue by giving her good example, and, in spite of the other girl's frequent opposition, she was kindness itself to her. All the time, she was waiting until she was able to influence this young person, and she did eventually succeed in exercising a very touching influence over her. I cannot remember her ever saying a word against anybody, nor ever complain of Mother Prioress's severity towards her. She always smiled at her and did her all sorts of little favours.

In the 1896 elections, Mother Gonzague was elected prioress by only a very slender majority. The Servant of God realised what a disappointment this was to her, and she did her best to comfort her with the most delightful tenderness and tact. She wrote her a marvellous letter, and the poor prioress took it very well.[8]

The Servant of God showed her charity, too, when she requested the prioress to allow her to take as her workmate a sister whose character, embittered by illness, must have caused her a great deal of suffering. She really showed great patience and zeal in this delicate situation. By a mixture of firmness and gentleness she succeeded in getting the upper hand of this poor soul, so that the latter latched on to her as to a comforting angel. This same sister once worked with me in the sacristy; whenever I found her difficult, all I had to do was hand her over to Sister Thérèse, who had such a way with her that it was no time before the poor soul was back again humbly asking me to forgive her.

Sister Thérèse's whole life is filled with this charity, so full of attention to the needs of others and so forgetful of itself.

Prudence

She displayed a prudence that was well in advance of her years. Though only fifteen when she joined us, she soon showed us that she was a child only in years. From the very beginning I was charmed by her self-possession. Later, in dealing with that difficult sister, she showed what prudence she was capable of, and she did her so much good.

The election of her sister Pauline as prioress created a very delicate situation for her with the ex-prioress, Mother Gonzague. But the Servant of God showed astonishing discretion when it came to avoiding friction. I was often in the parlour with the three Martin sisters when their uncle, M. Guérin, visited them. Whenever a misunderstanding arose about family affairs, her influence quickly dispersed the little clouds. She was an angel of peace for everybody. If someone needed advice, it was to her, the youngest, that her sisters turned, and her word was gospel. In counselling people, she liked to teach them what she called "her little way of surrender and childhood". This doctrine is full of simplicity, love and trust. She bequeathed it to ordinary people, but it is now attracting the admiration of people distinguished for both holiness and learning. A priest told me one day that when he read the Servant of God's writings he found light on a matter that had troubled him for a long time.

Justice

From her tenderest years the Servant of God found the cult of God, of the Blessed Virgin and the saints very attractive. In Carmel she liked to spend her moments of leisure decorating the statue of the Child Jesus and putting flowers in front of it. She had been told to do this, but she really loved it. At Christmas she took great delight in preparing the Crib, and sang the Divine Child's praise in poems that overflowed with tenderness and love. In the sacristy, she took great care with the preparation of the vestments, and everything else connected with divine worship, especially the ciborium and the hosts. In choir her whole bearing was so becoming and religious that she was obviously very conscious of the presence of God and of the grandeur of mental prayer and of the divine office. Her favourite saints, after our Lady and St Joseph, were our mother St Teresa, St John of the Cross, St Cecilia, St Agnes, Bl. Theophane Venard and Bl. Joan of Arc. She had an intense love of holy communion; the inability to receive it daily pained her deeply. She had in fact foretold that we would later enjoy this consolation, and her prophecy was fulfilled to the letter.

A feature of her piety that struck me particularly, because I had never heard it spoken of in Carmel or in the lives of the saints, was the role she attributed to flowers. For her, every flower spoke a language of its own, in which it revealed God's infinite love and perfections to her. She also used them to tell God of her own love and other sentiments. Late on a summer's evening, in the time of silence, and often on a feastday at recreation, she would strew flowers round the base of the Calvary in the cloister garth. She also penned some beautiful lines on the subject in her poem, "Jeter des Fleurs".

This plucking of petals from flowers was only a symbol of what she was doing for our Lord by means of the thousand and one sacrifices she made for him in every area of her life. Even near the end she was still plucking rose petals to perfume her crucifix with. That is what happened to the roses people brought to cheer her up. One day, when someone gathered up the petals that had fallen to the floor to throw them out, Sister Thérèse whispered: "Oh no; don't throw them out; they will be precious yet." I was told this by Mother Agnes and Sister Marie of the Sacred Heart; they were there at the time. On another occasion, when the community was gathered round her bed, Mother Agnes said: "What about throwing some flowers to the community!" "Oh no, Mother dear," she answered, "don't ask me to do that, please; I don't want to throw flowers to creatures. I would do it for our Lady or St Joseph, but not for anybody else."

Fortitude

The Servant of God's courage was revealed in the equanimity with which she bore the greatest interior and physical sufferings. When speaking of her love for her neighbour I mentioned the fortitude with which she bore their defects, and the sufferings that resulted from her father's illness and her own interior trials. When illness finally nailed herself to the cross, she still showed wonderful courage. She was always gentle and smiling; a heavenly smile was her only response to suffering —never a word of complaint. For the further adornment of her soul God permitted that our kind and devoted physician, who often came to see her, never thought of killing her pain with one of those analgesics that science has discovered, and which would have lightened her long martyrdom. She bore it to the end with heroic courage.

Temperance

The Servant of God was a model of mortification, but of a mortification that was authentic and free from any illusions of pride or self-love. Her spirit was inspired by that of God from childhood. To prepare herself for Carmel she had imposed numerous sacrifices on herself: she had trained herself to break her self-will and to render little services to those around her; that was all her youth would allow of. Once she was in Carmel, never did a complaint cross her lips, and I cannot recollect her ever asking for the slightest exemption from anything during her novitiate.

She found the cold very hard, but she never said a word to me about it; indeed, it was only lately that I discovered this. It would seem she suffered so much from it that it is a wonder she did not die of it. If only I had known! I would have done anything to remedy the matter. Today I say to myself: how heroic that dear child's virtue really was! Her mortification can be summed up in a few words: to suffer everything without complaint, whether it concerned clothing or food. She really had a lot to offer up where food was concerned. How often I have been moved as I saw that frail young girl deprived of the consideration and dietary concessions which she should have been generously granted! But God permitted that all too often she was given only left-overs or food that even a healthy stomach would have had difficulty in putting up with. It was the same with sleep, but the dear child never said a word, so happy was she to have these opportunities of suffering.

No matter how great the sufferings, she maintained an unchanging serenity. This caused surprise, but it was only later that the real reason for it came out: "When I am suffering a lot," she once said, "I answer with a smile instead of putting on a sad face. At first I did not always succeed, but now it's a habit, and one I'm happy to have contracted."

She was no less good at controlling her natural emotions. The generosity with which she mortified the natural instinct which would have made her prefer the company of her own three sisters to that of the others was noticeable time and time again. She adopted the opposite course of action. Here are some examples. After her long retreat she could have asked for permission to go and visit her sisters in their rooms, and this would have been easily granted. But she did nothing of the kind. They then thought their little sister would come looking for them at recreation and sit beside them, but she did not. That was how much the Servant of God feared to give in to nature's demands. When our foundress, Mother Genevieve, was told about this, she reprimanded her severely just to test her. She told her she had behaved like a heartless child, and that this was not the kind of perfection that religious life demanded.

Another time her beloved sister, Agnes of Jesus, was very hurt. Sister Thérèse had not gone to visit her, and this time she let her see that she was hurt. "But, Mother," said Sister Thérèse, "do the other nuns come to see you?"

"No," replied Mother Agnes.

"Then I must deprive myself, too," said Sister Thérèse.

That was her understanding of the degree of mortification of the heart required by religious perfection. On her deathbed, she said to Mother Agnes one day: "Mother dear, don't think that when I am dying my last look will be for you; it will be for Mother Gonzague and for those to whom I think it might be of some use. . . . Don't be upset . . . I only want to act supernaturally." It was Mother Agnes herself who told me this later.

Poverty

The Servant of God had a great love of poverty. I remember surprising her one day in the sacristy while she was removing the lace border from an altar-cloth. The lace was only tacked on loosely, and like a real poor person she was pulling out the thread carefully so that she could use it again. She could have done the job much more quickly by just cutting through it, but she saw this as an opportunity to practise poverty. Her poverty consisted above all in being satisfied with what she was given, in going without cheerfully, and in not saying anything when someone took something she had the use of. She did not see her time as belonging to her more than anything else, and she never took on a particular kind of work just because she liked it. She would have regarded that as too comfortable a way of life.

Chastity

Concerning this virtue I have only one thing to say about the Servant of God: she was an angel in a human body. Never did the slightest careless word cross her lips. She would have preferred to throw herself into a fire rather than expose herself to the slightest breath of anything that could tarnish her baptismal innocence. Her purity was reflected in her heavenly expression, always so calm, so kindly, and so dignified. Allied to this recollected exterior was a certain childlike quality which radiated candour and innocence. There was something about her that commanded respect, and seemed to say: don't touch me.

Her modesty was something that impressed all who met her. During the influenza epidemic our chaplain, Fr Youf, had to enter the enclosure several times to visit the sick and the dying. He noticed this modesty immediately, and remarked to me: "Not one of you can match young Sister Thérèse in that perfectly calm and religious bearing of hers." As she passed along the cloisters, even the gardener working in the cloister garth recognised her by the edifying way she carried herself, even though she had her veil down. In his own way he paid her this tribute: "Oh! That little Sister Thérèse; I never see her run." I think this angelic purity explains why God gave her such a wonderful insight into the Scriptures. That saying of our Lord's "Blessed are the pure of heart, for they shall see God" (*Mt 5:8*) was certainly true of her.

Obedience

The Servant of God was perfectly obedient. As a novice there was no thinking about it, just absolute docility. A short time ago, a nun who was in the novitiate with her said to me: "You remember what Sister Thérèse was like in the novitiate? Whenever you explained something to us or brought something to our notice, she never said a word. She always listened with deep respect." Nor did she ever make excuses when I corrected her, even when I was mistaken, as happened in the case of the broken vase, when I accused her of being untidy. She mentions that incident in her autobiography. While she was still a pos-tulant, I suggested an idea to her that I thought she might find helpful at mental prayer. Her sense of obedience made her try it out, even though it was a tiring effort. It was only afterwards I found out about this.

She had a great love of the Holy Rule, and nothing pained her so much as not being able to fulfil its prescriptions to the full on account of her youth.

I think she showed heroic obedience when she submitted in silence and without complaint the time that Mother Prioress refused her permission to go back and discuss the affairs of her soul with Fr Alexis, the retreat-master, because he had really understood her spiritual state and given her back her peace and joy.

I remember one very ordinary incident which showed the promptness with which she obeyed at the very first call. One winter's day, following a Carmelite custom, she had taken off her damp stockings to dry them by the fire during recreation, when someone came to tell her that she was wanted in the sacristy. Slipping on the cloth and cord slippers, which we call *alpargatas*, off she went across the cloisters with her legs bare, and not so much as a thought about how imprudent this could be for her. She could have said: "Just a moment, please," but as far as she was concerned she was answering the call of God himself, and she did so without a moment's hesitation.

Her convictions on the subject are well expressed in the autobiography: "How fortunate nuns are if they are simple! The will of their superiors is their only compass, so they are sure of never going astray. . . . As soon as one starts to ignore this infallible compass, the soul strays into arid paths and its water-supply of grace soon runs out."[9]

Humility

The Servant of God was like a hidden violet in this respect. She was so simple and self-effacing that, though one noticed something heavenly about her, she was taken for a child. She always put herself last, and tried to pass unnoticed by never voicing her opinion unless asked for it. This humility left her in the shade, so that today one continually hears nuns exclaim in astonishment at the wonders she has wrought since her death: "That little Sister Thérèse was so ordinary and hidden during her lifetime; how is it she is making so much noise now! Who would ever have believed that she could be so active all over the world!"

Her dedication and tact, her wisdom and her prudence, were often put to the test. She was richly endowed with all the gifts of heart and spirit, and she always employed these treasures for the glory of God and the service of those about her. She did all this quite naturally, with no ulterior motives, and with a simplicity that let her humility shine through. I could illustrate these characteristics with several anecdotes from her autobiography; they are well known.

When I reflect on the Servant of God's virtues, I compare her to the sky: the more you look at it, the more stars you see there.

23. I have been told that even before she became a nun people were struck by her angelic expression. When Sister Stanislas's nephew saw her out walking with her father, the venerable M. Martin, he said to his sister: "Look at Miss Martin! She's like an angel. You know something? I think you'll see her canonised some day." It was his sister who told Sister Stanislas this.

Miss Delarue, who prepared for her first holy communion at the Benedictine school together with Sister Thérèse, told me recently: "There is no expressing her air of purity, candour and innocence; nor the simplicity with which she gave answers that we could never have thought of."

Here in the convent we looked on her as a chosen person, amazing for her recollection and fidelity to duty. I am not aware that there is anyone in the convent who thinks differently about her.

24. Although I rarely saw the Servant of God during her illness, so as not to tire her, I saw her often enough to realise how heroic her courage was. I can confidently say that hers was the most beautiful death I have witnessed in Carmel. It was a harrowing experience to see her pain increase day by day. On the afternoon of 30 September we felt the end was near, and we all gathered at her bedside. At 4.30 p.m. her agony began, and

she thanked the community with a pretty smile for having come to help her with their prayers. She held the crucifix in her failing hands, a cold sweat bathed her brow, and she was shaking all over. Shortly before 7 p.m. Mother Prioress sent the community away, for the agony looked like dragging on for some time. Only Mother Prioress and her own three sisters stayed on. But we had hardly left when we were summoned back again. I was convinced this was the end. Back at the bedside, I saw her bend her head as she looked at the crucifix, and we heard her say: "Oh! yes, I love him . . . My God, I love you . . ." Suddenly she raised her head erect with surprising energy. She opened her eyes wide and gazed in a marvellous sort of way at a point above the statue of our Lady. We felt she was looking at something supernatural at that moment. I thought it must have been our Lord. Almost immediately afterwards, her head fell back on the pillow: it was all over. I shall never forget that look of hers, nor so beautiful a death.

27. It is marvellous to see how the Servant of God's "furore in the world" has gone on increasing since her death. The phrase I quote is the expression a religious used recently in the parlour. She seems to be everywhere—in communities, in seminaries, and in families. Every day we have letters telling us how much she helps priests and missionaries. In China, they tell us, she has converted whole villages.

In my own family I can see devotion to her growing steadily; they pray to her, they feel free to ask anything of her, and are always asking me for books, pictures, novena leaflets, etc.

We turn out these pictures by the thousand here, and still cannot meet the demand. Sometimes we receive as many as 100 letters in one day acknowledging favours and telling of the devotion they all have to the Servant of God. Some of these are read to us at recreation, and they establish beyond question her world-wide reputation for holiness.

29. The numerous letters from so many different quarters establishing the Servant of God's fame also prove that the faithful everywhere are confident of obtaining extraordinary temporal and spiritual favours through her intercession. There are numerous accounts of cures, conversions, and all sorts of favours. I am not very well informed about these, but I am sure it would be easy to collect a multitude of such attestations.

In our own convent, there have been numerous instances of sweet-smelling perfumes, which do not appear to have any natural explanation. Two or three months ago I learned of an extraordinary thing that happened to one of our young lay-sisters, Sister Jeanne-Marie of the Child Jesus, whom I regard as an angel of virtue and piety. A few days after the feast of the Immaculate Conception in 1910, she found that she was almost completely out of the little printed seals which Mgr Teil, the vice-postulator, had given her to stick on pictures and souvenirs by way of authentication. The sister who was helping her in this work, by cutting up sheets of them into individual seals, told her she did not have time to cut out any more just then. Sister Jeanne-Marie recommended herself to the Servant of God and went back to her room. To her great surprise and delight, she found her little box of seals filled up again. There were over 500 of them there. The matter was looked into, to see if any of the other sisters had done it to give her a surprise, but no one had done it. Besides, it was unlikely that they would have done so, because the work could not have been undertaken without Mother Prioress's permission, and also because we are forbidden to enter each other's rooms.

It was Sister Jeanne-Marie, too, who was similarly favoured last year, when she found a certain water tank inexplicably filled up for her at a time when she was doing her duty in spite of being very tired.

9   Martha of Jesus, O.C.D.

Désirée Florence Martha Cauvin was born at Griverville in the diocese of Evreux on 16 July, 1865. She lost both her parents at an early age, and spent her childhood and adolescence in orphanages, a fact that left a very definite mark on her character.

On 2 May, 1889, Désirée became Sister Martha of Jesus at the Lisieux Carmel, and made her profession there as a lay-sister on 23 September, 1890. At her own request, however, she was allowed to remain on in the novitiate under the guidance of Sister Thérèse.

By all accounts, Sister Martha was quite a difficult person. Due to the lack of maternal affection in her childhood, she was emotionally unbalanced. She was capable of very strong affection, such as that which she bore Mother Gonzague, but the emotion her sisters feared most was her violent temper, for then her tongue was at its sharpest. But then this same intensity of emotion heightened her good qualities too: she was a generous and tireless worker, and tried hard, with Thérèse's help, to overcome her temper in a genuine effort to be holy.

Typically, it was she who sometimes served Thérèse the dried-up left-overs from the kitchen, while in another mood she would invite her, solicitously but in vain, to come and warm herself there. She feared and admired Thérèse all at once: testing her with sarcasm, sulks and untimely visits, yet asking to be allowed to stay on in the novitiate to benefit by her guidance. Difficult material she may have been, but at least she was the first to admit it.

It is Martha that Thérèse has in mind when she speaks of the fellow-novice with whom she was allowed to "converse of spiritual matters from time to time," when she says that Jesus enabled her to enlighten this sister about her faults, particularly

216

the too natural affection with which she loved Mother Gonzague.

It was to please Sister Martha that Thérèse agreed to do her annual private retreat with her for three years. On these occasions Thérèse would adapt herself to the complicated accountancy by which the simple lay-sister kept track of her daily sacrifices and acts of virtue.

Sister Thérèse also wrote her several little notes, which show just how well she could understand and handle her, even in her blackest moods. It was for Sister Martha, too, that she wrote the "Prayer for obtaining humility", a birthday gift in 1897.

During the last years of her life, Sister Martha underwent a spiritual transformation, which became deeper and more obvious in the months of suffering that preceded her death on 4 September, 1916.

Her testimony, the fifteenth, was taken on 17-18 February, 1911.

The testimony

7. I have prayed to God that the way I give my testimony will cause him no offence. I love the Servant of God very much, but I would prefer to say nothing in her favour than to fail to tell the truth.

8. I entered Carmel only three months before the Servant of God, so I was with her in the novitiate. From that time onwards I was very attached to her because of her virtues, and the good she did my soul. This special bond of intimacy united us till the day she died. I will make use only of my own personal recollections in the testimony I am about to give.

17. The Servant of God entered the Lisieux Carmel in April 1888, and took the habit on 10 January, 1889. We did our novitiate together. She made her profession on 8 September, 1890; her profession had been delayed a while because our superior, Fr Delatroëtte, considered her too young. From the time the Servant of God joined us, I was aware that she was no ordinary person. But I found it very hard to understand how so young a nun could be as perfect as she was. What struck me most about her was her humility, piety and mortification.

18. Sister Thérèse's virtue gave her great influence over her companions in the novitiate, almost from the very beginning. Like myself, all the novices felt the need to have her opinion, to

be encouraged by her, and to follow her advice. Mother Prioress had given a general permission to consult the Servant of God in this way, so that in actual fact we used to deal with her as if she was a real novice-mistress.

In 1896 Mother Gonzague became prioress, and entrusted the training of the novices entirely to her, though she did not give her the title of novice-mistress. Out of humility the Servant of God wanted to remain in the novitiate, even when she had finished her training. I remained on there with her until 1895, and even after that I never ceased to consult her. Her guidance was firm, and she was extremely watchful and very sharp at seeing our defects and correcting us. She did this very conscientiously, and never sought the comforts that a less demanding zeal could have brought her. She loved us all equally with a strong, unselfish love that was purely supernatural.

19. I was well aware that in her latter days the Servant of God was writing something rather private, but I did not know exactly what it was; nor did I know the condition under which she wrote it. I received some short notes from her, exhorting me to fervour; I suppose she wrote similar ones to other sisters.

20. I do not know if I am putting this correctly, but I think heroic virtue is virtue that is not mean or paltry; it is something sublime and out of the ordinary. The Servant of God's virtue has always appeared like that to me. It is precisely because her holiness was not ordinary that I could not help being attracted to her.

21. *Faith*

No one who came into contact with Sister Thérèse of the Child Jesus could fail to be overwhelmed by a sense of the presence of God. Her way of speaking about spiritual matters was such that you would never tire of listening to her. She spoke with such feeling that you had the impression there was a fire ceaselessly devouring her. Everything about her commanded respect; when in her presence you felt that her soul was always united to God, that she never ceased to be conscious of his presence. The sight of her humble, modest, and recollected bearing in choir was also a source of edification: she seemed totally absorbed, or lost, in God.

One day she said to me: "There is only one thing I want,

and that is to become a great saint, because that is the only thing that is real on earth. I am determined to strive with might and main for this. I do not want to refuse Jesus the numerous sacrifices he asks of me; I want to deliver up my soul to him, so that he can possess it entirely and do what he likes with it. I am well aware that I cannot accomplish this without suffering, but what a joy it is to suffer for someone you love!"

She had not the slightest interest in the affairs of this world; everything left her indifferent except what concerned the glory of God and people's spiritual welfare. She said to me once: "You cannot afford to share your love if you want it to be pure and unselfish; Jesus must have it all. If you give it to a creature, what can you expect in return? A little token of affection, perhaps, but eventually a lot of disillusionment too. Whereas if you become attached to Jesus, you are sure of finding real happiness; he is a true and unchanging friend."

Love of neighbour

The Servant of God was always ready to do one a favour, and no matter what time of the day she was called upon. She never showed annoyance at being disturbed, but obliged even at the cost of real sacrifice to herself. Whenever she found it impossible to do what she had been asked to, she excused herself so charmingly that one went away as satisfied as if she had done the favour. One day she said to me: "One must never refuse anything to anyone, no matter what it costs. Just think it is Jesus that asks this little favour of you, and you will always cheerfully hasten to oblige."

In her great charity she always found an excuse for those who hurt her, by looking at their intentions, and always took care to be very nice to them. One day I asked her: "How come you always smile so sweetly when Sister X speaks to you? It cannot be because of any attraction because she is always making you suffer." She answered: "That is precisely why I love her, and why I show her so much affection; how could I prove I loved Jesus if I behaved otherwise towards those who hurt me?"

Once, a lay postulant accused Sister Thérèse and myself of trying to get Mother Prioress to send her away from the convent, which was completely untrue. Sister Thérèse said to me: "Let us pray a lot for her, and let's be nice and do something for her.

Then she won't be upset any more and will realise her mistake."

I must bear special testimony to the Servant of God's deal-ings with myself. She was kindness and charity itself to me; only in heaven will it be realised how much she did for me, and the lengths to which she carried her self-sacrifice on my behalf. I inflicted a great deal of suffering on her through my difficult temperament. But I can honestly say that she always remained calm and kind. I would even go so far as to say that the more I made her suffer, the more she seemed to show me preference and kindness. She never rejected me, in spite of the frequency of my visits; I never noticed even the slightest annoyance in the way she received me. Through her admirable virtues I came to love her dearly. Still, I was sometimes a bit jealous, and would get angry when she called attention to my shortcomings. On such occasions I used to go away and refuse to speak to her. But such was her charity that she always sought me out to try and help me, and her gentleness never failed to win me over.

One day I was upset and said some very hurtful things to her. She just went on talking calmly and gently, asking me to help her with some work she had to do. I gave in, still muttering to myself at the inconvenience she was causing me. Then I thought I would see how far her patience could be stretched, so, to try her virtue, I decided not to answer when she spoke to me. But I failed to upset her, and ended up asking her to forgive me for being so rude. Sister Thérèse did not scold me, nor did she say a word to hurt me; she just encouraged me to be more obliging in future, and taught me the error of my ways. Her charity towards me never ceases to amaze me, and I have often wondered what could make her so interested in a poor lay-sister. I can find no words adequate to express the self-sacrifice with which she attended to my spiritual welfare.

Prudence

The Servant of God was endowed with great prudence, especially where the training of novices was concerned. She did her best to find out what God wanted of each of us. She always kept a sharp lookout for the least fault, and missed nothing; indeed, she sometimes saw so clearly that she surprised me. She was very gentle in correcting people, but she was very firm. She never gave in to our failings, and never went back on her word.

of a Soul, and I was struck by the perfect way in which what she wrote agreed with what she had told me herself and with what little of her life I had been able to see for myself.

20. I have never done any studies, so I would not be able to explain very well what heroic virtue means. But I think I know what it means all the same. It is to push the practice of virtue beyond the ordinary. I honestly believe that Sister Thérèse's holiness surpassed that of even the most fervent nuns in this respect. What people, even her own sisters, say about her now seems to me to fall short of what I saw in her. Since she was always correcting my faults, I would have liked to find some imperfection in her, but I never could.

21. *Faith*

Anyone could see that Sister Thérèse never lost sight of the presence of God; the perfection and attention with which she did everything made it obvious. That she should be like this was rendered all the more meritorious by the fact that the community was in considerable chaos at the time, on account of the unfortunate administration of Mother Marie de Gonzague. She could have let herself slide like the others, and do things any old way. I have often thought to myself how well the words we say of certain saints, in the divine office, could be applied to her: "Blessed are those who could have transgressed, but did not" *(Eccl 31:10).*

She could not bear to see the slightest negligence on my part. One day I threw on the coverlet of my bed rather haphazardly. She saw it and scolded me for it. She said I could hardly be united to God and do things that way. "What are you doing in Carmel, if you don't behave spiritually?" she said. That was the way she used to scold me. But as soon as she saw that I admitted my faults, she would become more gentle, and speak like a saint of the merits of faith, and of the fidelity that Jesus expected of our love after all the signs he had given us of his.

In these relations with me during my novitiate, she never tried to win my affection by natural means, and still she won it entirely. I felt that the more I loved her, the more I loved God too; when my love for her sometimes grew rather cool, I felt my love for God diminishing too. I found that strange and could not understand it, until one day she gave me a picture, on the back of which she had written these words of St John of the Cross: "When our love for another person is wholly spiritual and based on God alone, then as it grows the love of God in our souls grows with it."[1] I cannot help believing that when she wrote that, she had read my thoughts.

I have never confided my troubles to her without reaping great spiritual benefit thereby. "The chief cause of your suffering and troubles," she used to say to me, "is that you look at things too much from an earthly point of view, and not enough from a supernatural viewpoint. You seek your own satisfaction in things to too great an extent. But you won't find any happiness until you stop looking for it."

Her faith in her superiors, as God's representatives, was remarkable. She respected and trusted them, no matter what they were like. "When you deal with them in a spirit of faith," she said, "God never allows you to go wrong." When Mother Gonzague was prioress, she would never let me criticise her. Sometimes I called her "the wolf", but Sister Thérèse always reprimanded me with that same spirit of faith.

One day she met me as I was going to Mother Prioress's room. She stopped me, and said: "Have you taken care to commend what you are about to God? It's very important to renew one's spirit of faith on these occasions, and to pray for light to see Mother Prioress's words as the channel of God's will for us. If you haven't done that, you are wasting your time."

When she was sacristan, I witnessed the spirit of faith with which she carried out that task. She told me how happy she was to have the privilege of touching the sacred vessels like the priests. She kissed them respectfully, and made me kiss the large host which was about to be consecrated. But her happiness was greatest the day she was bringing back the little gilded paten from the communion table, and saw that a fairly large particle had fallen on it. I met her in the cloister, carrying her precious treasure, and shielding it carefully as she went. "Follow me!" she said. "I am carrying Jesus." When she reached the sacristy, she placed the paten devoutly on a table, and had me kneel down and pray with her until the priest she had sent for arrived.

She had a burning desire for holy communion; the inability

to receive it daily was the greatest suffering she had to endure.
She would have suffered anything rather than miss going to
holy communion. One communion day she was very ill, and
had been ordered to take some medicine. Now it was customary
here to miss holy communion because of that. Faced with this
dilemma Sister Thérèse broke down and cried, but she pleaded
her cause so ably with Mother Prioress that not only was she
allowed to postpone the medicine until after Mass, but from
that day on the custom of missing holy communion in such
cases was abolished.

Hope

Sister Thérèse had made her own that saying of St John
of the Cross: "One obtains from God what one hopes for." It
was a saying she often repeated to me. I once asked her if our
Lord was displeased with me, seeing I was so imperfect. "Rest
assured," she said, "that he whom you have taken as your spouse
has all the perfections that one could desire, but, if I may say
so, he has one great weakness: he is blind! And there is one
branch of knowledge he is ignorant of—mathematics. If he were
able to see clearly and keep proper accounts, the sight of our
sins would make him annihilate us. But no, his love for us makes
him positively blind! Look at it this way. If the greatest sinner
on earth repented of all his offences at the last moment and died
in an act of love, God would not stop to weigh up the numerous
graces which the unfortunate man had wasted and the crimes
he had been guilty of; he counts only that last prayer and
receives him into the arms of his mercy without delay."

*Here the judge asked her to what extent her testimony
corresponded literally with the "Counsels and Reminiscences"
that were appended to the* Story of a Soul.

The "Counsels and Reminiscences" which were included in
the complete edition of the *Story of a Soul* were written up
mainly from notes I had made of my recollections; I used those
same notes to prepare this testimony.

The witness then resumed her testimony.

On a certain occasion the Servant of God was speaking
about the "little spiritual way" she had taught me, and, just
to test me, she said: "When I am dead, and you no longer have

anybody to encourage you to follow my 'little way of trust and love' you'll probably abandon it, won't you?"

"Certainly not," I answered. "I believe in it so firmly that if the pope himself were to tell me that you had been wrong, I think I could still believe in it."

"Oh! You should believe the pope before anybody else," she replied sharply. "But don't be afraid that he is going to tell you to change; I won't give him time to. If, when I get to heaven, I find that I have deceived you, I will obtain permission from God to come back straight away and tell you. Till then, believe that my way is safe and follow it faithfully."

One day I asked her how she prepared for holy communion. She said: "Just as I am receiving, I sometimes imagine my soul as a child of three or four who has its clothes and hair dirtied and in disarray from playing. These misfortunes happen to me from doing battle with souls. But our Lady immediately takes charge of me. She takes off my smock, tidies my hair, and puts a pretty ribbon or, maybe, a little flower in it. That's enough to make me sufficiently pretty again to take part in the angels' feast without any embarrassment."

"If you are sick," she would say, "just tell Mother Prioress about it; then leave it to God, and don't worry any more about it, whether they give you proper treatment or not. You have done your duty by informing the prioress of it, and that is enough. The rest is not your business, but God's. If he should permit you to lack something, that is a grace: it is because he is confident that you are strong enough to suffer something for his sake." As assistant infirmarian, I could see that this was the line of advice she followed herself. She would never admit that she was in pain unless forced to. She found nothing so hard as having people fussing about her. She told God how she was, and that was enough for her.

Here is an instance she gave me herself: "One evening the infirmarian came and put a hot-water bottle to my feet and tincture of iodine on my chest. I was already burning with fever, and could not help complaining to Jesus about such remedies. 'My Jesus,' I said to him, 'you can see that I am roasting, and they still add heat and fire. If only I had a glass of water instead! Jesus, your little girl is very thirsty, but she is glad of an opportunity to lack what she needs, so as to

resemble you more closely and save souls.' Soon afterwards the
infirmarian left and I didn't expect to see her again until the
following morning. To my great surprise, she returned a few
minutes later with a refreshing drink. How kind Jesus is! How
nice it is to trust ourselves to him!' "

Once, when I had some trouble in the family, she said:
"Put your trust in God and don't worry about it; everything
will turn out all right for them. . . . If *you* worry about it, God
won't; and you will deprive your relatives of the graces you
would have obtained for them by leaving it to God."

Love of God

Sister Thérèse transformed all her actions, even the least
of them, into acts of love. She continually urged me to do the
same, and suggested I offer myself as a victim to God's Merciful
Love, as she had done. I have often seen her shed tears as she
spoke to me of Jesus's love for us, of her own love for him, and
of the desire she had to make him loved.

One day I hurt her feelings when I would not admit the
faults she reproached me with. The bell rang just then, and
we had to go and join the community. On the way down I
began to be sorry for the way I had behaved, and I whispered
to her: "I was very naughty just now." I had not time to say any
more before I saw her eyes fill with tears. She looked at me
tenderly, and said: "I have never felt so keenly the love with
which Jesus receives us when we ask his pardon after offending
him. If a poor little creature of his like me could feel so much
love for you when you came back to me, what must God feel
when people come back to him?"

She had a knack of using everything to stoke up the fire of
love. One day I spoke to her about magnetism, and the extraordinary things I had seen in this connection. The following
day she said to me: "How I wish I could get myself magnetised
by Jesus! How gladly would I have handed over my will to him!
I wish he would take possession of all my faculties, so that I
could no longer perform personal, human actions but only
deeds that were wholly divine—inspired and guided by the
Spirit of Love."

One day I told her I was going to explain her "little way of
love" to all my relatives and friends, and get them to make the

"Act of Offering" so that they would go straight to heaven. "In that case," she said, "be very careful; our 'little way' could be mistaken for quietism or illuminism if it is badly explained." I did not know what these words meant, so I was rather taken aback, and I asked her to explain them. She told me then about a certain Mme Guyon who had strayed on to a wrong path, and added: "People must not think that our 'little way' is a restful one, full of sweetness and consolation. It's quite the opposite. To offer oneself as a victim to love is to offer oneself to suffering, because love lives only on sacrifice; so, if one is completely dedicated to loving, one must expect to be sacrificed unreservedly."

I am very sorry that I did not note down systematically all the lights which she received in prayer and passed on to me for the good of my soul. She had an extraordinary ability for interpreting the Scriptures. She was so good at discovering all the beauty of these holy books that it was as if they no longer held any secrets for her. One day during prayer she was particularly struck by the passage in the *Song of Songs* where the spouse says to his beloved: "We shall make you chains of gold, inlaid with silver" *(1:10)*. "What a strange thing for the spouse to say!" she said. "You would expect a silver chain inlaid with gold, or a gold chain inlaid with precious stones, because usually a piece of jewellery is inlaid with something more precious than itself. But Jesus has given me the key to the mystery: he has shown me that the gold chains are love, charity, but that he does not like them unless they are inlaid with the silver of childlike simplicity. God must value simplicity very highly to say he finds it fit to enhance the splendour of charity."

Another day she said to me: "I wanted to be very rich in order to have the joy of sacrificing to God all the pleasures which a fine fortune could have brought me. God, who is good enough to fulfil all my desires, fulfilled this one too. When the time came for me to make my profession, I learned that an enterprise in which my father had invested a lot of money was on the point of being successful. I was unspeakably happy to be able to sacrifice my expected fortune when I offered myself to Jesus."

Her love for God gave her a burning zeal for the salvation of souls, especially those of priests; she offered all her sacrifices for their sanctification, and urged me to do likewise. She called sinners "her children" and took her role as their "mother" very seriously. She was passionately fond of them, and worked for them with untiring dedication. One washing-day, I was sauntering along to the laundry, looking at the flowers in the garden as I went, when along came Sister Thérèse at a brisk pace, and overtook me. "Is that how one hurries with children to feed and work to do so they can live?" she said, and then, dragging me with her: "Come on, let's hurry; if we amuse ourselves here, our children will die of hunger."

Another time she said: "Before I entered, when I woke up in the morning I used to think about what the day might have in store for me, and if I foresaw annoying things I got up depressed. Now it's the opposite: the more opportunities I can foresee of bearing witness to my love for Jesus and of earning a living for my children, the poor sinners, the more joyful and courageous I am when I get up in the morning. The first thing I do is to kiss my crucifix. I then place it gently on my pillow while I dress, and I tell Jesus: 'Look, you worked and wept enough for thirty-three years here on earth; today you can take a rest, it's my turn to fight and suffer.' "

In her "Act of Offering to Merciful Love" she asked our Lord to remain always in her heart under the sacramental species, as he does in the tabernacle. Here are her own words: "I know, my God, that when you want to give us more, you increase our desires. My heart is full of immense desires, and I confidently invite you to come and take possession of it. I cannot receive holy communion as often as I would like to, Lord; but are you not all-powerful? Stay in me as you do in the tabernacle, and never leave this little host of yours."

I am personally convinced that this request of hers was granted. As she said herself on the subject: "If God has inspired me to ask this favour of him, it is because he wishes to grant it. . . . God will work wonders for his 'little victims of love', but they will be worked in faith, otherwise they could not go on living." In the canticle she composed for my profession (it has been printed with her poems under the title "I thirst for love") there is a verse which begins:

Thou, the great God whom heaven and earth adore,
Dost live *in me*, a prisoner night and day.

One of the sisters remarked to her that she must have slipped up here, that it should have been *for me*, etc. "No, no," she said, "what I have said is right," and she winked at me as much as to say: "We understand one another."

Love of neighbour

Sister Thérèse was very soft-hearted where other people's suffering was concerned, and she always showed it. She said to me: "Whenever I see one of the sisters suffering, and I have no permission to speak to her, I ask Jesus to comfort her himself." She invited me to do likewise, and assured me that this was very pleasing to Jesus.

I have remarked more than once that when the community worked together she would place herself next to the sisters who seemed downcast or depressed. Since she could not speak to them, she smiled affectionately at them and tried to be as obliging as possible. There used to be a sister (she has since left us) who had moods of the blackest depression. Nobody could ever work with her for long. Sister Thérèse took pity on this unhappy person and, seeing a great opportunity for sacrificing herself more fully for God's sake, she asked Mother Prioress to let her help this sister in her work. This heroic gesture brought her a great deal of suffering, but she bore it all with unfailing humility and gentleness.

For two or three months Sister Thérèse was assistant portress to an elderly nun who, though a very good religious, had a temperament that would try the patience of a saint. She was also exasperatingly slow and very eccentric in her ways. One day I lost my patience with her, and she retorted that Sister Thérèse never spoke to her like that. I told the Servant of God about this, and she said: "Be very gentle with her; she's not well. Besides, it's only charity to let her think she is rendering us a service, and it gives us an opportunity to practise patience. You are complaining after only a few words with her; what would you do if you had to listen to her all day, as I have to? Now, you can do what I do. It's really very easy. All you have to do is to mellow your soul with charitable thoughts; you then feel such peace that you no longer get irritated."

Another time she said: "It is perhaps at recreation more

than anywhere else that one finds opportunities for sanctifying oneself by the practice of charity. If you want to profit by it, don't go there for your own recreation; concentrate on making it a recreation for the others." And she literally practised what she preached. I noticed that her only care was to please others, and she did it so naturally that you would think she did it for her own enjoyment.

Whenever someone was needed for a boring or a tiring job, she volunteered. The laundry was where she was especially ingenious at renouncing her own will. One day I asked her which was better: to go out and rinse the clothes in cold water, or stay in the laundry and do it with hot water. "That's not difficult to decide," she said; "if you find it hard to go to the cold water, then so do the rest; so, you go. But if the weather is fine, you should preferably stay in the laundry. By choosing the worst places, you at once mortify yourself and practise charity towards others, because you leave the best places for them." After that I understood why she stayed in the laundry when it was fine, and in the stuffiest corner of it at that.

I also witnessed the heroic charity she demonstrated in the case of that holy nun she speaks about in her Life—the nun who had the knack of rubbing her the wrong way in everything that she did.[2] She showed such esteem and affection for that sister that one would have thought she had a special affection for her.

She wanted me to love my sisters, and especially Mother Prioress, with a wholly supernatural love. Once, I saw Mother Agnes speak to another nun and place more trust in her than in me. Expecting a bit of sympathy, I told Sister Thérèse about it. To my surprise, she said: "You think you love Mother Prioress very much, don't you?"

"Of course I do," I replied, "otherwise I wouldn't mind her showing preference for others."

"All right. Now I'm going to prove to you that you are absolutely wrong. It is not Mother Prioress that you love; it is yourself. When one really loves, one rejoices to see the beloved person happy. If you loved Mother Prioress for her own sake, you would be glad to see her finding some pleasure at your expense. Since you think she found you less pleasant to talk to than someone else, then you should not be hurt when you appear to have been passed over."

As she was speaking, I began to see for the first time what unselfish love was; I found out that until then I had never really known what it was to love.

Prudence

Sister Thérèse was so perfectly prudent that one would have thought she had years of experience behind her. Even so, the situation was often thorny enough: certain precautions were necessary to avoid offending the susceptibilities of Mother Gonzague, and there were other tensions in the community as well.

Whatever my difficulties, she always had an apt and sure answer; without the slightest hesitation she would show me clearly what I had to do to comply with God's will. One day I wanted to deprive myself of holy communion because of a fault for which I was bitterly sorry. I wrote her a note informing her of my decision, and this is the answer I got: "Dear little flower of Jesus, that is enough! Though the humiliation of your soul is making your roots eat earth . . . you must open or, rather, raise up your petals for the bread of angels to come like a divine dew to strengthen you and give you everything you lack."[3]

At the end of one retreat I told her about my resolutions and the new fervour I was then fired with. But she said: "Be careful. I've always noticed that hell seems to be let loose against someone who has just finished a retreat. The demons unite to make us fall as soon as we take the first steps, so as to discourage us. In fact, once we fall we say: 'How can I keep my resolutions, if I've fallen so soon?' If we allow ourselves to think along those lines, the devils have won. So, each time they are successful, you must get up again without surprise, and humbly say to Jesus: 'They may have knocked me down, but I'm not beaten. Here I am, standing again and ready to go on fighting for love of you.' Then Jesus will be moved by your goodwill, and will himself be your strength."

One day I wanted to omit mental prayer because of urgent work. She said: "Unless the necessity is very great, never ask to be dispensed from community exercises for the sake of work, no matter what it is. That kind of dedication cannot be pleasing to Jesus. Real dedication is to never waste a minute, and to give oneself fully during the hours set aside for work."

I was so sensitive that I cried often and for very trivial reasons. Sister Thérèse waged constant war on this impressionableness and tried in every way to make me strong.

One day I was looking for a little appreciation for having behaved virtuously. "A pity you should do that!" she said. "When you think of all the lights and graces Jesus gives you, it would have been rather poor of you to have acted otherwise. What's that compared to what he has a right to expect of you? You should rather be humbling yourself at the thought of all the opportunities for virtue that you have let slip." Her retort was a salutary lesson; even now it stops me from being complacent when I do anything good.

On some feastday or other, they forgot to serve me with dessert at dinner. Afterwards, I went to the infirmary to visit Sister Thérèse and found the sister who sits next to me in the refectory there before me. I skilfully let her know that I had been forgotten. Sister Thérèse heard me and made me go and bring it to the notice of the sister who had served the desserts. I implored her not to make me do this, but she said: "No, that's your penance; you're not worthy of the sacrifices God asks of you. He asked you to do without dessert, because it was he who permitted you to be forgotten. He thought you were generous enough to make this sacrifice, and you disappointed him by drawing attention to the fact." Her lesson bore fruit and cured me entirely.

When I went to the Servant of God for guidance, I could not help admiring her tact and delicacy. She never asked an annoying or merely curious question, even on the pretext of doing me good. More than once I was able to see for myself the truth of that passage in her Life: "When I speak to a novice, I am careful to mortify myself. I avoid asking her any questions that would satisfy my curiosity . . . because I don't think any good can come of self-seeking."[4]

Justice

The divine office held a very special place in Sister Thérèse's devotion. One of the things she was most insistent on was the way we carried ourselves in choir. She never tired of telling me that since I was there in the presence of the King of kings, I ought not to permit myself the slightest carelessness. And I noticed how her own bearing was above reproach. She moved as little as possible, and touched neither her face nor her garments. "God appreciates these little expressions of submission," she used to say. "He is pleased to notice the attention and respect shown him."

She had great devotion, too, to the Holy Face of Jesus, and she spoke to me constantly of her desire to resemble him. She was so happy to see that Sister Genevieve, who was in the novitiate with me, and I shared this devotion that she composed an act of consecration to the Holy Face just for the three of us, as well as a hymn on the same subject.[5]

She also liked the Stations of the Cross. As she said herself: "The soul reaps so much benefit from doing them, and the souls in purgatory so much comfort, that I would like to be able to do them every day."

Her devotion to Mary was quite touching; she had recourse to her in all her difficulties, and had me do likewise. In our counselling sessions, if there were things that I found rather hard to tell her, she would bring me over to the miraculous statue that had smiled at her when she was a child, and say: "It's not me you're going to tell what's worrying you; you'll tell it to the Blessed Virgin. So, get on with it." She listened in to all I said, and when I had finished she would tell me to kiss our Lady's hand. Then she gave me her advice, and peace returned to my soul.

She also had a filial love of St Teresa and St John of the Cross. The latter's writing especially filled her with love. But it was the Scriptures, and the Gospel above all, that she constantly cited, and to such good effect that you might say her conversations were a commentary on the Bible.

She was also particularly devoted to the angels. She used to tell me that out of respect for them we should always carry ourselves with dignity. She could not bear to see the least contraction on my face, such as frowning, for example. "The face reflects the soul," she used to say, "so it must always be calm, like the ever-happy face of a little baby. That holds good even when you are alone, because you are always in the sight of God and his angels."

She loved all the saints, too. She looked on herself as their child, and liked to ask them for their "double love" (Cf. 2 Kings,

That happened to me every day, and this command became a
real torture for me. Whenever I had a stomach-ache, I would
have preferred to be flogged rather than go and tell her, but out
of obedience I did it every time. The novice-mistress eventually
forgot that it was she who had told me to do this, and she would
say: 'Poor child, you'll never be healthy enough to observe our
Rule; it is too much for you.' Or if Mother Gonzague were
asked for a remedy, she would get annoyed and say: 'For goodness sake, that child is always complaining. We come to Carmel
to suffer, and if she cannot bear her little indispositions let her
go home.' Even at the risk of being sent away, I obediently continued to report my stomach-aches for a long time afterwards,
until God finally took pity on my weakness, and permitted them
to free me from this obligation."

Poverty

Sister Thérèse would keep for her own use only what was
strictly indispensable, and the uglier and poorer these were, the
happier she was. She used to say that there was nothing sweeter
than to lack what was necessary, because then you could say you
were really poor. She urged me never to ask for anything to be
bought without first assuring myself that there was no other
alternative, and I was then to choose unhesitatingly what was
cheapest, like the really poor people do. It was out of a spirit of
poverty, too, that she chose closely-lined stationery. Though it
was inconvenient, she wrote on every line so as to use less paper.
The same motive made her keep the wick of her lamp as low as
possible, so as to receive only the bare minimum of light she
needed. In the refectory, too, I noticed that if she took a little
too much salt she did not throw it away; she kept it carefully
under her napkin until the next meal.

Chastity

My close relations with Sister Thérèse enabled me to collect
some examples of her angelic purity. Our chaplain at the time
was Fr Youf; he suffered from cerebral anaemia and could not
bear to be asked for spiritual direction outside of confession. On
the other hand, Mother Gonzague's temperament was not the
kind to encourage me to go to *her*. While in this predicament I
was troubled one day about something to do with purity, and I

decided to broach the matter to Sister Thérèse. "I'm afraid you won't understand anything about my problems," I said. She smiled and replied: "Do you think purity is a matter of being ignorant of evil? You needn't be afraid to tell me anything you want to; nothing will surprise me." After she had comforted me and restored my peace of soul, she made this admission: "There is only one thing that I have not experienced, and that is what is called pleasure in this matter." And another time this person who was so pure said to me: "When I am alone, whether it is getting up or going to bed, I am always very careful to be as modest as if I were in the presence of others. After all, am I not always in the presence of God and of his angels? This modesty has become such a habit with me by now that I would be incapable of behaving otherwise."

Humility

Sister Thérèse always urged me to become more and more humble and little. "What a grace humiliation is!" she would say. "If people could only understand what substantial nourishment it is for the soul they would seek it avidly." Very often, at recreation or elsewhere, when I asked her: "What are you thinking about? Tell me something!" she would answer with that angelic expression of hers: "What am I thinking? Oh! just that I would like to be unknown and to count for nothing. I wish my face was hidden from everyone but Jesus, so that nobody here on earth could recognise me."

One day I was telling her about something that happened to me, something I considered an injustice. She said: "It is only just that we should be looked down upon by others, that people should be lacking in esteem for us; they only treat us as we deserve."

She never used her work as an argument or an excuse for anything, and she never spoke of her difficulties. To help me accept a humiliation, she once confided to me: "If I had not been accepted in Carmel I would have entered a Refuge and lived out my days there, unknown and despised among the poor penitents. I would have been happy to be taken for one of them, and would have become an apostle among them, telling them what I thought of God's mercy." When I asked her how she would have hidden her innocence from her confessor, she answered: "I would have told him I had made a general confession before coming in, and that I had been forbidden to go over it again."

One elderly nun could not understand how so young a person as Sister Thérèse could be put in charge of the novices, and she made no secret of her opposition to her. At recreation one day she said some bitter things to her, among others, that "she would be better off directing herself than directing others." I was watching them from a distance. The Servant of God's angelic meekness contrasted strongly with the passion of the sister speaking to her, and I heard her answer: "Yes, sister, how right you are! Indeed, I'm much more imperfect than you think."

I have noticed that in the poems she composed for me she always proposes Christ's humility as the model. Take this one, for instance:

> For me, on a foreign shore,
> What scorn you have borne!
> I wish to hide myself on earth,
> To be last in everything
> For you, Jesus.[8]

On 30 November, 1895 she told me of her "Act of Offering as Victim of Love," of which she speaks in her Life.[9] I showed a great desire to imitate her in this. She approved, and it was decided that I would offer myself the following day. But when I was alone again I thought of how unworthy I was, and I decided that I needed a long preparation. I went back to Sister Thérèse and explained my reasons for postponing the event. Her face immediately lit up with joy. "Yes," she said, "this act is more important than we could imagine, but do you know the preparation God requires of us? To humbly admit our unworthiness. So, since he has done you this favour, give yourself up to him without fear."

What she called her "little way of spiritual childhood" was a constant subject of conversation between us. She used to repeat to me that "Jesus reserved his privileges for the little ones". She never stopped talking about the trust, self-surrender, simplicity, uprightness, and humility of the child, and always proposed it to me as a model.

One day when I expressed a desire to be stronger and more energetic, in order to practise virtue better, she said: "If God wants you to be as weak and powerless as a child, do you think your merit will be any the less for that? Resign yourself, then, to stumbling at every step, to falling, even, and to being weak in carrying your cross. Love your powerlessness, and your soul will benefit more from it than if, aided by grace, you were to behave with enthusiastic heroism and fill your soul with self-satisfaction and pride."

The incident which I am now about to relate proves that it was only out of obedience that she wrote the account of her life. Shortly before she began it, I said to her: "The story of my vocation is so interesting that I am going to write it down, so as not to forget it. When I read it later on, it might do me some good."

"Beware of doing anything of the kind!" she said. "Anyway, you cannot do it without permission, and I advise you not to ask for it. I certainly would not like to write anything about my life without a special order to do so, and an unasked-for order at that. It is more in keeping with humility to write nothing about yourself. The great graces of life, such as a vocation, cannot be forgotten, and they will do more good when recalled to mind than when read about on paper."

22. One thing that struck me very forcibly about Sister Thérèse was that she could read what was happening in my soul. When I entered here, after spending over two years in a Paris Carmel, I found it hard to get used to the difference in customs. I was always comparing the two Carmels, and this made me unhappy. The Servant of God saw clearly that thoughts like these would ruin my vocation, and she fought against them with all her strength. Whenever I indulged in them I was sure to be reprimanded by her without my saying a word. On the other hand, whenever I resisted them she showed me how glad she was. When I asked her how she could possibly know what I was thinking, she said: "My secret is this: I never pass any remarks about it without first invoking our Lady. I ask her to inspire me to say what is best for you. After that, I admit that I am often surprised myself at some of the things I say to you without thinking. I just feel that in saying them to you I am not mistaken, and that Jesus speaks to you through me."

More than once I have been immediately and marvellously comforted through the power of her prayer. Before my profession, I was very upset one day—broken, weary and crushed by interior sufferings. That evening, before prayer, I wanted to say a few words to her, but she cut me off with: "The bell is ringing for prayer; I haven't time to comfort you. Anyway, I can see clearly that I would be wasting my time; God wants you to suffer alone for the present."

I followed her in to prayer in such a state of discouragement that, for the first time, I doubted my vocation. I was on my knees only a few minutes, crushed by sad thoughts, when suddenly, without my having started to pray or even expressed a desire for peace, I felt a sudden change in my soul. I understood the attraction of suffering, and I left prayer that evening completely transformed.

The following day, I told Sister Thérèse what had happened. She seemed quite moved, so I asked her why. "How good God is!" she replied. "Yesterday evening I had such pity for you that at the beginning of prayer I kept on asking our Lord to bring about a change in your soul and to show you the value of suffering. He heard me."

Before Mother Agnes of Jesus finished her term of office in 1896, she was to have professed Sister Genevieve and me, for our period of novitiate had expired. But the difficulties raised by Mother Gonzague at the time were so great that my profession was postponed until after the elections. I had a presentiment about this trial, and it was in vain that Sister Thérèse, to whom I had confided my apprehension, tried to dispose me to make the sacrifice.

One evening I was so depressed that I just cried and cried. Then, suddenly, my whole thinking changed. I imagined that it was the Last Day. I saw that God would not ask me if I had made my profession before such and such a date, but whether I had loved him dearly and availed myself of the opportunities to prove it. Next day, I asked the Servant of God if she had prayed for me. "Yes," she said, "I felt a strong urge to do so yesterday evening during silence." The time she had prayed for me was exactly the time that grace had flooded my heart.

Sister Thérèse foresaw that she would be a model for a

host of ordinary people (lit. "little souls"). She often said so, with charming simplicity. One day I said to her:

"I would like you to die during your thanksgiving after holy communion."

"Oh, no!" she replied. "That's not how I want to die. That would be an extraordinary grace and would discourage ordinary folk, because they could not do likewise."

She spoke to me several times of her hope "to spend her heaven doing good on earth". In her last "recreational composition", written in January or February 1897, she puts into St Stanislas Kostka's mouth what she thought on this subject. Afterwards she said to me: "What I like best about that piece is that I succeeded in expressing my certainty that it is still possible to work on earth for the salvation of souls. St Stanislas was admirably suited for giving expression to my thoughts and inspirations on this subject."

Here is a copy of the text of the dialogue between St Stanislas and our Lady. She has just told him he would soon die.

St Stanislas: I have no regrets about anything on earth, but I do have one desire, a desire so great that I could not be happy in heaven if it were not fulfilled. Tell me, Mary, if the blessed can still work for the salvation of souls. If I cannot work in Paradise for the glory of Jesus, I would prefer to remain in exile and go on working for him.

Our Lady: You would like to bring greater glory to Jesus, your only love; in the heavenly courts you shall win great victories for him. Yes, my child, the blessed can still save souls: the gentle flames of their love attract souls heavenwards.[10]

St Stanislas: Oh! How happy I am! Dear Queen of Heaven, I pray you that when I am with you in your heavenly home, I may be allowed to *return* to earth to protect holy souls, souls whose long career here will complete mine. That way I can, through them, present the Lord with an abundant harvest of merits.

Our Lady: Dear child, you shall protect souls struggling in the world; the more plentiful their harvest, the brighter you shall shine in heaven.

Another time I was looking up at the sky, and I said to Sister Thérèse: "How happy we shall be when we are up there!"

"True," she replied, "but as far as I'm concerned, if I want to go to heaven soon, don't think it is to rest. I want to spend my heaven doing good on earth till the end of the world. Only then will I enjoy it and take my rest. If I did not firmly believe that this desire of mine could be fulfilled, I would prefer to go on living till the end of time, in order to save more souls." She spoke these words as if inspired, and with great conviction.

About 1895 or 1896, before she wrote her manuscript, the Servant of God told me privately about the prophetic vision she had had as a child of the trials that would accompany her father's last years. She also told me how the Blessed Virgin had miraculously cured her of a strange illness, and how on that occasion the statue of the Blessed Virgin had disappeared from her sight and was replaced by a clear vision of the Mother of God herself.

23. During her life in Carmel, the Servant of God passed almost unnoticed in the community. Only four or five nuns, including myself, got close enough to her to realise the perfection that was hidden under the humility and simplicity of her exterior. For most of the nuns, she was a very regular religious, always above reproach.

The jealousy felt by a considerable section of the community towards the four Martin sisters brought her a certain amount of suffering. It was Mother Gonzague, when she was prioress, who waived the rules, and obtained permission for the four sisters to enter. But once this was done, she was the first to feel that antipathy I have spoken of. On the other hand, she told me herself several times (and in this she echoed the sentiments of the others): "If a prioress were to be chosen from the whole community, I wouldn't hesitate to choose Sister Thérèse, in spite of her youth. She is perfect in everything; her only drawback is the presence of her three sisters."

As for the little group that observed her more closely and without prejudice, I can sum up their impressions by giving my own. I have always considered Sister Thérèse's holiness to be heroic, and I have had no cause to change my mind since her death. From the beginning of 1896, when I saw she was ailing, I took care to collect souvenirs of her, particularly her hair. I did not do this for myself or out of ordinary affection; I did it because I was convinced that these things would be needed as relics after her death.

24. During the last months of her life, I was not able to get near her very much, because I had ceased to be infirmarian by the time she was put in the infirmary. One day I wrote and asked her if the thought of her approaching death brought her any joy. She wrote me this note in answer to mine:

"You want to know if I'm glad to be going to heaven? I would be very glad *if* I was going there, but I am not counting on my illness to get me there; it's too slow. I don't depend on anything but love any more. Ask Jesus to ensure that all the prayers that are said for me will serve to stoke the fire that must consume me."[11]

On 12 August, 1897, my twenty-third birthday, she wrote shakily on the back of a holy picture: "May your life be filled with humility and love, so that you may soon come where I am going . . . into the arms of Jesus."

After the last spring-cleaning of the convent before her death, I went to see her; she had been in greater pain than usual. She smiled and said: "I'm glad I was so sick today; it makes up for the hard work I have not been able to share in with you. That way, I have no reason to be envious of the rest of you."

Seeing her so sick, I said to her one day: "How sad life is!" "But life is not sad," she replied. "If you had said 'the exile is sad', I could understand. People make the mistake of calling what must come to an end 'life', but it is only to heavenly things, to what will never end, that one should really apply the word. And in this sense, life is not sad; it is gay, very gay."

Three days before she died, I saw her in such pain that I was heartbroken. When I drew close to her bed, she tried to smile, and, in a strangled sort of voice, she said: "If I didn't have faith, I could never bear such suffering. I am surprised that there aren't more suicides among atheists." Seeing her so calm and strong in the midst of such a martyrdom, I could not help telling her that I thought she was an angel. "Oh, no!" she said, "I'm not an angel. They are not as happy as I am." She wanted to make me understand that they did not have the privilege of suffering for God as she had.

The day of her death, I returned to the infirmary after Vespers to find the Servant of God in the throes of a terrible last agony, which she was bearing with invincible courage. Her hands were purple and joined together in anguish, and she was crying out in a voice rendered loud and clear by the acuteness of her pain: "O God, have mercy on me! Mary, help me! . . . My God, how I am suffering! . . . The chalice is full, full to the brim. I'll never be able to die."

"Courage," said the prioress, "you are nearly there, just a little more and it will all be over."

"No, Mother, it isn't over yet. I feel it; I am going to suffer on like this, maybe for months yet."

"And if it was God's will to leave you a long time on the Cross, would you accept it?"

" Yes, I want it," she said, in a tone of extraordinary heroism.

Then her head fell back on the pillow, and she looked so calm and resigned that we could not hold back our tears. She looked just like a martyr waiting for further torture. I left the infirmary; I could no longer bear to assist at so painful a spectacle. I returned only when the community did during her last few moments, and I witnessed the long and beautiful ecstatic look on her face at the moment of death. It was 7 p.m. on Thursday, 30 September, 1897.

27. I am amazed at the volume of mail received here every day; it comes from all over the world. I am obliged to keep abreast of it, because it is my responsibility to deal with orders for books and pictures. The way devotion to the Servant of God is increasing daily is quite remarkable; I know this from the way the mail keeps on increasing. At the moment we are getting an average of 100 letters a day.

Everybody has recourse to her with touching confidence, and she disappoints nobody. Some do not have their prayers heard the way they expected to, but they admit that the spiritual graces they receive instead surpass the material favours they have been refused. All of them desire to see her glorified soon, and many priests even offer up Masses for this intention. In short, it is rare to see a saint so universally loved. Nor is this love a passing enthusiasm; it continues to increase and shows no signs of abating.

There were some who did not appreciate Sister Thérèse at first, and who spoke scornfully of her as "a child" or "a little rose-water saint", but when they studied her life and her little way of spiritual childhood more closely they became her warmest admirers and most fervent friends.

In my own personal correspondence from relatives and friends there are often expressions of gratitude to Sister Thérèse for noteworthy favours. Fr Charles, of Bagnolet parish in the Paris diocese, who was my spiritual director before I became a Carmelite, wrote on 1 July, 1908: "I do my spiritual reading in these two precious jewel caskets, the *Story of a Soul* and *Pensées de Sr Thérèse*. They contain very precious pearls, and I reap much spiritual benefit from them. Anything that one could say in praise of them would still be an understatement. We find in them a perfect exposition of how to put the evangelical counsels, etc., into practice, in a simple way that is within everybody's reach."

29. I have always found the memory of the virtues practised by Sister Thérèse a real stimulant. Whenever I wish to urge myself on to do good, I have only to ask myself what she would have done in my place. I know immediately what is the most perfect line of action for me to take. I have such confidence in her that I say this little prayer to the Child Jesus every day: "Impress on me your childlike virtues and graces, so that on the day of my birth in heaven the angels and saints will recognise in your little spouse the faithful likeness of my dear Sister Thérèse of the Child Jesus."

Whatever the situation, I have recourse to her, and I gratefully acknowledge that I have never done so in vain, either on my own behalf or on that of others. If her power does not always show itself in temporal favours, it makes itself felt in spiritual graces that are infinitely more precious.

Here are some favours I received myself. For the sake of convenience, I had made a large pleat in my habit so that I would not have to adjust it every morning when I put my cincture on. It was firmly sewn with a lock stitch. I told the Servant of God about this a few days before she died, and she told me to unstitch it, that it was contrary to our custom. I left it as it was, nevertheless, putting off the job of unstitching it till some other time. The day after her death I could not get this blessed pleat out of my mind. I said to myself: "She sees I still have it, and maybe it grieves her." So, I said this prayer to her: "Dear sister, if you find this pleat displeasing, undo it yourself, and I promise never to re-make it." Imagine my amazement when on getting up the following morning I found it was no longer there! My feelings were a mixture of terror and consolation. It was a warning to me to put all her counsels and recommendations into practice.

On 28 February, 1909, she suddenly cured me of an abdominal ailment which had resisted every treatment for over two years, and was growing steadily worse. It had reached the point when I felt I should soon be forced to abandon the austerity of the Rule. Distressed, but full of faith, I rubbed my stomach with some oil from the lamp that burned before ·the statue of our Lady—the one that had smiled at the Servant of God as a child. At the same time, I asked Sister Thérèse to have pity on me and to cure me, so that I could continue to observe the Rule. All discomfort ceased immediately, and I have been perfectly well ever since.

Sister Thérèse has favoured me with perfumes several times: a scent of violets, especially one day after I had made an act of humility; a scent of roses: this emanated one day from the cupboard where her books and pictures are kept; a smell of incense on certain occasions when I was about to perform some service in connection with her.

On 15 September, 1910, I went to the turn at six o'clock to pick up a package from Bar-le-Duc. I noticed a piece of damp and ·rotten wood lying on the table. As I approached, I found that this old piece of wood, which I thought was for the rubbish heap, exuded a strong, sweet smell of incense. I immediately thought it must be a fragment of the coffin that had been exhumed nine days previously. I went to inform Mother Prioress so that she, too, could enjoy this marvel, but she smelled nothing. We told a novice about it, and she found a smell of incense. When Mother Prioress saw that, she fetched another sister but did not tell her what she wanted her for: she too found the smell of incense.

Mother brought this precious relic to recreation to show it to the community, but the other sisters smelled only damp, rotten wood even though they had been told it was a piece of

I

the Servant of God's coffin. It was actually from the side of the coffin, near the head. It had fallen off and could not be found. We showed it to Doctor La Néelle, one of the experts called to witness the exhumation, and he recognised it for what it was.

It is worth noting that these incidents never occur when one might reasonably expect them. The day of the exhumation, for instance, the entire cover of the coffin and some fragments of clothing were brought to the convent, and no one experienced anything like scent emanating from them.

I have also had visible evidence of her help in the trials that befell my family. She did not free them of any suffering or humiliation, but she obtained for them the grace to bear these trials as Christians, so that all of them benefited spiritually.

I also attribute to the Servant of God's protection the complete and very necessary conversion of my younger sister, and her subsequent vocation to Carmel. Here is what she wrote to me last year: "I can't get over the change in myself. I would like to live in indifference as before, but I just cannot. And to think that all this happened as a result of a novena to Sister Thérèse of the Child Jesus! Little by little I have come to love God, and I have felt loved in return. That's the mystery of my conversion, etc., in a nutshell."

The incoming mail I deal with here daily is full of testimonies to the Servant of God's holiness, and many of the letters contain accounts of spiritual and temporal favours received through her intercession. During 1909 I counted 1,830 such acknowledgements from many different countries. In 1910 and 1911 I have had to stop counting because of the immense pressure of work which this correspondence entails.

11 Mary Magdalen of the Blessed Sacrament, o.c.d.

This witness was a lay-sister and a novice of Sister Thérèse's. Born on 9 September, 1869, Melanie Marie Françoise Lebon grew up amidst poverty and hardship. She entered Carmel on 22 July, 1892, the feast of St Mary Magdalen, and took the name of this saint as her religious name. She was professed on 20 November, 1894. It was on this occasion that Sister Thérèse composed the poem "The Story of the Shepherdess who became a Queen"; it was sung at recreation in honour of the newly-professed sister.

As a novice she was entrusted to Sister Thérèse, and soon became a real problem to her on account of her touchy and sullen temperament. Indeed she was a problem for everybody, not just for Sister Thérèse. Fr Piat says she was "dour, sullen, and withdrawn, to such an extent that the community thought of sending her away".[1] But on the other hand, she was intelligent and hardworking. Sister Thérèse, for all her heroic efforts, was never able to win this sister's confidence. As she humbly admits in her testimony, Sister Mary Magdalen avoided Sister Thérèse as much as possible: she was just too perfect for her, and she felt that Thérèse knew what she was thinking about.

Later, after Thérèse had miraculously healed her leg, she underwent a change for the better and served the community devotedly in the kitchen until a year before her death, which occurred on 11 January, 1916.

She was the eighteenth witness, and testified on 16 March, 1911.

The testimony

8. I knew Sister Thérèse from the time I entered Carmel until her death. I watched her a lot and my testimony is composed from what I remember myself. I have read the *Story of a*

Soul, and I think what Sister Thérèse says there about herself agrees completely with what I saw for myself, but I shall not make use of that book in my testimony.

9. I have great devotion to the Servant of God, because I feel she obtains favours for me and protects me. I pray to her every day, and I offer little sacrifices for the success of the proceedings for her beatification.

18. At the beginning of 1893, six months after I had entered, Mother Agnes of Jesus became prioress and Sister Thérèse of the Child Jesus, novice-mistress.

Asked by the judge if it was not rather Mother Marie de Gonzague who then became novice-mistress, she replied:

Yes, it was Mother Gonzague, the ex-prioress, who was officially appointed novice-mistress, but that was only to have some peace. She was not able to train novices properly, so Sister Thérèse was given the unofficial task of supplying for her as discreetly as possible in this service of training. I think she had all the qualities necessary to guide us and make saints of us. One noticed that she did everything she said, and that inspired people to imitate her. Whenever she was asked anything, she always paused a moment before answering. She always arranged things with a view to pleasing God. Her decisions were clear and fair. She put a lot of unselfish zeal into our training. As she said to one of my companions: "Whatever the consequences, I will tell you the truth. I would prefer to be forced to leave the community than to leave someone in her ignorance. If you don't want to practise virtue, go back to the world."

19. Like the rest of the community, I knew she composed poems for recreation, but it was not until after her death that I learned she had written her autobiography.

20. From the moment I entered Carmel I was aware that Sister Thérèse was not like the other nuns. It is true that when I entered the Lisieux Carmel, I found the community in a very disappointing state. I used to think all Carmelite nuns were saints, but I gradually became aware that at that time there were a lot of very imperfect nuns. They were noticeably lacking in silence, regularity and especially mutual charity, and there were some lamentable divisions among them.

The community's general orientation was in the direction of these disorders, but in this unedifying environment Sister

or finding what people say of her sanctity exaggerated. In fact, they love her with all their hearts and pray to her with utter confidence. I know about her reputation outside the convent only from what I hear at recreation. The unanimity we have on the subject ourselves, I think, stems from the certainty we have acquired through experiencing the efficaciousness of her protection and of her intercession with God.

29. I was an eye-witness to something very unusual that happened in the kitchen in the summer of 1910. I had to fill a boiler that takes four large pitcherfuls. Sister Jeanne-Marie offered to help me. She began by emptying the boiler completely. I filled one pitcher at the pump, and Sister Jeanne-Marie emptied it into the boiler. When she went back to pour in the second, she found the boiler full up. I am sure of three things: 1, that the boiler had been emptied; 2, that I had pumped only one pitcherful; 3, that the boiler, which I filled twice daily, takes four pitcherfuls. Sister Jeanne-Marie told me that since she had a lot to do and was tired, she had prayed to the Servant of God to come to her assistance.

In September 1907 I was confined to bed in the infirmary with a bad leg, which got steadily worse over a period of eight months. The ailment consisted of an uninterrupted series of abscesses or boils (35 in eight months) coupled with a kind of withering of the leg. In the middle of May 1908, Mother Marie-Ange, the then prioress, suggested I pray to Sister Thérèse of the Child Jesus and ask her to enable me to resume my work in the kitchen. We made a novena and the leg got worse. We then started a second one and I was completely cured. The first Sunday of June I resumed my duties and I have never since had to interrupt them.

12   Marie-Elisa-Jeanne Guérin

Jeanne Guérin was a first cousin of Sister Thérèse's: her father, Isidore Guérin, being Mme Martin's brother. Born in Lisieux on 20 February, 1868, Jeanne married Dr Francis La Néelle on 1 October, 1891. Her marriage was childless, and this was very upsetting for her. But she bore her cross in a truly Christian spirit. Sister Thérèse tried to encourage and console her in her suffering, and also urged her to surrender herself entirely to Divine Providence.[1]

Thérèse had to comfort her cousin, too, when the latter's sister, Marie, entered Carmel and became Sister Marie of the Eucharist (1870-1905). Jeanne lost her husband in 1916, and she then devoted her energies entirely to charitable work. She died on 24 April, 1938.

The interest of her testimony is twofold. During her childhood and adolescence Jeanne and Thérèse were almost sisters, and her testimony also includes letters from Sister Marie of the Eucharist during the last months of Thérèse's life.

Mme La Néelle was the twentieth witness; she testified on 28 March, 1911.

The testimony

8. I was with the Servant of God from the time of her arrival in Lisieux (1877) until she entered Carmel (1888). When she came to Lisieux after her mother's death, she was four and a half and I was nine and a half. Our contact during this time was continual; M. Martin's chief motive in coming to Lisieux after his wife's death was to be near our family. His wife was my father's sister.

After she entered Carmel I spoke to her only rarely, and our relationship became of necessity less intimate. I will make no use of the *Story of a Soul* in my testimony, though I have the impression that what she says there is true. I shall draw chiefly on my own memories and on the correspondence between her and members of my family.

9. I pray to the Servant of God, but I notice she sends me more crosses than consolations. For some years now, many graces have been received by people on all sides through her intercession, and I conclude from that that Providence intends her to be beatified. I admit that in the years immediately following her death I did not foresee this supernatural expansion; it has revealed to me a sanctity that I did not know was so great.

14, 15. When she was little, Thérèse was a very pious and an extraordinarily good child. I cannot remember ever seeing her disobey or tell the tiniest lie. She was reared entirely by Pauline; it was she who engraved the imprint of all the virtues on her. Our little saint had a very special love for Pauline, whom she had chosen to replace her mother. My parents loved her as if she were their own daughter, and she returned their affection, as her letters to them testify. We have preserved them all like a treasure. I cannot recall her ever offending my father or mother in the slightest; they were full of admiration for her virtues and angelic life. I often heard people around me say things like: "This child won't live long; she is too angelic." And indeed her expression was truly that of an angel.

I must note, however, that on account of the difference in age between us I probably did not know the Servant of God as well as my younger sister Marie did. I was five years older than Thérèse, and that is a lot between children. Besides, she always went round with my young sister, while Céline and I were always together.

The Servant of God was not expansive; in fact, she spoke very little. I can remember only very few occasions when I saw her enjoy playing games. She frequently complained of headaches at that time, and I thought it was the pain that made her so serious. I would never have suspected then that she was so holy. She was very impressionable and cried for nothing.

At the age of ten she was seized by a terrible illness. We attributed it to the great sorrow that Pauline's departure for Carmel had caused her. I remember very clearly that she was most upset and quite inconsolable. All the stages of this illness are still vivid in my memory. The doctor who attended her said it was St Vitus's dance, but I remember he was not too sure of his diagnosis, and he gave the impression that there was more to it than just that. Just what, he did not know himself; if he had known he would have told my father.

16-18.   When I saw Thérèse enter Carmel at fifteen, I was edified by her virtue, of course, but deep down I thought she had done so to be reunited with Pauline, whom she loved so much. My father and mother disagreed with me on this. My father had been very much involved in the details of this entry into Carmel, and I heard my parents say that this child was predestined.

It was chiefly during her religious life that her virtues shone brightest. I was married in Caen, and I saw Thérèse only in the convent parlour whenever I came to Lisieux. Or rather I should say that I guessed she was present, for I neither saw nor heard her. The inflexible Rule condemned me to sit in the parlour in front of a completely closed grille, and I could hardly ever hear our little saint, because she completely effaced herself to let her sisters do the talking, and said very little herself.

The Mother Prioress, Mother Gonzague, wrote to my parents, and this is what she said about Thérèse: "I could never have believed that a fifteen-year-old could be so mature. There is no need to say a word to her; everything is perfect."

My young sister Marie entered the convent in 1895, and lived there for two years with the Servant of God. I often heard my parents say how happy they were that Sister Marie of the Eucharist (that was my sister's name in religion) would have her as a model at the beginning of her religious life. The letters I have from my parents and sister bear witness to their admiration for Thérèse's virtues. And the letters we received from the Servant of God herself, too, show the degree of perfection to which she had been raised.

24.   When she was very ill (1896-97) I heard from the nuns and from other people who visited her that she was most resigned, and was in a hurry to go off with God. She longed to die of love. During this last illness she was always in a great deal of pain.

Once she was dead, I was so sure that she was with God that I was convinced she would grant me anything I wanted. I have preserved a whole lot of letters written by my parents and sister at this time. Here are the most noteworthy passages from that correspondence:[2]

Sister Marie of the Eucharist to M. Guérin, 8 July, 1897:
    "Thérèse is very much changed, much thinner; but she is as calm as ever and still jokes. She is happy to see death approaching, and isn't a bit afraid of it. It will sadden you, papa, and that's understandable, as we are going to lose our greatest treasure. But there is no need to be sorry for her: loving God the way she does, she is sure of a warm welcome up there! She will certainly go straight to heaven.
    "When we spoke to her about going to purgatory ourselves, she said: 'Oh, what an awful thing to say! You insult God by thinking that you will go to purgatory. There can be no purgatory for those who love.'
    "Some time ago Mother Prioress gave M. de Cornières (the doctor) her poem 'Vivre d'amour'. She was not yet ill at the time, just a bit bronchial. When he had read it, he said to Mother Prioress: 'I'll never be able to cure her for you; she was not made for this world.' "

Sister Marie to Mme Guérin, 18 July, 1897:
    "There is no need to feel sorry for our little sister, she is so happy. She is so well prepared. She will be a great source of protection for us when she reaches heaven . . . Yesterday our Father Superior said to her: 'How can you speak of going to heaven soon? Your crown isn't ready yet; you have only just begun to make it.'
    " 'That's true, Father,' she said, 'I have not made my crown; God has made it for me.' Yes indeed, her crown is ready. It is up to us now to make ones as beautiful as hers. When you have known so beautiful a soul, it would be very wrong not to follow in her footsteps."

Sister Marie to M. Guérin, 21 July, 1897:
    "The Father Superior came at six o'clock and anointed her; then he brought her God. . . . It was a moving sight, I can assure you, to see our little patient still so calm and pure. I have never seen anyone dying so calmly. 'What do you expect?' she

said. 'Why should death make me afraid? All I've done, I've done for God.'

"When anyone suggests she will die on such and such a feast, she says: 'I don't need a feastday to die on; the day of my death will be my greatest feast.' "

Same to same, 17 August, 1897:
". . . You must not think her desire to go to heaven is some emotional thing. No, it's something very calm. This morning she said to me: 'Don't think I would feel let down if they told me I was going to be cured. I would be just as happy to live as to die. I long to go to heaven, but it is chiefly because I feel very peaceful and happy. I am not bursting with joy, but peaceful, and that is why I am happy.' "

Same to same, 27 August, 1897:
". . . And now, dear father, you are waiting impatiently for news of your little queen. It's the usual: she's getting weaker and weaker, and she cannot bear the slightest noise around her, even the rustling of a paper or speaking in a low voice. There has been quite a change since the Assumption. It has come to the point when we wish for her deliverance, because what she is going through is martyrdom.

"Yesterday she said: 'Fortunately I did not ask God for suffering; if I had, I would be afraid of not having enough patience to bear it. But since it comes solely from God, he cannot refuse me the grace and patience I need for it.'

"The congestion is still giving her trouble. Yesterday she said: 'I tell God to apply all the prayers that are offered for me to sinners, and not to the relief of my pain.' "

25, 26. The letters and reports they receive at the convent establish that the Servant of God's holiness has become known the wide world over. I know the gist of that correspondence from my Carmelite cousins. And, besides, I get a lot of visits and letters myself asking me for souvenirs, relics, pictures, etc., because of my being related to Sister Thérèse. My husband, Dr La Néelle, has bought Les Buissonnets, where the Servant of God spent her childhood, and I know that people come to visit the house out of devotion.

28. I have never heard the Servant of God's holiness criticised or opposed. Many, like myself, have had to admit that her reserve and simplicity prevented them from recognising the heroism of her virtue while she was alive. What they have heard since her death has been quite a revelation to them, but they would not dream of questioning the truth of this perfection.

Her account of some favours received has been omitted.

13   Godefroy Madelaine, O. PRAEM.

Victor Madelaine (1842-1931) was born at Le Tourneur in the diocese of Bayeux. He joined the Norbertine, or Premonstratensian, Canons at the Abbey of Mondaye (Calvados), taking the religious name of Godefroy, and was professed there on 7 February, 1864. After ordination he became a well-known preacher throughout Normandy, and was prior of his abbey from 1879-99.

During these years he visited the Lisieux Carmel several times, and was highly thought of there as a preacher and spiritual director. He preached the annual retreat in 1890, 1892, and 1896. On these occasions he spoke to Sister Thérèse, and as an old man he could still recall with admiration his conversation with her in 1896, when she told him so calmly about her great trial concerning the faith. He was happy to be able to follow the various stages of her glorification.

Unlike many of the witnesses, he had a high regard for Mother Gonzague, and she, too, thought very highly of him. So when, less than a month after the Servant of God's death, she decided to publish the manuscripts of her life, it was to Fr Godefroy that she turned for help.

In his testimony he recounts the part he played in editing and publishing the Story of a Soul. *This is the most important part of the testimony, and the only part we are retaining in the present edition.*

Fr Godefroy testified before the tribunal on 23-24 May, 1911, the twenty-fourth witness to do so.

The testimony

19. On 29 October, 1897, only a few weeks after the Servant of God's death, Mother Marie de Gonzague, the prioress, told

me she had some autobiographical notes written by Sister
Thérèse. She asked me to examine them. Here is an excerpt
from her letter:

"The recent events here (Thérèse's death) have left me
almost lifeless; I don't know whether I'm coming or going. The
death of our angel has left me with a void that will never again
be filled. The more aware I become of the perfections of this
blessed child, the greater my sorrow at having lost her. Out of
obedience, she left me some beautiful pages which I have just
taken up again with Mother Agnes of Jesus, and I think we
could make them known. This is just for yourself. Would you
correct it (the text) for us or, if you are too busy, have it corrected. No one knows about this, not even the community,
except the Father Superior, whose permission I obtained."

I studied the manuscript for about three months. I divided
it into chapters, and made a few little corrections, just a few
literary touches, nothing affecting the substance. The Reverend
Mother has sent me back the letters I wrote her at the time. To
put the history of this manuscript on record, it will be enough
to quote from some of them.

1 March, 1898: "Dear Reverend Mother, I have read the
whole manuscript and the poems. I am holding on to it because
I must read it again. I shall then mark with blue pencil what I
think should be omitted from the published edition. All of it,
absolutely all of it, is precious for *you*. But there are some details that are so intimate and out of the ordinary, that it would
be better, I think, not to print them for the public. There are
also slight mistakes in grammar and style; these are only slight
blemishes and can easily be made to disappear. Finally, we have
also noticed a certain repetitiousness; for the public it would be
better to suppress some of these repetitions. I shall mark them.
That's the critical part of the work. But, Mother, I can scarcely
tell you the pleasure and spiritual delight with which I read
those pages, so totally permeated by the love of God. I hope to
send you back the manuscript, with my remarks, before Easter.
You can then start preparing the copy for printing."

On 8 March, 1898 I wrote: "Dear Mother, you can put your
mind at rest about the *imprimatur:* we've got it. Yesterday I saw
the bishop and, after listening to my report, he granted it."

What had happened was this. When the bishop heard of a

ᴍanuscript by Sister Thérèse, his first reaction was one of distrust of the female imagination. But I was able to assure him in all conscience that I had studied the matter carefully and that I had been forced, in the present instance, to recognise that this whole manuscript bore evident marks of the Spirit of God, and that I had been unable to find any doctrinal error in it. On the strength of this testimony, the bishop granted his *imprimatur*.

Here is a passage from a letter I wrote some months later (3 January, 1899):

"Dear Reverend Mother, three days ago in Bayeux, one of the most intelligent of the canons told me he had read the *Story of a Soul* three times, and that it gets better each time. He added that the students at the major seminary are devouring the dear book. Deo gratias! Those beautiful words 'I will spend my heaven doing good on earth' are coming true." (Providence has ordained that that canon is today the president of the tribunal examining her Cause).

As for the value of this manuscript, I think it is the most authoritative account of her interior dispositions. I observe that she undertook and carried out this work only at her superiors' behest. Moreover, I find it an expression of such candid humility that it guarantees the truth of what is said there. "It is for you alone, Mother," she says, "that I am going to write the story of the little flower picked by Jesus. This thought will enable me to write freely, without worrying about style, or about the numerous digressions I shall make. If a little flower could speak, I think it would just say what God had done for it; it wouldn't try to hide his gifts."[1]

A third thing I would like to draw attention to is her detachment about what happened to the manuscript. "If you burn this manuscript before my eyes, without even reading it, I won't mind in the least."[2] I have found the teaching contained in this manuscript so sublime and accurate that she must have had some supernatural enlightenment. Without going into all the details, I can mention the happy way she always uses Sacred Scripture, and her marvellous discourse on fraternal charity.

Should anyone raise the question of the veracity of what is contained in this manuscript, my own opinion would be that one must accept everything in it as perfectly accurate, because

1. Sincerity, a horror of lies, and a need to be absolutely frank

were qualities apparent in the Servant of God since early child-hood (as a child she found no peace until she had revealed her little peccadilloes). 2. The study of her life shows that she was not given to flights of fancy and that she had no leanings towards illuminism. Her whole account is simple and reasonable.

14 Marie of the Holy Rosary, o.s.b.

Marguerite-Léonie-Augustine Leroy was born in Lisieux on 27 June, 1867. She went to school with Thérèse for two years, but was not in the same class. After Thérèse's death she became a Benedictine nun in Lisieux, and made her profession as Sister Marie of the Holy Rosary on 2 July, 1900.

Sister Marie was the thirty-second witness; she testified on 12 August, 1911.

The testimony

8. I knew the Servant of God because I was at school with her for about two years. I was about six years older than her, so we were not in the same class. In my testimony I shall make use only of what I saw myself.

9. I have a sincere devotion to the Servant of God; I hope she will be beatified. The study of her life makes me think she is a saint, and the good her protection does my soul makes me think her intercession with God is very powerful.

11. I often saw M. Martin and his daughters after their arrival in Lisieux. He inspired his children with great veneration. Indeed, as a Christian he was a model for the whole parish.

13. Before I became a nun I knew the Martin family well. In the eyes of the world, which judges superficially, the tender affection shown to the Servant of God may have looked like she was being spoiled. But I observed them closely, and I can testify that it was not so. M. Martin's children, Thérèse as much as her sisters, received a very serious Christian upbringing and were not allowed to do as they liked. Indeed I would say obedience was rather strict in the family.

14. During the two years that I knew Thérèse Martin at the Benedictine school (1882-4) I found her shy and sensitive. Because of that, and also because I was six years older than her,

I left her with the "little ones" and did not establish any close relationship. But I still saw in her, without being too clearly aware of it, an exceptional delicacy of conscience which inspired one with real respect for her.

I remember her asking me one day (she was nine at the time) if she could talk to me during playtime. I was president of a kind of sodality in the house, and, as such, the younger girls used to sometimes ask me for advice or encouragement concerning their conduct. I expected something similar on this occasion, but to my surprise and, indeed, embarrassment, she said: "Marguerite, I would like you to teach me how to meditate." I remember this incident clearly. I am almost certain it was then, too, that she told me, as she later told one of the teachers, that at home she used to shut herself in behind her bed to "think", which meant think about God.[1] This story has been told so often in our community that I have begun to doubt whether or not it was to me she said it.

I had left the school before the time Thérèse made her first communion.

In her autobiography, Sister Thérèse gives us to understand that she suffered during the time she spent at the Benedictine school. I think I can give the reason for this: it was the contrast between the exquisite delicacy and forms of piety that existed in her home, and the roughness of a certain element attending our school at that time.

27. All the nuns in our community have studied the *Story of a Soul,* and they almost unanimously regard it as the life of a saint.

28. There is one sister, however, who tries to dampen our enthusiasm whenever we express our admiration for Sister Thérèse. She does not give any specific reasons for her opposition, and I think she does it more out of a habit of contradicting people than out of any real conviction.

29. I cannot give any instances of temporal favours received in my own case, and anyway I've never asked her for any. But reading her life has awoken a great desire for perfection in me; the influence is quite definite. Moreover, I am convinced that when I pray to her I obtain very precious help towards putting these good desires into practice.

15 Aimée of Jesus, O.C.D.

All the witnesses we have heard from so far were called by the promoter of Sister Thérèse's Cause. This witness was called by the promoter of the faith.

Born on 24 January, 1851, Sister Aimée of Jesus entered the Lisieux Carmel on 13 October, 1871, and made her profession there on 8 May, 1873. She was a strong, active woman, with a disconcerting brand of realism—a pragmatist who wanted no artists in the community, just practical people like good seamstresses, nurses, etc. She was an uncompromising opponent of Céline's entry into the Lisieux Carmel. She did not want to have four sisters living in the same community, and Céline's particular talents were not to her liking either.

It is well known that Thérèse asked God for a sign to know if her father went straight to heaven. "If Sister A. of J. gives her consent to Céline's entry or does not oppose it," she wrote, "that will be an answer to say that papa went straight to you."[1] And that is what happened. Under her rough and gruff exterior, however, Sister Aimée had a really generous heart.

In a very honest testimony she reveals from the outset that she " was not particularly intimate with Sister Thérèse", and she humbly admits that she "was one of the instruments God had used to sanctify her". In her opinion, Sister Thérèse "would have made an excellent prioress; she would have always acted prudently and charitably, and never abused her authority."

Sister Aimée gave her testimony on 17 March, 1911.

The testimony

8. I was in the convent when the Servant of God entered it in 1888, and I lived with her till her death. Still, we were not particularly intimate, and for that reason many details of her life must have escaped me.

9. I esteem and love the Servant of God as a very holy person, but not with any enthusiasm or natural liking.

The interrogator passed on immediately to Q. 21, which was the question that had caused this witness to be called.

21. I was one of the instruments God made use of to sanctify her. The charitable way she bore with my defects brought her to an outstanding degree of holiness. Her fraternal charity was unselfish and supernatural. I thought her behaviour towards the voting sisters heroic, for when Mother Agnes of Jesus was elected prioress in 1893, the votes were very divided. The secrecy of the vote was not kept as well as it ought to have been, but Sister Thérèse did not show the slightest animosity towards the nuns who did not vote for her sister.

Even when she was dying, she had the courage to suffer rather than upset others. I remember the Sunday before she died, one of the portresses came to stay with her during Mass. The sister placed herself against the bed in a way that aggravated the difficulty she then had in breathing. The Servant of God pretended nothing. It was only after the portress had gone away and she had an attack of congestion that the dear patient was forced to admit the cause of it.

As I've said, I did not have many personal dealings with Sister Thérèse. I must even have appeared quite indifferent to her. And yet, in our infrequent meetings I felt the warmth of her affection for me and a charity that flowed from her ardent love of God and her deep humility. Only once during her illness was I able to render her some little service: I shall never forget the sweet look with which she thanked me, nor the angelic smile that accompanied it.

Her fortitude was heroic during the trial of her venerable father's illness. She showed admirable resignation, and attended the community acts punctually, even when her sisters were discussing family matters. I saw her at recreation then, when her sisters were absent, and she spoke to us perfectly calmly though the big tears in her eyes showed us that she was not indeed unmoved by these sufferings.

From the very beginning of her stay in Carmel her religious comportment was remarkable. In spite of her youth, there was nothing childish or frivolous in her behaviour. She gave no opening for becoming the plaything of the community; her seriousness insured that she would not be treated as a child.

Her serenity was imperturbable. In the annoyances of everyday life, she let her sisters get worked up, but she remained unruffled herself. Only once did I see Sister Thérèse lose this calm just a little. Her sister Céline (Genevieve of St Teresa) had a violent upset some weeks before her profession, and she could not hide it. The cause of it was Mother Gonzague, the novice-mistress. I did not know exactly why Sister Genevieve had been humiliated, but I remarked in a general kind of way to Sister Thérèse: "Mother Marie de Gonzague has a right to test Sister Genevieve, so why be surprised?"

She retorted with some feeling: "There are some ways in which people should not be tested, and this is one of them."

This answer surprised me at the time, and I thought it sprang from a love that was too natural. But I was not sure, because I did not know what exactly had happened. For a long time now, I have been convinced that she answered like that out of a spirit of discernment.

I am sure she would have made an excellent prioress; she would always have acted prudently and charitably, and never abused her authority.

I noticed the delicacy of the Servant of God's humility in the way she never said a word to make us feel grateful for the many gifts bestowed on us by her family. The natural and supernatural gifts God so richly endowed her with were never used to mortify another person. She was so good at effacing herself that one had to be close to her to appreciate her virtue. To my own shame, I admit that I did not come to appreciate soon enough the rare qualities God had endowed her with.

23. The Servant of God was very simple and modest. She was so careful to disguise her virtue that while she lived the community was not as aware as it is now of how perfect her life was. Nevertheless, I can assure you that even when she was alive all the nuns considered Sister Thérèse an exceptionally virtuous person, particularly remarkable for her humility, charity and gentleness. Apart from the little imperfection I mentioned (and maybe it was not an imperfection at all) I have never noticed the slightest defect in her.

In Sister Thérèse's time we had a chaplain called Fr Youf. I would like to remember him here, and pay a tribute to his esteem for this little sister. One day I felt I had reason to complain about her elder sisters, but he said: "Don't complain! Even if you do have something to suffer from one side, surely you must also be very happy to have a treasure like the younger sister. She is first class, and is making enormous strides in virtue. If only she were known, she would be the glory of this Carmel." Fr Youf said that to me towards the end of her life. The presence of four sisters and a cousin of theirs was liable to cause some friction and unfavourable judgments from time to time. But never to my knowledge was the perfection of Sister Thérèse of the Child Jesus called in question.

I have omitted her account of a favour granted to a niece of hers in 1902.

Notes

For my own convenience, I have translated all quotations from St Thérèse's autobiography and letters myself. For the reader's convenience, I refer in the notes to the following translations:

R. KNOX, *Autobiography of a Saint*, London, 1958.
J. CLARKE, O.C.D., *Story of a Soul*, Washington, 1975.
F. SHEED, *Collected Letters of St Thérèse*, London, 1949.

It is to be noted that in some instances the text used by these translators is not identical with that quoted by witnesses in 1910–11.

I Agnes of Jesus, O.C.D.

1. KNOX, 112-13; CLARKE, 83.
2. KNOX, 156; CLARKE,123.
3. SHEED, Letter 18.
4. KNOX, 194–5; CLARKE, 158.
5. KNOX, 312; CLARKE, 259.
6. KNOX, 270; CLARKE, 224.
7. KNOX, 81; CLARKE, 57.
8. KNOX, 218–19; CLARKE, 179.
9. In this decree Pope Leo XIII laid down that it was the confessor, and not the reverend mother, who was to decide how frequently nuns could receive Holy Communion.
10. KNOX, 253–6; CLARKE, 211–13.
11. KNOX, 99–100; CLARKE, 73.
12. KNOX, 211; CLARKE, 174.
13. KNOX, 219; CLARKE, 180.
14. KNOX, 128; CLARKE, 99.
15. KNOX, 135–6; CLARKE, 104–5.
16. KNOX, 192–3; CLARKE, 157.
17. SHEED, Letter 207.
18. Lit. "little souls". "Little" here and in the phrase "little way", is contrasted with the "extraordinary", i.e. visions, revelations, etc. (Tr.)
19. KNOX, 71–3; CLARKE, 45–7.
20. KNOX, 145; CLARKE, 112.
21. SHEED, Letter 233.
22. What Mother Agnes presented to the tribunal was what we know as *Novissima Verba*. We refer the reader to the English translation published by Gill and Son, Dublin, 1953.

2 Thomas Nimmo Taylor

1. At the end of his testimony, Fr Taylor noted that he meant "purity" here in the sense of "moral beauty and simplicity".

3 Marie of the Sacred Heart, o.c.d.

1. KNOX, 56; CLARKE, 33.
2. KNOX, 53; CLARKE, 28.
3. KNOX, 53; CLARKE, 29.
4. KNOX, 120; CLARKE, 88.
5. KNOX, 135; CLARKE, 104.
6. SHEED, Letter 70.
7. SHEED, Letter 92.
8. SHEED, Letter 176.
9. KNOX, 236–7, 241–2; CLARKE, 196, 200.
10. KNOX, 295–6; CLARKE, 247–8.
11. KNOX, 155–6; CLARKE, 123.
12. TAYLOR, *St Thérèse of Lisieux* (1947 ed.), 383
13. Cf. KNOX, 268; CLARKE, 222.
14. KNOX, 156; CLARKE, 123.
15. SHEED, Letter 28.
16. KNOX, 228–9; CLARKE, 188.
17. Cf. KNOX, 71; CLARKE, 45–6.
18. KNOX, 155–6; CLARKE, 123.
19. TAYLOR, 389–423, including many favours of a later date.

4 Genevieve of Saint Teresa, o.c.d.

1. English translation, London, 1926.
2. KNOX, 110; CLARKE, 81.
3. KNOX, 118; CLARKE, 87.
4. KNOX, 112; CLARKE, 82.
5. KNOX, 126; CLARKE, 97.
6. KNOX, 127–8; CLARKE, 98–9.
7. Cf. KNOX, 177; CLARKE, 141, but Céline does not quote literally.
8. KNOX, 142; CLARKE, 109.
9. KNOX, 147–151; CLARKE, 114–18.
10. KNOX, 237; CLARKE, 196.
11. KNOX, 203–4; CLARKE, 168–9.
12. SHEED, Letter 14, where the two sentences are in reverse order and far apart.
13. KNOX, 158; CLARKE, 125.

14. KNOX, 254–7; CLARKE, 211–14.
15. SHEED, Letter 107.
16. SHEED, Letter 128.
17. SHEED, Letter 98.
18. KNOX, 211; CLARKE, 174.
19. SHEED, Letter 86.
20. SHEED, Letter 40.
21. SHEED, Letter 122, dated 18 July, is the nearest to this adapted quotation of Céline's.
22. SHEED, Letter 102.
23. KNOX, 187; CLARKE, 152.
24. SHEED, Letter 114.
25. SHEED, Letter 73.
26. SHEED, Letter 146.
27. SHEED, Letter 63.
28. SHEED, Letter 121.
29. KNOX, 147; CLARKE, 114.
30. KNOX, 167; CLARKE, 132.
31. SHEED, Letter 16.
32. SHEED, Letter 18.
33. SHEED, Letters 58 and 59.
34. KNOX, 181; CLARKE, 143.
35. KNOX, 132; CLARKE, 101.
36. KNOX, 43; CLARKE, 21.
37. KNOX, 195; CLARKE, 158.
38. KNOX, 46–7; CLARKE, 24–5.
39. SHEED, Letter 109.
40. KNOX, 113; CLARKE, 83.
41. SHEED, Letter 124.
42. KNOX, 248; CLARKE, 207.
43. SHEED, Letter 122.
44. KNOX, 86–94; CLARKE, 60–66.
45. SHEED, Letter 146.
46. KNOX, 258; CLARKE, 215.
47. SHEED, Letter 233.

7 Teresa of Saint Augustine, O.C.D.

1. Cf. KNOX, 268–9; CLARKE, 222–3, where St Thérèse speaks of this nun, without naming her.

8 Marie of the Angels and the Sacred Heart, O.C.D.

1. KNOX, 186; CLARKE, 151.
2. KNOX, 192; CLARKE, 156.

3. KNOX, 129; CLARKE, 100.
4. KNOX, 308; CLARKE, 255–6.
5. *Story of a Soul*, ch. 12. This is not in the modern edition.
6. KNOX, 165–6; CLARKE, 131.
7. KNOX, 241; CLARKE, 200.
8. SHEED, Letter 170.
9. KNOX, 263; CLARKE, 218.

10 Marie of the Trinity, O.C.D.

1. Cf. *Dark Night of the Soul*, Book 1, ch. 4.
2. Cf. KNOX, 268; CLARKE, 222–3, and testimony No. 7 of this edition.
3. SHEED, Letter 214. The text as quoted by Sister Marie differs a little from that translated by F. SHEED. (Tr.).
4. KNOX, 303; CLARKE, 252.
5. Cf. TAYLOR, 450-51 for the prayer.
6. Cf. KNOX, 236; CLARKE, 195.
7. KNOX, 253; CLARKE, 210.
8. From the poem "I thirst for love".
9. KNOX, 220; CLARKE, 180–81. CLARKE gives the text of this prayer on pp. 276–7. (Tr.)
10. Our Lady's words are versified in the original. (Tr.)
11. SHEED, Letter 213.

11 Mary Magdalen of the Blessed Sacrament, O.C.D.

1. S. J. PIAT, O.F.M., *Sainte Thérèse de Lisieux à la découverte de la voie d'enfance*, Paris 1964, p. 171.

12 Marie-Elisa-Jeanne Guérin

1. Cf. SHEED, Letters 110, 159, 227.
2. I have retained only the letters of Sister Marie of the Eucharist; pressure of space compels me to omit those of her parents. (Tr.)

13 Godefroy Madelaine, O.PRAEM.

1. KNOX, 36; CLARKE, 15.
2. KNOX, 304; CLARKE, 253.

14 Marie of the Holy Rosary, o.s.b.

1. Cf. KNOX, 101; CLARKE, 74.

15 Aimée of Jesus, o.c.d.

1. KNOX, 216; CLARKE, 177–8.